GREAT WESTERN AUTO TRAILERS

PART ONE

GREAT WESTERN AUTO TRAILERS

PART ONE
PRE-GROUPING VEHICLES

JOHN LEWIS

WILD SWAN PUBLICATIONS LTD.

© Wild Swan Publications Ltd. and John Lewis 1991
ISBN 0 906867 99 1

FOR CHERRY

ACKNOWLEDGEMENTS

My thanks are due to all those that have helped and encouraged me in this book, including: Geoff Balfour, Gerry Beale, Sean Bolan, Steve Bromhall, Roger Carpenter, David Castle, Colin Chapman, D. G. Coakham, John Copsey, Tony Fairclough, Ian Forsythe, Pat Garland, David Geen, John Hodgetts, Peter Korrison, Mike Morton Lloyd, Ian Pope, Peter Rance, S. Rickard, Dick Riley, David Rouse, Jack Slinn, Colin Strevens, Chris Turner, Ralph Tutton, Steve Vincent, H. F. Wheeller, B. Y. Williams, Stephen Williams, and M. Yarwood. I must also thank the Great Western Museum Trust, Didcot, for access to the late Eric Mountford's records (these are now with the Welsh Industrial & Maritime Museum, Cardiff); Pendon Museum Trust, Long Wittenham; and The Keeper of the Public Record Office, Kew, in whose charge are the GWR registers of condemned coaches.

The GWR coaching stock registers and some other papers are in the National Railway Museum Library, York, and my thanks go to Phillip Atkins, John Edgington, Jane Elliott and Lynne Thurston of the NRM.

Finally, I would particularly like to thank Paul Karau and June Judge for all their help and hospitality.

Title page: A Diagram U trailer between Symonds Yat and Monmouth on 20th September 1951.
(D. W. Winkworth)

Designed by Paul Karau
Printed and bound by Butler & Tanner, Frome

Published by
WILD SWAN PUBLICATIONS LTD.
1–3 Hagbourne Road, Didcot, Oxon OX11 8DP

CONTENTS

A '517' class 0-4-2T with Diagram A9 (left) and U trailers at Northolt Junction c.1925/6.
COLLECTION R. C. RILEY

Introduction	. . . .	1
Chapter One	HISTORICAL OVERVIEW	3
Chapter Two	PURPOSE-BUILT MATCHBOARDED TRAILER . . .	51
	59ft 6in Trailer No. 1: Diagram A	51
Chapter Three	PURPOSE-BUILT 70FT TRAILERS	53
	70ft Trailers Nos. 2–6: Diagrams B1, B, V, W, X, A4 .	53
	70ft Trailers Nos. 9 & 10: Diagrams D, A11 & A12 .	65
	70ft Trailers Nos. 11–13: Diagrams E & F . .	67
	70ft Trailers Nos. 25–8: Diagrams K1, K, Y & A5 .	71
	70ft Trailers Nos. 29–34, 42–7 & 53–70: Diagram L .	73
	70ft Trailer No. 48: Diagrams O & S . . .	87
	70ft Trailers Nos. 49–52: Diagram P . . .	91
	70ft Trailers Nos. 71–4 & 93–8: Diagrams Q & R .	93
	70ft Trailers Nos. 75–80: Diagram T, and Nos. 81–92: Diagram U	97
Chapter Four	PURPOSE-BUILT 59FT 6IN TRAILERS	111
	59ft 6in Trailers Nos. 7 & 8: Diagram C . . .	111
	59ft 6in Trailers Nos. 19–24: Diagrams J1 & J . .	115
	59ft 6in Trailers Nos. 36–41: Diagram N . . .	119
Chapter Five	EARLY CONVERSIONS TO TRAILERS . . .	123
	4-wheel, 28ft Low-roof Driving Trailers Nos. 560 & 598 .	123
	52ft Clerestory Trailers Nos. 14–17: Trailer Diagrams G, G1 & H	124
	54ft Clerestory Trailers Nos. 18 & 35: Trailer Diagrams 1, A8, M & M1	127

v

COLLECTION PAUL STRONG

Chapter Six	LOW ROOF CONVERSIONS TO TRAILERS 1912–1914/1931	129
	51FT DRIVING TRAILERS	129
	Nos. 3331/32/35–40: Trailer Diagrams A2 & A3 – 'Clifton Downs' Stock	129
	THE 'CLIFTON DOWNS' INTERMEDIATE TRAILERS	138
	45ft Intermediate Trailers Nos. 2293/4: Diagram C1 'Clifton Downs' Stock	138
	51ft Intermediate Trailer No. 6734 (later 3273): Coaching Stock Diagram E56/C42 'Clifton Downs' Stock	138
	51ft Intermediate Trailer No. 7173 (later 3390): Coaching Stock Diagrams E59/C41 – 'Clifton Downs' Stock	139
	50ft Intermediate Trailers Nos. 7169–72 (later 3274–6 & 3387): Coaching Stock Diagrams E58/C40 – 'Clifton Downs' Stock	139
	'Clifton Downs' Trailers – Allocations	141
	46ft 6in Composite Driving Trailers Nos. 7026/8: Trailer Diagram A1	143
	56ft Composite Intermediate Trailer No. 7216: Coaching Stock Diagram E120	145
Chapter Seven	CONVERSION OF THE STEAM RAIL MOTORS	147
	MATCHBOARDED TRAILERS CONVERTED FROM SRMs	148
	59ft 6in Trailers Nos. 99–104: Trailer Diagram Z	148
	57ft Trailers Nos. 105 & 106: Diagram A6 (ex-SRM Diagrams A & A1)	154
	59ft 6in Trailers Nos. 107–112: Diagram A7 (ex-SRM Diagrams D & D1)	157
	59ft 6in Trailers Nos. 113–124: Diagram A9	163
Chapter Eight	THE CONVERSION OF WOOD-PANELLED SRMs TO TRAILERS	167
	70FT GANGWAYED TRAILERS	167
	Nos. 126 & 127, Diagrams A13 & A14	167
	70ft Trailers Nos. 134–137 and 148: Diagrams A15, A17, A18 and A25	170
	70ft Trailers Nos. 138–140: Diagram A19	177
	70ft Trailers 146, 197 & 198: Diagram A23	178
	70ft Trailers Nos. 149–158, 181–186, 199–201, 206, 210, 212–218: Diagrams A26 & A29	181
Chapter Nine	59FT 6IN TRAILERS: EX-SRMs	193
	59ft 6in Trailers Nos. 125, 128–133: Diagram A10	193
	59ft 6in Trailer No. 147: Diagram A24 (ex-SRM Diagram L)	196
	59ft 6in Trailers Nos. 202–205, 207–209, 211 and 219: Diagram A31	197

*Part Two will cover
Post Grouping and Absorbed Vehicles*

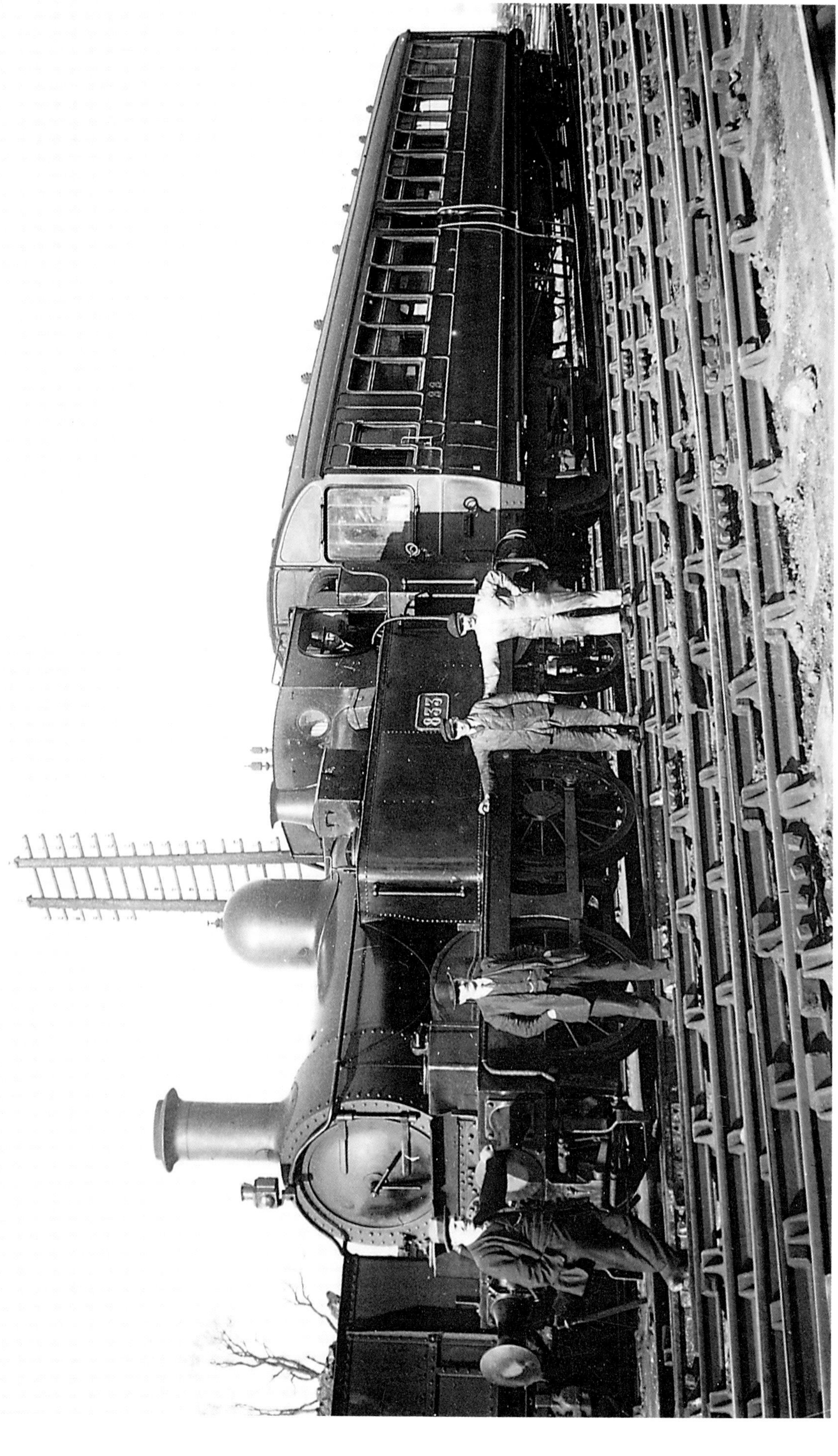
833

INTRODUCTION

At the turn of the century, the managements of the various British railways were actively seeking ways of improving the economics of local train services. In most cases the era of railway expansion was over, and accommodation had been reached with rival railways over the control of territory. This had left the railway companies saddled with some branch lines of doubtful profitability through countryside that probably had insufficient population to support a railway, in spite of the near-monopoly of transport the railways enjoyed at this time. They also owned urban and suburban lines which did not cater well for existing passenger traffic flows, either because they went in the wrong direction, or were circuitous, or they were at a disadvantage with a rival line. The principal rivals of railways had been canals, coastwise shipping and, mainly in large towns, horse drawn vehicles; but things were changing, especially in the larger built-up areas, where the new tramways were seen as a major threat to some railway services.

Amongst the solutions considered by railway management were electric train services on 'proper' railways, the use of self-contained steam-powered coaches (steam railmotors), and the use of internal combustion engines to propel coaches.

However, there were problems with all of these. Electric train services required a large investment in traction equipment, cabling, and power supply; electrical technology was quite basic, too. Railway vehicles were much more strongly and heavily-constructed than their road equivalents, and needed more power to start (and stop). The internal combustion engine was still in its infancy, and for various reasons, petrol engined railcars were not very successful.

One solution which avoided these particular problems was the steam rail motor, which in effect incorporated a (very) small steam engine as a single unit into one end of a passenger coach. The theory was that by having small, dedicated units of this kind, running and capital costs could be lowered. The trains would be capable of fairly rapid acceleration to about 30–40 mph, so they were suitable for services having frequent stops. Since these motor units could be driven from either end, turnround times could be drastically reduced, improving their utilisation, and allowing their use on intensive services. Open passenger saloons were provided, so that the guard or a conductor could issue tickets on the train, and the stations served could be unstaffed (or have their staff reduced). Effectively, a steam powered equivalent of a tram had been produced, but one that was constructed to allow it to be freely used on ordinary railways.

Steam railmotors (SRMs) introduced their own problems. There was a tendency to go too far in reducing the size of the steam traction unit (firebox/boiler/cylinders), so that on some railways the SRMs were grossly underpowered, being deficient in tractive effort and/or boiler steaming capacity. The GWR's rail motors were amongst the most powerful of their type, and were stated to be capable of hauling two 70 ft trailers or four horseboxes; in these circumstances, however, time-keeping was liable to suffer badly.

SRMs were often used on routes where the frequency of service after their introduction had generated increased traffic. As a result, they were liable to be a victim of their own success. The passenger accommodation was strictly limited, and to increase it, a coach had to be attached. If this was the case, the coach had to be a special one so that the SRM could be remotely-driven from it, otherwise the SRM would have to run round the coach at the end of each journey, and the advantages of quick turn round would be lost. The GWR soon found that such trailers were necessary.

SRMs were notorious for their vibration when running. This was caused by the thrust of the pistons, aggravated by the short wheelbase of the power unit and the outside-cylindered engine portion; this effect could not be dampened by buffing and drawgear as on an ordinary train, because the power unit was integral (or articulated) with the passenger accommodation. It has been said that when an SRM came into sight accompanied by a trailer, knowledgeable passengers immediately made for the latter.

Because the SRM had a locomotive portion semi-permanently attached to the passenger accommodation, it meant that the whole unit had to go into locomotive sheds and to coaling stages, all of which made it very hard to keep the passenger accommodation acceptably clean. It also meant that when work had to be done on the power unit, the passenger saloon was also unavailable for traffic. The GWR did in fact keep a small 'float' of SRM power units, but since they ran as an integral portion of the SRM, built into the coachwork, removal of the power unit was a major exercise. The services of a breakdown crane were usually required because the boiler had to be lifted out through the SRM's roof before the power bogie could be removed.

The GWR initially took up the concept of SRMs enthusiastically, and before long had 99 in operation. (No. 100 was a petrol-electric powered railmotor.) But as a result of the disadvantages listed above, the GWR eventually either converted its SRMs to ordinary trailers, or it sold or scrapped them.

Having introduced the concept of an auto trailer, it was a short step to the realisation that there was another way of producing a steam-powered train with the advantages of an SRM, but without most of its disadvantages. Instead of having a special built-in (or permanently attached) engine unit, the solution was to use a separate, conventional steam locomotive, specially equipped for remote control from a trailer, which was able to be coupled to one or more such trailers. The specific advantage of this idea was that the locomotive would be available for other duties when not required for auto train work.

Normally, it would have been a much more expensive proposition to provide a new locomotive and trailer than to build a new SRM. However, around 1905 the GWR found itself with a surplus of small tank engines, which were financially fully depreciated but were capable of further economic life. So it was decided to equip some with the necessary apparatus to enable them to be controlled by the driver from a trailer that was being propelled by the locomotive.

This concept was also taken up with enthusiasm by the GWR, and the trailer fleet increased quite rapidly, although it did not outnumber the SRM fleet until about 1913. The purpose-built trailer feet was supplemented from time to time by conversions from ordinary coaches which usually kept their original 'non-trailer' running number. In due course, during BR days, the trailer numbering series reached 256.

Eventually, the use of auto trains (consisting of a locomotive plus one or more trailers) ceased, either as the result of the introduction of diesel multiple units or the closure of many of the branch lines over which they operated. The last GWR-type auto-fitted locomotive was withdrawn in 1964.

Ironically, although the use of 'proper' auto-trains with steam locomotives died out, the principle of auto train working never has, perhaps the closest analogy in some cases being a rail motor + trailer(s). For example, the Southern Railway used two-car electric multiple unit trains where one coach was a driving motor car (equivalent to an SRM) and the other a driving trailer. BR still uses this arrangement, which was also used for some first generation diesel multiple units. Other examples included the Glasgow & Edinburgh trains with a class 47 diesel at one end and a driving trailer at the other, and even the original Bournemouth & Waterloo express electric trains, where a four-car power set pulled or pushed up to 2 four-car trailer sets. The 1980s saw further extensions of the 'Pull and Push' system of working, notably on the Euston to Birmingham service, and this is now the normal method of operating the East Coast main line.

Quite a number of GWR and BR(W) auto trailers have been preserved, and rides in them can still be enjoyed.

A pair of Diagram L trailers and 0–4–2T No. 574. The trailer nearest the camera is in the pre-1908 'full' brown and cream livery.

COLLECTION J. E. KITE

CHAPTER ONE
HISTORICAL OVERVIEW

LENS OF SUTTON

BY the time that the first trailer was built by the GWR in September 1904, there were 26 steam railmotors in existence, all in the matchboarded style. The first two had flat ends, the remainder having the prominent bow-ends that were to be a hallmark of the SRMs and purpose-built trailers of GWR design until the last GWR-type trailers were built by British Railways.

The first trailer was in the matchboarded style of the existing SRMs, with bow ends, 59 ft 6 in in length and 8 ft 6 in wide. The second trailer, which entered service in December 1904, was in the wood-panelled style, and 70 ft long and 9 ft wide, matching subsequent SRMs and trailers in form. These trailers had open-plan passenger accommodation. The passenger seating was arranged partly with longitudinal benches, and partly in seating bays arranged conventionally across the carriage, with a centre corridor. This type of arrangement was adopted for the vast majority of trailers.

By the end of 1905, the SRM fleet had reached 60 carriage units; all those built during that year were in the wood-panelled style. Nos. 15 and 16 were non-standard, but as they never became trailers, they can be ignored. During this period, 70 ft SRMs, as well as 59 ft 6 in examples, were produced; the width was increased to 9 ft.

During 1905, the trailer fleet reached 21 coaches, but Swindon appears to have been too busy to construct 19 completely new trailers; and so, between July and September of that year, six gangwayed clerestory coaches were altered to become trailers, as were two rather old 4-wheel, third class, low-roof coaches, only 28 ft 0¾ in long. These four-wheelers dated back to the 1870s, when they had been built as 6-wheel coaches, and formed quite a contrast to the 70 ft trailers in general production in 1905! Possibly because of their origins, these two coaches kept their original third class running numbers, whilst the clerestory coaches were renumbered into the trailer series.

The clerestory coaches were originally corridor third class, lavatory stock, about 12 years of age. They were presumably chosen as having an open saloon (the smoking accommodation of the original coach), and a side corridor to the other compartments, enabling the guard to issue tickets, if required. The GWR did have examples of 'open' hauled carriages; these were gangwayed clerestory coaches built for the New Milford boat trains. Although quite unpopular with their intended passengers, these coaches were only 4–5 years old, and remained in main line service.

As trailers, the 4-wheel examples were unusual (apart from their size) in having all the passenger accommodation in compartments. They remained unique in this respect until 1912. Originally they had five compartments, but one was altered for use by the driver.

Included amongst the earlier trailers were Nos. 3–6, which were notable in being modified at an early date to run in pairs, which meant fitting through regulator gear. Trailers Nos. 7 and 8, which were built to run on the Lambourn Valley Railway, were originally not fitted with any control gear; this meant that they could only be used as conventional coaches!

1906 and 1907 saw the SRM and trailer fleets grow steadily, until SRM No. 99 was built in February 1908; this was the last SRM to be built by or for the GWR. During this period, the general style remained the same, and they continued to be produced in both 59 ft 6 in and 70 ft lengths. The year 1906 was significant in that the first trailers to be lit by incandescent gas lamps were built. Earlier vehicles had flat-flame burners, which were not as efficient, and were mostly altered in due course.

Trailers continued to be built to the same dimensions as the SRMs, and still in the wood-panelled style, until 1913. There were a number of variations between these trailers, and some alterations were made to them; some were given gangways, so that they could be used with SRMs, or together.

There was one experimental trailer, No. 48, which was built with seating across the carriage, compartment fashion, but without the partitions. There were narrow gangways down each side of the coach for use principally by the guard, and each seating bay was served by sliding doors on each side, giving the vehicle the external appearance of a 'concertina' coach. The guard operated the sliding doors by turning a windlass arrangement. This coach was not a success in its original state, and was soon rebuilt into a conventional example.

Between 1912 and 1914, more 8-wheel coaches were converted into trailers. The coaches concerned were all compartment-type, with low roofs; 8 brake thirds built in 1898, 2 all-thirds constructed in 1879, and 6 composites built in 1897–8 were altered for the Bristol, Clifton Downs & Avonmouth service (being collectively known as the 'Clifton Downs' type). The brake thirds were given a driver's compartment and became driving trailers, whilst the others became intermediate trailers. Two low-roof brake composites were also altered to trailers, but for general service. The composites were amongst the few GWR trailers offering first class accommodation.

These trailer conversions were not renumbered into the trailer series. The driving trailers were, however, given new trailer diagrams which were included in the trailer diagram book, but the intermediate trailers were not issued with new diagrams. During 1913/4, the four-wheel trailers were withdrawn, leaving the trailer stock totalling 108 units.

From 1915 onwards, most of the SRMs were altered to conventional driving trailers; this involved an appreciable amount of work as the engine units were built into the bodies. The matchboarded SRMs were dealt with by early 1920, after which the conversion of the wood-panelled vehicles commenced; the process was not completed until 1935. Some SRMs were scrapped or sold without being altered.

With the grouping in the early 1920s, the GWR acquired a number of trailers from the amalgamated and absorbed companies in South Wales. These included some 'trailers' from the Taff Vale, which were really lightweight ordinary coaches designed to be hauled by the Taff's SRMs. A number of trailers were 'adopted' by the GWR, given standard control gear, and otherwise altered. Some of these were given GWR trailer diagrams and were numbered and indexed into the diagram book, but retained their hauled coaching stock numbers. Of the remaining absorbed trailers, some continued using their original control gear for a short while before being scrapped, or else it was removed, and the vehicles continued as hauled coaches.

In December 1928, the building of new trailers recommenced; a dozen 59 ft 6 in vehicles were constructed in the contemporary steel-panelled style. They were followed by another 22 in 1930–3 which were to the new length of 62 ft 8 in. These were the last conventional, open plan trailers built by the GWR.

The last SRM to be converted to a trailer was No. 64, in December 1935, when it became trailer No. 216. At this time the highest trailer number in use was 219 (rebuilt from SRM 76 in October 1935), and no more coaches were numbered into the trailer series until 1952.

In 1936, two suburban brake thirds were altered to trailers, and two brake composites were built as such (the former were practically new vehicles). They were 57 ft long, steel-panelled, with flat ends, with the passenger accommodation arranged in compartments. A further four very similar brake thirds were built as trailers in 1939. None of these coaches were numbered into the trailer series, although they were given diagrams in the trailer book. They were the last trailers to be built by the GWR.

In 1952, British Railways (Western Region) built a further 15 trailers of the traditional type, followed by 10 more in 1954. These were steel panelled, 63 ft long and had the usual deep bow ends. They could be distinguished from the genuine GWR article by having large windows to the passenger areas, with deep sliding windows at the top giving ventilation, instead of toplights. These were numbered in the GWR trailer series as W220W–W244W.

In 1953/4, eighteen compartment-type steel-panelled thirds were altered to trailers for the South Wales interval services. These were flat-ended coaches similar to the 1939 trailers, and like them were not numbered into the trailer series.

Finally there were trailers W245W–W256W, which were also conversions, this time from brake thirds; again, they were flat-ended steel-panelled compartment coaches. These conversions took place in 1955, and were the last.

Apart from the two 4-wheelers, and some absorbed trailers in the 1920s and the 30s, withdrawals of these coaches were confined to conversions until the 1950s. Most went during that decade, with a few surviving past 1960.

An unidentified 'Metro' 2–4–0T with a Diagram U trailer at Lostwithiel in the 1930s. E. E. BANKINS

Historical Overview

HALTES

The brand new 'Trumpers Crossing Halte (for Osterley Park)'. This was situated on the Brentford branch and served by auto trains to and from Southall. 'Trumpers' refers to Trumpers Way which still exists. The trailer, No. 4 of Diagram B1, is propelled by '517' class 0–4–2T No. 1165. No. 4 is in 'as built' condition. A classic example of a 'written off' loco being given an extended life as the motive power for an auto train instead of using a steam rail motor with a specialist power unit.
COLLECTION J. E. KITE

In developing their local services against competition from whatever source (especially tramways), the GWR exploited the ability of SRMs and trailers to serve simple stations with minimal facilities. Because these vehicles were not compartmented inside, and had a limited number of entrances for passengers, they were particularly suited to services where tickets were issued on the train. Most were also designed with retractable steps, so that passengers could board and alight from rail level.

This gave the GWR the opportunity to introduce auto trains to serve places which were convenient for potential passengers. If the numbers using the facility grew and improvements were required, then these could be effected. On the other hand, if the new stop was not well used, the costs of serving it would not be great, so the service could continue. If the worst came to the worst, and the service could not be sustained, then little capital expenditure would have been lost.

The GWR designated these 'basic' stopping places 'haltes', introducing them in the early years of the century especially for auto trains; the title was later amended to the more familiar 'halt'. In some places, they were called 'platform'. In its basic form, a halte consisted of a gravel surface, perhaps retained by wooden baulks at the lineside, adjacent to a level crossing or road bridge. More sophisticated haltes were sometimes provided, with a raised platform, usually of timber, and frequently with a basic shelter for passengers. The well-known GWR, corrugated iron 'pagoda' was commonly used for this purpose. Haltes were illuminated by one or two oil lamps, probably as much to show the driver where to stop as to provide illumination for passengers. It was usually the duty of the guard of the last train of the day to extinguish the lamps of haltes when the last passengers had gone.

The general concept of haltes was very successful, and the GWR opened a large number, especially before the Great War, continuing at a reduced rate thereafter where there appeared to be a suitable demand. For example, some twelve halts, as they were now usually called, were opened in 1934 alone. Although some did not survive changing circumstances, in particular the Depression and wartime, most survived for 50–60 years, until the Beeching 'Axe' fell on so many local services. Some do, however, still exist, although it is British Rail policy not to use the term 'halt'.

Sarsden Halt on the Banbury & Cheltenham line.

FRANK PACKER

Historical Overview

Pentrecourt Halt, with its pagoda shelter and the lightly constructed wooden platform, was on the Newcastle Emlyn branch. It is shown here on the day of opening, 1st February 1912.
LENS OF SUTTON

Waterloo, Great Western style, was a halt on the ex-B & M Machen–Caerphilly line at a point where the up and down lines were some distance apart. Waterloo Halt was on the up line; the approximate equivalent on the down line was Fountain Bridge Halt.
COLLECTION J. E. KITE

This picture again shows the simple nature of the construction of many halts with their rough timbers construction and corrugated iron shelters. The solitary oil lamps on each platform were positioned by the access steps up the side of the embankment. It is believed that the full name of this station was actually 'Old Hill High Street Halt' and it was on the Old Hill–Blowers Green branch in the West Midlands.
W. A. CAMWELL

Historical Overview

Poyle Halt for Stanwell Moor on the West Drayton–Staines branch reached from the overbridge. LENS OF SUTTON

Castle Bar Halt with No. 1426 propelling an A26 or A29 and a Diagram U trailer towards Ealing on the frosty morning of 18th December 1954.
B. Y. WILLIAMS

Teigl Halt on the Bala–Festiniog branch. COLLECTION R. C. RILEY

White Hart Halt was also on the Machen–Caerphilly line at a point where the up and down lines diverged and ran at different levels. This is the up line stopping point; the down line is apparent above the station nameboard. White Hart opened in May 1947 and closed in June 1952. Waterloo was the next halt towards Caerphilly (see page 7). L & GRP, CTY. DAVID & CHARLES

Historical Overview

DEFINITIONS AND TERMS

Trailer
Auto trailers are variously referred to as 'auto cars', 'auto trailers', 'trailers', 'control trailers' and 'autocoaches'. In this book, they will be referred to as 'trailers', and defined as 'a coach having apparatus to enable a suitably-equipped locomotive pushing it to be controlled by a driver in the trailer, or in another trailer coupled ahead of the coach in question.' Ordinary coaches will be referred to as 'hauled' coaches.

Auto fitted locomotives and Auto Engines
A locomotive equipped with the apparatus necessary to enable it to be controlled from a trailer will be referred to as 'auto-fitted' or as an 'auto engine' as appropriate.

Auto Train
A train consisting of one or more trailers, coupled to an auto-fitted locomotive or to an SRM, with the regulator control apparatus connected up and working, will be referred to as an 'auto train'. The alternative term used elsewhere is 'Motor train'.

Branch and Suburban trailers
The GWR tended to divide trailers into two types: 'Branch' trailers, which had luggage accommodation, and 'Suburban' which had no such provision. In the event, some trailers without a luggage compartment were normally run together with trailers containing one, as a regular pairing.

Driving and Intermediate trailers
The majority of GWR trailers were designed so that they could be driven from one end, with a compartment or vestibule reserved for the driver; GWR driving trailers could *only* be driven from one end. Where it is necessary to differentiate between types of trailer, these will be referred to as 'driving trailers'. The GWR owned a few 'intermediate trailers', which were not equipped with the driver's part of the control apparatus. These intermediate trailers were designed to run with a driving trailer ahead of them, and could not be used as the leading coach when being propelled.

Matchboarded style
The first trailer to be built (No. 1) was styled in a similar fashion to the first SRMs, having sides covered in vertical matchboarding below the waist. These will be referred to as 'matchboarded'. Until the early SRMs were converted to trailers, there was only the one vehicle in this style.

Wood-panelled style
The majority of purpose-built trailers (and many of the ex-SRM conversions) were in the 'wood panelled' style, as distinct from the later steel-clad coaches. These wood-panelled trailers had external mouldings covering the joints in the wood panelling sheets and were characterised by high-domed roofs and bodies.

It was common practice from the Great War onwards for all types of wooden-bodied coaches to have areas of the panelling sheeted over with metal where damage or deterioration had occurred. In some cases, this sheeting covered the toplights of a trailer which considerably altered its appearance.

Clerestory and low-roof coaches
There were a few early conversions from gangwayed clerestory coaches which also had wood panelled bodies, but their roof enables this style to be distinguished. There were also a number of conversions from local, non-corridor coaches built in the 1890s and earlier; these again had wooden-panelled bodies similar to the clerestory coaches, but without the clerestory roof. These coaches had 'turn-under ends', and a body height of 7 ft 3 in or 7 ft 6 in, hence the term 'low roof' trailers.

Steel-panelled trailers
Later designs had steel-panelled bodies from new, and will be so identified.

THE CONTROL APPARATUS

This photograph of No. 530 of the '517' class shows the trailer control apparatus quite clearly. To the left of the vacuum pipe hose is the bell circuit cable; to the right of the coupling hook is the TRG connector and universal joint; below the buffer beam is a 'T' shaped bracket with the TRG cranks and rodding. The main TRG rod under the locomotive is just visible in places. The photo seems to have been taken in Old Oak Common engine shed c.1906.   E. POUTEAU

The requirement that a locomotive could be controlled from the driving compartment of a coach it was pushing gave considerable scope to the Victorian and Edwardian inventor, and all sorts of apparatus were designed. These ranged from somewhat bizarre-looking arrangements of ropes and pulleys, sometimes attached to the chimney of the auto engine (eg TVR, LSWR), through mechanical rodding devices, to compressed air control (eg LBSCR, SR), usually employing Westinghouse air pumps (to the grave concern of the Westinghouse company which did not want the reliability of their air brakes to be compromised).

The GWR adopted a mechanical system to control the locomotive's regulator, a valve in the brake pipe to control the automatic vacuum brake, and a standard handbrake. These were supplemented by electric bell communication between the driver, the guard and the fireman. A whistle cord was provided to operate the whistle on the SRM or locomotive. This was found to be ineffective as a warning system when the trailer was being propelled, and a warning gong was fitted onto the front of driving trailers.

GWR driving trailers had a regulator in the driver's compartment pivoted above the end

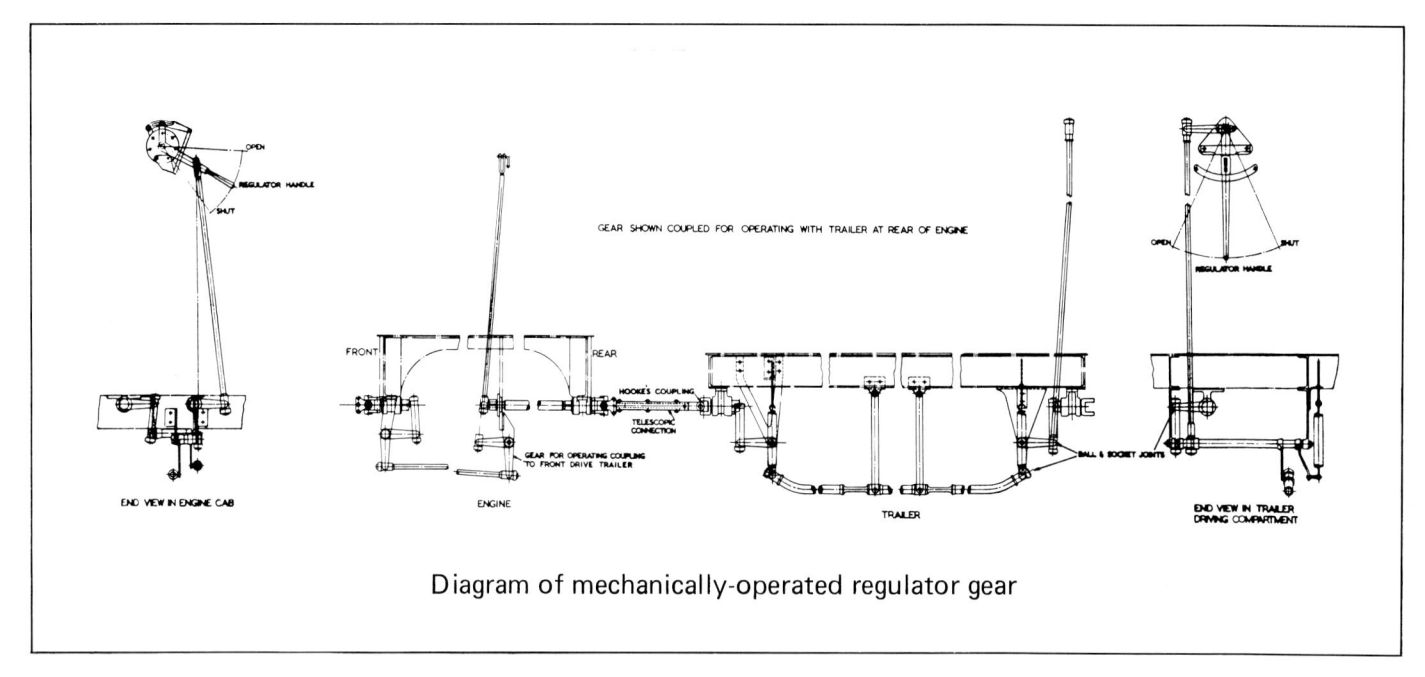

Diagram of mechanically-operated regulator gear

windows. The position of the pivot could be identified externally by a small triangular plate on the end of the trailer. From this, a system of levers and rodding led down underneath the coach, where a crank caused a stout rod running longitudinally underneath the coach to move; sometimes, this longitudinal control rod was divided into two lengths, coupled by levers. At the locomotive end of the trailer, some more cranks and levers caused a square-section rod to rotate. This rod had joints in it to compensate for curves negotiated by the train, and to enable the rod to be folded against the coach end when not in use.

When the trailer was coupled to an auto engine (or SRM), the square-section rod was fitted around an eye on the engine, and provided a longitudinally-sliding joint that allowed for compression of the buffers and drawgear. From this, further rods and levers transmitted the motion to the regulator on the footplate.

Notable features of the GWR system included:

1. A locomotive had the same eye fitting front and rear, so that a trailer could be attached at either end, with its driver's compartment facing away from the locomotive.
2. An SRM did not have a regulator coupling at the power unit end, so a trailer could only be coupled to the opposite end.
3. An intermediate trailer had a locomotive coupling at one end and a standard trailer type at the other, so as to provide a 'through regulator'.
4. It would appear that, until about 1910 driving trailers could only be used as the leading carriage of a train when propelled, as they were not fitted with a regulator coupling socket at the driver's end, and therefore could not act as an intermediate trailer. Thereafter it became standard practice for driving trailers to be fitted with a locomotive-type coupling eye at the driver's end. It was then possible to have two driving trailers facing the same way, coupled together, with the regulator connected right through to the locomotive. With this fitting at the driver's end, they were recorded as having 'through regulator gear' (TRG).
5. Because of the limitations of the mechanical control gear (principally due to friction and lost motion), the number of trailers that could be propelled by a locomotive with the TRG coupled up was limited to two.

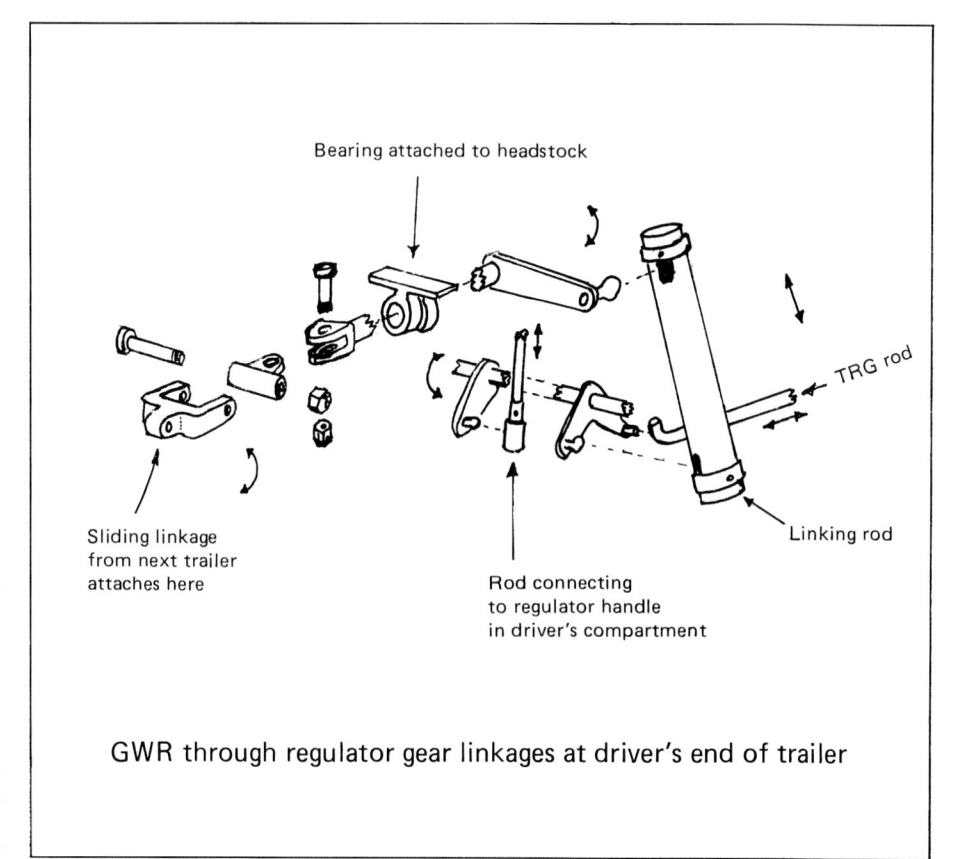

GWR through regulator gear linkages at driver's end of trailer

Historical Overview

TRG on an autocoach at Didcot (Great Western Society).

N. M. WRIGHT and AUTHOR

NUMBERS

The GWR, being a railway with a strong central organisation, had a tendency to classify everything it owned that moved, and much that did not. In the Victorian era at least, it also had an inclination to give each class its own separate numbering series. Trailers were originally numbered into the SRM series, but a separate sequence for trailers only had been set up by January 1905, when trailer No. 4 was built. Trailers Nos. 1–3 were originally numbered 53–5 in the SRM series, but they were rapidly renumbered into the trailer series, and SRMs carrying the released numbers 53–5 appeared between September and October 1905.

At the end of 1905, there were separate numbering series for steam rail motors, trailers, and for each class of coach. Thus, in December 1905, there was an SRM, a trailer, a third class coach, a second class, a composite, a first class coach, and a saloon, (a Royal) each numbered '1'. In addition, there was a No. 1 passenger brake van, a No. 1 horsebox, and other vehicles also carried the number although they were not coaching stock.

It was realised that this system created confusion, and in 1907 a single series was issued for all passenger coaching stock, except SRMs and trailers, each of which kept their own separate series.

The 'ordinary coach' series of numbers were organised on the basis of the coach class, and the renumbering was basically carried out by adding the appropriate number of thousands to the original coach number. Third class coaches kept their original numbers, and were allocated the range 1–4,999. Second class coaches had 5,000 added to their numbers and occupied the 5xxx range. Composites began at 6,000 and ran through to 7,999, whilst first class coaches had 8,000 added, and were renumbered into the 8xxx series.

In 1909, saloons, restaurant cars and sleeping cars were completely renumbered into the 9xxx series from the original numbering system their class of accommodation had placed them in.

Also in 1909, second class was abolished on the GWR, and this was followed by a renumbering of most second class coaches into vacant numbers within the third class series. At the grouping, the GWR found itself with some second class coaches once more, but the class (in South Wales) was quickly abolished.

Although most purpose-built GWR trailers were numbered in the trailer series, an appreciable proportion of the trailers converted from ordinary hauled coaches retained their original numbers. A few trailers from absorbed railways were renumbered into the GWR trailer series at the grouping, but most were allocated numbers in the hauled coach series.

It was a common practice from time to time for new coaches to be given the running numbers vacated by condemned coaches. However, this did not apply to the SRMs, as none were scrapped or converted until their building had ceased, and the practice was not applied to the trailer series either, though some absorbed trailers were given vacant numbers in the hauled coaching stock series.

DRAWINGS AND DIAGRAMS

The GWR had numerous drawings of its rolling stock. These ranged from 'general arrangement' drawings of the whole vehicle through sectional drawings to detail drawings which gave all the small dimensions of individual parts. There were also what are known as 'Diagrams'.

A general arrangement drawing, as its name suggests, sets out the general arrangements of the parts of a whole. The most common rolling stock drawings show vehicle bodies, normally a side elevation, sometimes with an end view and/or a floor plan. Occasionally sections or part sections were included; these often carried a significant amount of detail and dimensions. There were also general arrangement drawings of underframes, bogies and brakegear. In this century, GWR coach body general arrangement drawings did not usually give more than an outline of the underframe, bogies and wheels.

The GWR's 'diagram' drawings were normally based on body general arrangement drawings, and sometimes carried the same drawing numbers. Diagrams were simplified when compared with the parent GA drawing, and were to much smaller scales (the GA drawings could be up to 1 in:1 ft, or even 1½ in:1 ft, which made them quite large when a 70 ft coach was illustrated). Diagrams were issued in a range of sizes, the smallest being about 8 inches in length. At these small scales, it was not possible to give any dimensions of details, but they normally included overall measurements, and/or over-body dimensions, internal compartment sizes, the wheelbase, door spacing dimensions, the seating capacity and the tare weight of the coach. One side elevation, an end view, and a floor plan were the normal components of the drawing; sections were not shown. Diagrams were reproduced to varying scales to get the vehicle onto a standard page.

Diagrams were issued to parts of the organisation needing the information they contained, in particular the traffic department, the civil engineer and the signalling department. At some time around 1907–9, a selection of the coaching stock diagrams were grouped together into looseleaf binders for convenience. In order to index them, each diagram was illustrated on a separate page and was given a page number (this should not be confused with the diagram drawing number). The diagram index numbers (usually shortened to 'Diagram No.') were in alphanumeric code. There were separate coaching stock diagram books for ordinary hauled coaches, SRMs and trailers.

The hauled coaching stock book diagram numbers had a letter which indicated the class of coach, followed by a number to differentiate the different types of coach of that class. Thus, diagram S14 was the 14th diagram in the all-third class 4 or 6-wheel coach section. The diagram index letters and their meanings included:

A: First Class   8 wheel coaches
C: Third Class   ,, ,,
D: Brake Third   ,, ,,
E: Composite   ,, ,,
S: Third Class   4 and 6 wheel coaches

The steam railmotor diagram book was organised on different lines: the diagrams were numbered sequentially A, B, C (etc), and variations on the original design illustrated in diagrams were usually indicated by a suffix, e.g. Q1.

The trailer diagram book was similar to the SRM one, although trailer designs were more numerous, if only because of the conversions from SRMs. Consequentially, the number series ran from A to Z (with several '1' type diagrams being issued, e.g. K1, which sometimes illustrated the original design). The series then started again at A1, and eventually reached A44.

There are a few points to note regarding the diagram books.

1. Diagrams were in existence before the diagram books were first introduced.
2. Only the diagrams that were considered relevant and depicting current rolling stock with a reasonable life expectancy were normally included in the diagram book, and index.
3. A number of diagrams exist which were not included in the diagram books (or at least were not allocated an index number).
4. Not all coach variations were illustrated in separate diagrams.
5. Diagrams were not intended to be an 'as constructed' record of the coaches illustrated; a few

Historical Overview

of them are known to be less than 100% accurate.
6. A diagram could be altered to take into account alterations in the coaches illustrated; alternatively a new diagram, with a new diagram number, might be issued.
7. Whilst all trailers numbered in the trailer running number series were eventually given diagrams that were included and indexed in the trailer diagram book, the converse was not true. There were trailer diagrams included and indexed in the trailer diagram book of trailers which had (and kept) running numbers in the ordinary carriage numbering series. Further, some trailers for which no trailer diagram was issued at all were numbered in the ordinary carriage stock series.
8. It is uncommon to find stock absorbed from pre-grouping companies in any of the GWR rolling stock diagram books, but there were several examples in the trailer diagram book.

DETAILS

In this section, we shall look at the development of details on the trailers, from a general historical viewpoint.

WINDOWS

The first purpose-built trailers had large, fixed windows throughout, with ventilation provided by opening toplights (which were hinged at the bottom), arranged in pairs above each large fixed light. These hinged toplights were apparently inadequate as ventilators, particularly in smoking areas, and most of these trailers soon had some of their fixed lights replaced by strategically-placed pairs of droplights. Later examples had droplights from new.

Traditional coach building practice from the 19th century (and into the 20th) had the window glass retained in place by external mahogany bolection mouldings. Each window was normally dealt with separately, but you could often tell which droplights were not originals, because the replacements did not have bolection mouldings. From about 1909, a design was evolved for new construction, where the fixed light plus its toplights were treated as a single unit, and the whole assembly was fitted into the coach side with a single bolection moulding round it. The change was visually quite subtle, but noticeable.

The first two lots of trailers built between the wars (in 1929 and 1930) had steel-panelled bodies, but the windows still had wooden frames. These frames were let into the bodysides so they appeared flush, and as a result, the window glazing was recessed. The 1933-built trailers, however, had flush glazing (with the glass only *slightly* recessed). Later trailers were also built with this style of glazing, but the 1939 vehicles were really compartment coaches, and the windows did not have toplights. The BR-built ones also had flush glazing but differed in having sliding opening windows incorporated in the main window unit, instead of in the toplights.

No. 41 (Diagram N) with round section underframe truss bars, bolection mouldings around droplights (Diagram C did not have these mouldings) and 8ft American bogies. The white lines on the end windows and driver's droplight show well here. HMRS

Original pattern windows on trailers with bolection mouldings round each window.

Later pattern windows as used on Diagrams Q, R, T and U 70ft trailers. In this case the window and its toplights are one unit enclosed with a bolection moulding. The toplights are hinged and move together. J. H. RUSSELL

GREAT WESTERN RAILWAY.
JP.

Chief Mechanical Engineer's Department,

Divisional Locomotive, Carriage & Wagon Superintendent's W. Office,

Newton Abbot.

Telephone:
Newton Abbot 551 Three Lines.

Your reference:—

Tuesday 15th October 1935.

Please quote this reference:—
244135.

Dear Sir,

Reflection from windows of luggage compartments of trailers through engine cab windows.

Referring to mine of February 2nd last, according to the returns the following trailers still remain to have the tops of the end windows in the luggage compartment painted black to a depth of 17":—

Nos.	2.	3	6	7	8	10	12	14	15	16	17
	18.	23	28	34	35	49	51	60	61	67	69
	71.	72	75	76	78	87	91	(93	94)	95	102
	105	106	126	131	135	139	143	144	145	153	
	162	163	171	174	181	189	202	203	204	205	
	206	207									

It may be that some of these vehicles have already been dealt with and, if they are working in your district, I shall be glad if you will ascertain if this is so and the numbers, also arrange for any still outstanding to receive immediate attention, advising me.

Yours truly,

FOR A. W. H. CHRISTISON.

Mr. Whereat, Taunton.
Mr. Whereat, Exeter.
Mr. Lewis, Newton Abbot.
Mr. Saturley, Plymouth.
Mr. Tully, Truro.
Insp. Taylor, Newton Abbot.
L. G. Morris, Esq., Newton Abbot.

Historical Overview

END WINDOWS

Almost all GWR purpose-built trailers had three large windows at each end, the exceptions being the Diagram C intermediate trailers, Nos. 7 and 8 (which had wooden panels at the locomotive end of the carriages), and the 1939 batch (which had a single window at the driving end, and steel panelling at the non-driving end).

By the early 1930s, it was common practice to paint a narrow white line horizontally across the glass of the end windows at the driving end only. The purpose of this line was apparently to remind locomotive crews that there was glass there, particularly when coaling an adjacent locomotive. The line was painted on the inside of the windows and was positioned towards the top, the actual location varying between trailers. Some trailers carried a white horizontal vertical line on the driver's vestibule droplights.

It appears that reflections from the locomotive (luggage compartment) end windows of trailers caused problems for locomotive crews, because at the beginning of 1935 instructions were sent out that the top 17 in of these windows were to be painted black. This was presumably done on the outside of the glass, but photographs showing this feature are rare. A reminder, listing 55 trailers still to be dealt with, was sent out in October 1935; this implies that about 160 had been dealt with by that date.

Following this, it was evidently decided that no worthwhile purpose was served by having end windows in the locomotive-end of trailers, and these were plated over. Unfortunately, no modification dates have been recorded in the registers, but the process seems to have been largely complete by BR days. There were, of course, exceptions: No. 169 had not been dealt with by the late 1940s, and No. 6, together with No. 4303 (ex-

0-4-2 tank engine No. 835 at Kingham with Diagram A9 trailer, possibly No. 119, on 29th August 1919. This is one of the earliest photographs showing white lines on the trailer windows.
J. N. MASKELYNE

Diagram L No. 47 at Tetbury c.1952 in what appears to be brown and cream livery with a white line on the end windows and the driver's droplight. The height of these lines could vary.
ROYE ENGLAND

A maroon liveried A28 trailer with a prominent vertical white line on the driver's droplight, but no white lines on the end windows. 3rd September 1954.
S. RICKARD

Dean 8ft 6in bogie.

Special 9ft American bogie on trailer 57.

9ft olute spring bogie.

Collett 7ft bogie.

9ft coil spring bogie.

9ft 'heavy duty' bogie.

9ft 'fish-belly' bogie (this example was built by a contractor).

9ft pressed steel bogie.

Ordinary 9ft American bogie.

Historical Overview

Barry Railway) still had these end windows in BR days.

BOGIES

Trailer No. 1, like the earlier SRMs, had Dean 8 ft 6 in wheelbase suspension bogies. These can easily be identified by their external suspension links attached to the coach solebars. The clerestory conversions of the following year had both 8 ft 6 in and 10 ft wheelbase bogies to Dean's design.

The purpose-built trailers from No. 2 to those constructed at the end of 1905 had 8 ft or 9 ft plate-frame bolster bogies (Dean's units did not have bolsters). Identifying features of these bogies were the volute springs over the axleboxes, and the nests of volute springs on the bolsters. The springs over the axleboxes could not be seen, but were protected by curved metal plates.

Unfortunately, these volute spring bogies gave an unsatisfactory ride, and they were quickly changed; the replacements were very similar in appearance, but had volute springs in place of coil. Some trailers were built with the 9 ft coil spring version in 1906, and six built by the Bristol Carriage & Wagon Co. in 1906 had that company's plate-frame bogies; known officially as 'Bristol' or 'Gloucester', depending on the contractor that supplied the coaches concerned, they were most generally known as 'fishbelly' bogies because of the shape of their frames. The GWR produced a similar-looking bolster bogie from 1910, which was also known as the 9 ft light duty bogie.

From 1906, however, the coil spring bogies were mostly supplanted (on new coaches) by 9 ft wheelbase 'American' bogies, so called because the type was in common use in the USA. Officially, however, they were described as coil and elliptical spring bogies with equalising beams. They were particularly notable by having no springs above the axleboxes, a relatively light bogie frame, and sprung equalising beams between the axleboxes. There were both 8 and 9 ft American bogies in common use, but the 9 ft type was normally favoured for trailers. It became policy in the 1920s to replace the coil spring bogies, and the 9 ft American bogies were often used as a substitute, although by then they were no longer usually employed on new stock.

The GWR built no more new trailers between 1913 and 1929, but quite a number of conversions were made, including low-roof stock which had both 8 ft 6 in and 6 ft 4 in wheelbase versions of Dean's suspension bogies.

In the years leading up to 1935, most of the SRMs were altered to trailers. This gave rise to some problems, as they only had one conventional coach bogie each; the other was part of the power unit, and was of course unsuitable for conversion. The result was that only about half of them retained the same carrying bogies when converted to trailers. Replacement bogies, as far as is known, are recorded under details of the trailers later, but the 9 ft American, the 7 ft Collett heavy duty and the 9 ft heavy duty types were all used.

The 1929 and 1930-built trailers all had Collett 7 ft wheelbase bogies, but the 9 ft heavy duty units were fitted to the 1933-built examples. The 1939 and BR-built examples had the GWR pressed-steel 9 ft wheelbase bogie.

WARNING DEVICES

The drivers of the early auto trains were able to operate the engine whistle from their compartment in the leading trailer using a connecting cord which ran through the handrail along the inside of the coach, and was connected to the loco. This cord emerged from the non-driving end of the trailer immediately below the roof, just to the left of centre when viewed from the loco.

At the driving end of the trailer, the cord emerged to the right of centre, just above the regulator bearing plate. This was a later adaptation, made at the same time as the fitting of through regulator gear to the trailer; there would have been no requirement for a cord at the driving end until the coach could act as an intermediate trailer.

The use of the locomotive whistle to warn platelayers and others of the approach of the auto train proved unsatisfactory, as the sound was too easily masked by lineside features. After all, the whistle was over 150 ft behind the front of the train when two 70 ft trailers were being propelled. In due course, therefore, the use of the engine whistle was supplemented by an external, pedal-operated gong at the driving end of trailers. The only dates known for the fitting of these are to trailers Nos 1 and 72 in June 1927 and Sep-

Fair Rosamund – perhaps the most famous auto engine of them all. The whistle cord can be seen between the cab and the trailer. This photograph was taken about 1930 at Oxford. No. 1473 was the regular Woodstock branch engine until its withdrawal in 1935.
COLLECTION R. S. CARPENTER

The driver's cab of No. 231, preserved at Didcot, showing the pedal and cable which operates the warning gong. AUTHOR

tember 1925 respectively. Slip coaches were also given gongs instead of their warning horns from about this time.

Most gongs were placed above the driver's window (the left-hand pane, when facing the front of the trailer), with the right-hand edge of the gong approximately in line with the right-hand edge of that window. There were, of course, exceptions. For example, trailer No. 4 (which normally ran as an intermediate trailer) had a gangway connector at the driver's end; consequently, the gong was placed *below* the driver's window.

Most of the clerestory trailer conversions also had the gong fitted below the right-hand driving end windows, there being no room above, because of the roof profile. On the other hand, the clerestory conversions for the Glyncorrwg branch had the gongs below the left hand window ...!

The low-roof 'Clifton Downs' driving trailer conversions had the gongs below the left-hand end windows, rather like No. 4, as did the ex-TVR trailer GWR No. 2521.

The GWR conversions from steel-panelled compartment stock (and those built in the same style) had flat ends with a single, large window for the driver. In these cases the gong was below the waist, a little to the left of centre.

SANDBOXES

Some trailers were equipped with sandboxes at the driving end from about 1913, possibly as an experiment. However, from the mid 1920s it seems to have become policy to fit sandboxes to trailers at the driving end following criticism from an Inspecting Officer after an accident at Snow Hill, Birmingham (see Appendix*). The sandboxes were attached to the bogie frame, and the pipe curved down to the rail just ahead of the first wheelset. Unfortunately, this is one of the subjects in which official records are incomplete. Curiously, some intermediate trailers are recorded as being fitted with sand apparatus.

Commencing with the 1928/9 batch of trailers, new driving vehicles were fitted with sanding gear as standard.

BLUE AXLEBOXES

On Collett's instructions, from mid-1927, carriage stock axleboxes were to be painted blue; this was to indicate modified axleboxes, and had the effect of brightening-up the lower regions of coaching stock so treated. Not all trailers are recorded with their axleboxes painted blue.

ELECTRICAL COMMUNICATION APPARATUS

From the introduction of trailers, the driver was able to communicate with both the fireman (on the footplate) and the guard by means of an electrically-operated bell circuit. The cable for this appeared to be armoured,

*See Part 2.

and emerged from the bottom of the trailer body, just above and to the left of the right-hand buffer (viewed from the locomotive). The cable terminated in a connector, and seems to have simply hung down from the coach when not in use.

After the fitting of TRG to trailers, it was necessary to fit a similar cable to the driving end of the coach. This one was in the mirror image position, that is, just above and to the right of the left-hand buffer of the trailer (when facing the end of the vehicle). The cable at this end of the coach had a similar fitting to that on locomotives.

With the fitting of the GWR's automatic train control system to trailers (during the 1940s, in most cases), the electric cabling was altered to a twin cable system with a different

---

GREAT WESTERN RAILWAY.

NOTICE TO DRIVERS AND FIREMEN.

INSTRUCTIONS TO BE OBSERVED BY DRIVERS AND FIREMEN IN WORKING RAIL MOTORS OR AUTO TRAINS WHEN THE ENGINEMAN IS DRIVING FROM THE VESTIBULE END AND THE FIREMAN REMAINS ON THE FOOTPLATE.

(1) It is essential that there should be a proper understanding between the driver and fireman as to the working of the engine and the following General Instructions should always be observed.

(2) The driver should satisfy himself that the fireman properly understands the working of the reversing gear, vacuum brake, lubricator and sanding gear, and the management of the fire and boiler.

(3) On receipt of a signal to start from the guard, the driver must sound the whistle which the fireman must acknowledge, and the driver must not start until the fireman has acknowledged his signal. Before acknowledging the driver's signal the fireman must satisfy himself that the brake is off and that the reversing lever is in the correct position.

(4) When approaching signals or terminal stations, the fireman must be on the look out and be prepared to act in case of emergency from any cause.

(5) If a fireman discovers any fault in the working of the engine he must inform the driver at the first stopping place, but if the fault is such that it is necessary to stop before reaching the stopping place the fireman must call attention of the driver by applying the vacuum brake.

(6) The fireman must not leave the footplate or the engine room without the consent of the driver.

(7) The following is the code of electric bell signals between the driver and fireman and guard:—

1 ring	... ...	To start.
2 rings	... ...	To stop.
3 rings	... ...	Fireman to blow brake off.

C. B. COLLETT.

CHIEF MECHANICAL ENGINEER'S OFFICE,
SWINDON.
October 1929.
Circular No. 4940.

A close-up of the driving end of No. 37 (Diagram N) c.1935 showing bell circuit cable hanging down next to the tail lamp. This is the pre-ATC arrangement.
R. BROOKMAN

GREAT WESTERN RAILWAY.

O. B. COLLETT,
Chief Mechanical Engineer.

Telegrams: LOCO. SWINDON.
Telephone: SWINDON 711: Ext.........

Chief Mechanical Engineer's Department,
SWINDON, WILTS.
July 28th 1936.

Your reference:— Circular No. 5720.

Please quote this reference:— 17719
1

Dear Sir,

Revised General Appendix.
Auto-Car Instructions.

Attention is directed to the amended code of bell signals to be used in connection with the working of Auto-trains shewn on page 131 of the revised General Appendix.

It is desired that the amended code should be adopted on and from the 1st proximo, concurrently with the new appendix, and I shall be glad if you will instruct your staff accordingly.

Will you please arrange to remove, before Saturday next, the cast-iron plates shewing the existing code from the cabs of Auto engines and from the drivers and guards compartments of all trailers and other vehicles concerned, and return them to Stores as scrap.

It is not intended to perpetuate these plates, but in order to call attention to the altered code I am sending you under separate cover a supply of gummed paper slips to be used immediately in temporary replacement.

Please advise me when the matter is in order.

Yours truly,

C.B. Collett

P.S. This alteration is in order to conform with the general practice — Rule 117.

1 Ring,   Start

2 Rings, Brakes off

3 Rings, Stop

Historical Overview

pattern of connectors. (One cable carried the communication signal, the other the ATC circuit.) The cables now no longer hang down from the ends of the trailer, but the connector fitted into a socket just above the buffer beam, to the right of centre at the non-driving end and to the left at the driving end of the trailer. There would have been some problems during the changeover period, and some trailers retained the old system even fitted with the new. These are indicated in the records as having 'dual bells' ATC circuits.

CHAIN COMMUNICATION APPARATUS

During the early 1900s, the GWR introduced into its coaching stock the present system of emergency signalling, by which passengers could inform the train crew that something was amiss by pulling an internal chain; this was connected to the automatic vacuum brake system, and thus made a partial brake application. However, the apparatus was not fitted to trailers until the late 1920s or early 1930s. Presumably the GWR thought it unnecessary in an open coach in which the guard (often) rode. The apparatus appears to have been removed from the clerestory coaches as they were being converted to trailers (in 1905), but it was refitted to them in the 1920s and 1930s.

The presence of the chain communication apparatus was revealed by the 'tell-tales' and associated rodding at one end of the coach. The apparatus consisted of a rod system across the coach with the 'tell-tale' discs at the outer ends.

When the chain was pulled, the rod was rotated through 90°, the discs clearly showing the coach in which the 'emergency' occurred. The rods were connected to a valve enclosed in a small rectangular box, which in turn was connected to the vacuum system by means of a vertical pipe that ran to the main vacuum pipe near to where the connector hose was fitted. The exact arrangements varied between coaches, depending on the arrangement of the vacuum pipe. In some cases a 'swan's neck' vacuum pipe arrangement was used, and only a short vertical pipe was necessary; in others, the vacuum hose simply hung from the solebar, and the pipe to the chain apparatus had to descend right to the coach underframe. The rodding across the end of the coach was normally in the GWR's standard five-part arrangement, with a raised central section that could clear a gangway connector, should one be fitted in due course. The 'Clifton Downs' conversions, being compartment coaches, had the alternative 'straight across' arrangement which was retained after their conversion to trailers.

The end at which the external apparatus was fitted also varied; normally it was at the non-driving end, or, in the case of an intermediate trailer, the locomotive end. However, a number of trailers had the equipment at the

Trailer 192 at Ashburton. HUGH BALLANTYNE

Trailer 56 of Diagram L in BR plain maroon, showing the communication alarm mechanism. Note how the rodding is raised at the centre and the pipe comes down to the 'swan neck'.
AUTHOR'S COLLECTION

Trailer 244 at Ashburton in 1956 showing the final arrangement of the alarm gear.
AUTHOR'S COLLECTION

Left: Diagram L No. 44 in BR plain maroon, 1951-style, showing the traditional position for the warning gong. On Diagram L trailers the chain alarm apparatus was at the luggage end. Centre: The driving end of a Diagram U trailer in BR maroon and cream. Note how the chain alarm rodding is raised over the central window and a pipe leads down from the 'box' to the right of the gong to the vacuum pipe. Right. No. 89 at Woodstock. Diagrams U and T trailers were unusual in having the alarm apparatus at the driver's end. Having a boarded-up window, this example, No. 89, shows the pipework fairly clearly. No. 183 (below) had a low level vacuum pipe and a longer pipe from the alarm apparatus.

AUTHOR'S COLLECTION, R. H. G. SIMPSON and DR. G. D. PARKES

driving (outer) end of the coach, often, but not exclusively, on those with gangway connectors.

The record of the fitting of chain communication apparatus to trailers is incomplete (it does not seem to have been recorded at all in the case of hauled coaches).

SMOKING/NON-SMOKING ACCOMMODATION

Most trailers had their passenger accommodation divided into two or three areas by partitions across the coach. Up until 1928, one of the smaller saloons was usually allocated to smokers (as usual with the GWR, there was at least one exception!). Starting in that year, the rules were changed, and the larger (or the largest) saloon was allocated to smokers instead.

Also dating from this time was the practice whereby a pair of gangwayed trailers were semi-permanently coupled together, one of them being allocated to smokers, and the other to non-smokers.

The 'Clifton Downs' trailers, which were compartment stock, originally had two smoking compartments in the driving brake thirds, and two third class compartments plus one first class for smokers in the intermediate composite trailers. By the end of the second war, the arrangement seems to have been changed to one non-smoking compartment in the driving trailers, and two (or possibly three) in the intermediate trailers.

The 1939 trailers had one non-smoking out of five compartments in the driving brake thirds, and one first class plus one third class non-smoking compartment out of two first and four thirds in the composite vehicles.

Smoking compartments were indicated by a SMOKING sign, originally transfers on the window glass, with non-smoking compartments being unmarked. Later stick-on labels were used. Sometimes these were supplied by tobacco companies and had advertising slogans facing the interior of the coach. By about 1930, the triangular 'NO SMOKING' signs had appeared on the latter.

SEATING

As trailers were mostly 'open coaches' there was considerable scope for varied arrangements of seating. Typically, a GWR-built trailer would have at least three distinct seating areas; these would be of two types of seats, and often there would be partitions between at least two of them. The seating on most GWR-designed trailers was upholstered, which was not always the case in the third class accommodation in some of the absorbed vehicles. The following types were found:

Longitudinal bench seats
These were ordinary bench seats with low backs placed along the trailer sides, leaving a wide, central 'gangway' between them along the coach.

Seating bays
This arrangement provided seating arranged across the trailer; one pair of seats were positioned to face another pair, forming a seating bay on one side of the central gangway. Another seating bay would be provided in

Driving end detail of auto trailer No. 183 at Ealing Broadway in 1933.
H. F. WHEELLER

Historical Overview

the same position on the other side of the gangway. These seats all had fixed backs.

Walkover seats
This was a variation on the seating bay arrangement. In this case, the seats had pivoted backs that could be swung over the seat base, allowing the passenger to face the direction of travel (or the opposite) by simply pushing the backs to the alternate position. They were popular with some tramways where, at the terminus, the conductor would walk through the vehicle and push all the seat backs over before the start of the return journey.

In the GWR trailers, these seats were arranged in pairs to give 2+2 seating either side of the central gangway, but the seat the passengers 'faced' did not necessarily face them.

Note that:-
1. The end pairs of seats against a partition or the end of longitudinal bench seats had fixed backs, but to avoid confusion they will be regarded as walkover seats if they faced other walkover seats, instead of forming part of a normal seating bay.
2. Walkover seats can be identified on diagrams because the intermediate seats were not arranged back-to-back with the adjacent seats to form bays.

Normal seating bays

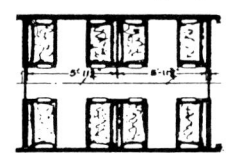

Walkover seating bays

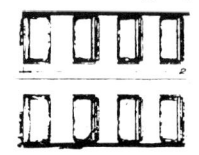

In the example, there are four sets of walkover seats (counting along the coach). Unlike normal seating bays, there could be an odd number of sets, and if the space available was sufficient, there could be more walkover seats than seating bays. The GWR did not use half-bays.

Workmen's coaches
It was common practice, particularly in South Wales, to provide 'workmen's' coaches for miners and steel workers. These vehicles had wooden seats (without upholstery), normally with slats along the seating; this design enabled the seat to be easily cleaned. The GWR inherited some trailers from the TVR with this type of seating in the third class areas.

No. 48
70ft trailer No.48 (of Diagram O) was an experimental high-capacity design, which had wooden seats arranged centrally across the trailer, with narrow gangways at the sides. In this case, the seats were of wood sheeting rather than slats. For further details, consult the section on that trailer.

Compartment seating
Compartment-type trailers had standard coach seating. Where first class accommodation was provided, the seats had upholstered arm rests to each seat.

CARRIAGE LIGHTING
The vast majority of GWR-built trailers were gas lit. The first vehicles were illuminated by flat flame burners, but from 1906 the more efficient incandescent burners were used; the earlier trailers were eventually converted to this later form of lighting. The clerestory trailers also had flat frame burners, but these were changed to incandescent soon after conversion into trailers. The two four-wheel trailers never received incandescent burners. Those SRMs that were built with flat flame burners all seem to have been altered to incandescent units before they were rebuilt to trailers.

Coaches with flat flame burners could be distinguished from those with incandescent lamps because the former had one gas supply pipe to each lamp, whilst the latter had two: one for the pilot light (which was kept burning more or less continuously), and a second for the main gas supply.

A Diagram N trailer in BR plain maroon at Coryton Halt in May 1954. This picture shows the twin pipes along the roof, serving the gas lamps. COLLECTION R. S. CARPENTER

No. 1421 with the Cowbridge branch train c.1950, showing the gas piping on the roof. The trailer is in newly applied BR crimson and cream livery. W. A. CAMWELL

At the grouping, the GWR acquired a number of trailers with electric lighting from the ADR, the Barry Railway and the Rhymney Railway; these had Stone's system of lighting. The GWR had a number of carriages with this type of electric lighting, but its standard was Lucas-Leitner.

GWR trailers built from 1929 were electrically-lit on the Lucas-Leitner system, and a number of older trailers were altered from gas lighting to electric at this period. Most of these were GWR-built, many of which were used in the Plymouth area, but some ex-TVR trailers were also given electric lighting.

AUTOMATIC TRAIN CONTROL

The GWR was, quite rightly, very proud of its 'Automatic Train Control' system (ATC). This comprised a metal ramp laid between the rails, which was contacted by a shoe on a locomotive passing over it. If the signal controlling the ramp was at caution or danger, an electric circuit on the locomotive was broken, and an electromagnet released a lever which operated a valve in the vacuum brake, allowing air to enter the vacuum pipe and to partially apply the brakes. The air entering the system did so via a siren, thus giving the driver an audible warning. He had to cancel this, or the train would stop. If the signal was at 'All Right', a current in the ramp from a battery maintained the current in the electromagnet's circuit, and the brakes remained off. Instead, a bell was rung to let the driver know that the next signal was 'off'.

A four-coach auto train fitted with ATC could have up to five sets of the apparatus; one in each of four trailer driving compartments, as well as that on the engine. Of these, only that in the leading driving compartment (when propelled) and on the engine would be attended by someone competent to cancel a warning indication. The problem was, therefore, to ensure that only one of the instruments was 'alive' at any one time.

In November 1934, two trailers, Nos.179 (of Diagram A28) and No.194 (of Diagram A30), together with Collett 0–4–2T No.4844, were fitted with a modified form of the standard ATC apparatus. In this arrangement, only the loco had the pick-up shoe, and the apparatus in the trailers was connected electrically to that in the loco by cables. Both ends of the trailers had cables and connectors, so that two trailers could be pushed by the loco, with only the instrument in the front trailer in use. The operating voltage was increased from 4 to 8 volts by using an additional battery on the loco, and the ATC apparatus' coils had to be modified to work at the higher voltage.

In order that only one of the instruments on the train was 'alive' at any one time, 'locks' were fitted, into which a large steel 'key' could be inserted. This brought the ATC into use, and operated the vacuum valve on the trailers. If the key was not inserted properly, the vacuum gauge would not work for the brake test, and the only way the vacuum brake could be controlled was by using the emergency brake setter. On the locomotive, the key operated a lock on the ejector, which was arranged so that the ejector could only be used to blow up a vacuum if the key was inserted in the lock on the engine or in a trailer. The use of this 'ATC key' was seen as analogous to the use of a token in a single-line working.

Comprehensive tests were carried out on the main line between Didcot, Swindon and Chippenham, and the apparatus was found to work satisfactorily. In May 1935, the train was transferred to Reading to cover the Reading 'B' 2-car auto set working. This rather complicated diagram involved trips between Reading, Basingstoke, Didcot, Marlow and Henley, and covered nearly 1,200 miles each week.

In 1935, it was estimated that the cost of fitting a trailer with ATC was £55, and a locomotive with the new apparatus, £42. Loco No.4847 was also given the apparatus, so that it could be used in place of 4844 when necessary.

The apparatus continued to function satisfactorily, but it was considered that it was rather expensive. In March 1938, therefore, it was replaced by equipment based on that used in the GWR diesel railcars which, although they could not work in multiple, did have a driver's cab at each end of the unit. The principal difference was that the key and its 'lock' were replaced by a double pole electric switch, the spindle of which operated the vacuum valve, as before. On the engines, the key and lock were dispensed with altogether, so the ATC was continuously 'active', and the fireman had to cancel any warning signals. If the driver forgot to switch the ATC out of use when the auto train reversed, he could drive the train normally until an adverse signal was encountered. Then the ATC he had forgotten would bring the train to a standstill, and he would find that he could not create a vacuum until he had walked to the back of the train and switched the ATC out. Drivers did not often forget!

The experimental train retained separate cables and two-way couplers for both the ATC circuit and the communication bell circuits. However, it was found possible to use a single four-way electrical coupling instead, and to integrate the bell circuit so that it was operated off the loco's ATC batteries, thus obviating the need for a separate battery to be carried on each trailer. This arrangement cost more, as it included rewiring the bell circuits. In June 1939, costs were estimated as:

Bell wiring, Connectors	Existing, 2 way connectors	New, 4 way connectors
Manufacture trailer apparatus	£12/10/0	£12/10/0
Install & wire up trailer	£15/10/0	£17/ 0/0
TOTAL per trailer	£28/ 0/0	£29/10/0
Modify existing loco apparatus	£ 2/ 0/0	£ 2/ 0/0
Wire up loco	£10/ 0/0	£14/15/0
Additional 4v 3 cell battery	£ 7/ 0/0	£ 7/ 0/0
TOTAL per locomotive	£19/ 0/0	£23/15/0

Historical Overview

The auto train with the experimental ATC system. The second cable for the ATC is visible on the end of trailer No. 194.
NATIONAL RAILWAY MUSEUM

The revised apparatus worked satisfactorily, and it was decided to fit ATC apparatus to auto trains that normally used main lines equipped with the system. At this time, the Running Department estimated that only 69 trailers, formed into 34 trains, were used mainly on lines equipped with ATC. The Drawing Office recommended that 100 trailers and 68 auto engines should be equipped with ATC, at a cost of £4,092, or £4,565 if the integrated cabling was used. In practice, the Locomotive Committee was asked to approve the equipping of 60 auto engines (£1,425) and 90 trailers (£2,655), at a total cost of £4,080, using the integrated wiring. Approval was given. New Work Order 5269 was issued to cover this work on 7th July 1939, and according to the order form, the work was completed by 29th July 1941; however, a Drawing Office memorandum dated 12th February 1943 stated that six of the trailers still had to receive attention.

ATC was fitted as the trailers came to the works for repair, but only the bell circuits were given (two-way) connectors. When the whole train had been equipped with ATC, the local C & W Department out-station fitted the new four-way ATC + bell couplers instead, thus bringing the ATC into use.

Some confusion seems to have arisen, because the Carriage Works were issued with the original list of 100 trailers, and in January 1941 were working to it!

Amongst the original list of trailers to be given ATC were Nos.7, 8, 3276 and 3390, all of which were intermediate trailers, and never carried a driver. Nos.3276 and 3390 received through wiring only, and presumably the other two did as well.

Some Southall drivers soon complained via their union, ASLEF, that auto trains were frequently running with their communication bells inoperative, because trailers with four-way electric couplers were being attached to trailers with the old two-way system.

To try and reduce this problem, the Drawing Office recommended (in January 1941) that the additional 10 trailers and 4 engines in the original submission should be fitted with ATC. They also pointed out that 27 trailers were kept as spares, available to replace any others sent to Swindon for overhaul, and recommended that these 27 should be provided with both four-pin and two-pin electric couplers and circuits, but not the actual ATC apparatus, so that they could run between a locomotive and any other trailer. The problem of non-ATC fitted trailers being in the same train as an ATC-fitted loco (or vice versa) does not seem to have been addressed. This wiring is recorded in the register as 'Dual bells'.

In March 1941, it was suggested that, to save the guard worrying about which bell circuit was in use on the 'dual-bells' fitted spare trailers, the bell pushes should operate switches on *both* circuits. The cost of the

Trailer driving cab No. 231 at the Great Western Society, Didcot, showing the ATC instrument with bell, handbrake and vacuum brake setter.
AUTHOR

Conduits for ATC wiring are visible on No. 4842. LENS OF SUTTON

additional 4 conductor wiring was estimated at £17/10/0 per trailer, plus £2/5/– for each bell push. The Locomotive Committee agreed (in May 1941) to the spare trailers being fitted with the additional circuits, at an estimated cost of £540 (an average cost of £20). New Work Order 7638 was issued to cover the task; 16 trailers had been dealt with by February 1943, but it took until 10th October 1946 for them all to be done. These trailers are recorded in the register as having 'Dual Bells'. Many of the entries are dated February 1945, which seems to have been the date on which the records clerk was informed.

However, the provision of the 'dual bells' wiring on the spare trailers failed to solve the problem of inoperative bell circuits, as the Running Department were still unable to fulfil their undertaking not to mix incompatible trailers in the same train. Further complaints ensued from the Union, and the GWR General Manager gave approval, on 5th August 1943, to the fitting of all auto-engines and trailers with ATC, at an estimated cost of £9,000.

Unfortunately, this was not the end of the matter, as it transpired that the number of trailers to be dealt with had been understated by an estimated 34 (those with hauled stock running numbers had probably been forgotten), and the total cost should have been £10,500. In January 1944, Mr Hawksworth agreed that work should proceed, and approval for the remaining 34 should be

The front of Diagram U trailer No. 84 at Ross-on-Wye on 1st July 1951. No. 84 is in brown and cream with two waist lines, and is fitted with 'dual bells' ATC. It has the old single cable and the new pattern twin cable which appear above the left-hand buffer. The chain communication apparatus is also visible behind and below the gong. ROYE ENGLAND

sought when the work on the remainder was nearing completion.

It is questionable if the costs were correct even at this stage, as the 27 'spare' trailers being fitted with the dual bells circuitry were not included in the numbers to be fitted with ATC. Further, the numbers of trailers in service was quoted as 248 when it should have been 250, and only 12 intermediate trailers were identified, whereas the correct number was between 14 and 16 (it is not now possible to be more definite). As Mr G. E. Scholes of the Drawing Office said in a paper dated 1943, '... some difficulty was experienced in compiling the portion showing trailers and autocars...'

In 1944, the GWR were investigating two versions of 'simplified' ATC apparatus, which did away with the need for batteries to be carried on the locomotive. One of these had been developed as far as the production of drawings showing how it applied to auto trains, but this system was rejected, because batteries would still have had to be carried on the auto engine for the bell circuits and, more importantly, a three wire connecting cable was to be used, once again raising questions of compatibility.

The latest fitting of ATC to an existing trailer recorded in the registers is 1950. The equipping of the spare trailers with ATC is not recorded, although later photographs of some show only the four-way connector, so they may have received the apparatus.

Historical Overview

A new 54XX 0−6−0T loco showing the bell cable looped around the vacuum pipe and the TRG below the coupling hook.

NATIONAL RAILWAY MUSEUM

This type of retractable steps was only used on trailer No. 1 and some of the early SRMs. The treads sloped downwards unless the steps were fully 'out'. When the SRMs with these steps were converted to trailers, they were given the later pattern. The drawings on the opposite page show the later type of retractable steps which were used on the later SRMs and all trailers except No. 1. In this design the treads always remained horizontal.

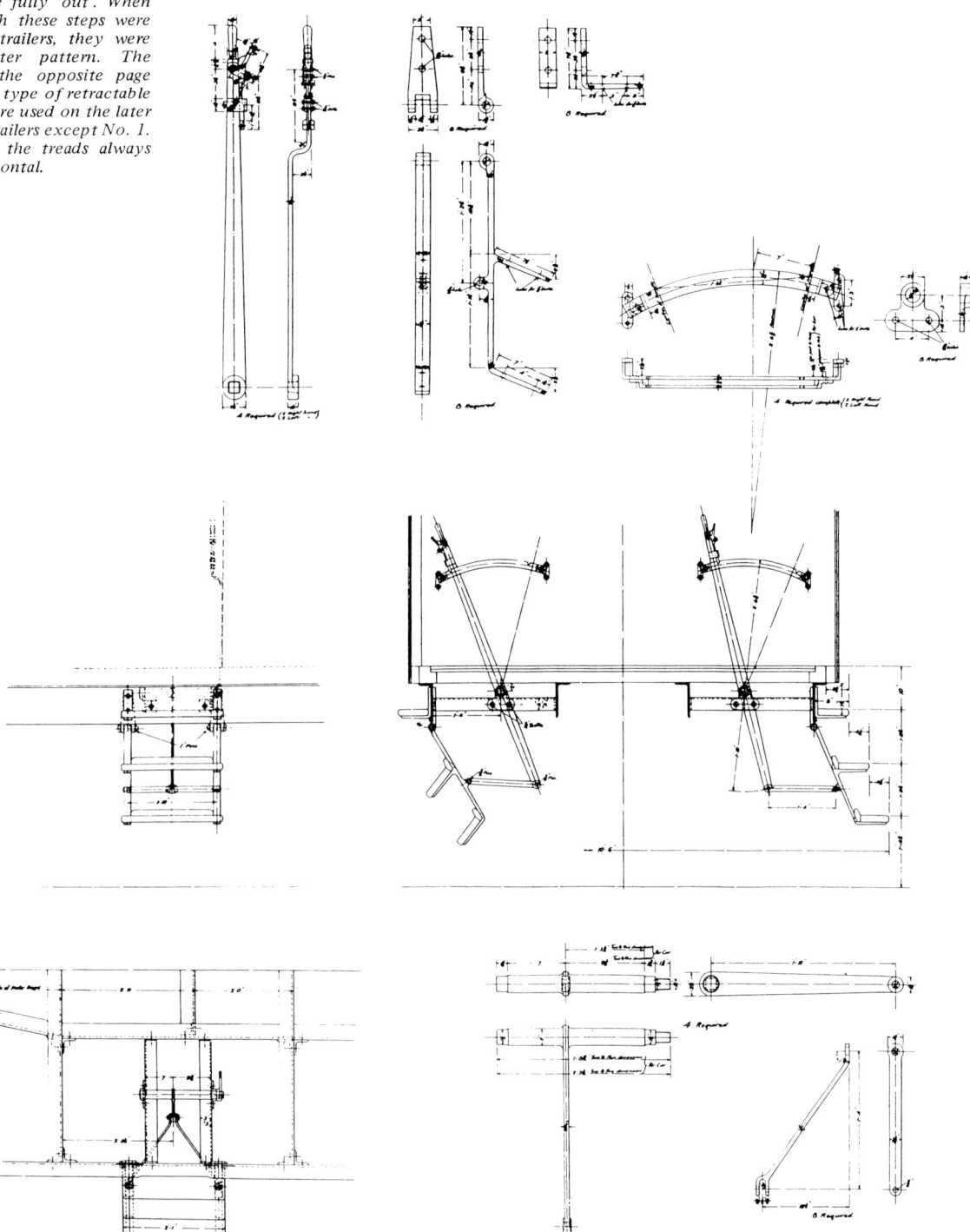

G.W.R. SWINDON

ARRANGEMENT & DETAILS OF STEPS

STEAM MOTOR CARS LOT 1063

AUGUST 1904

Nº 25650

LOT 1108

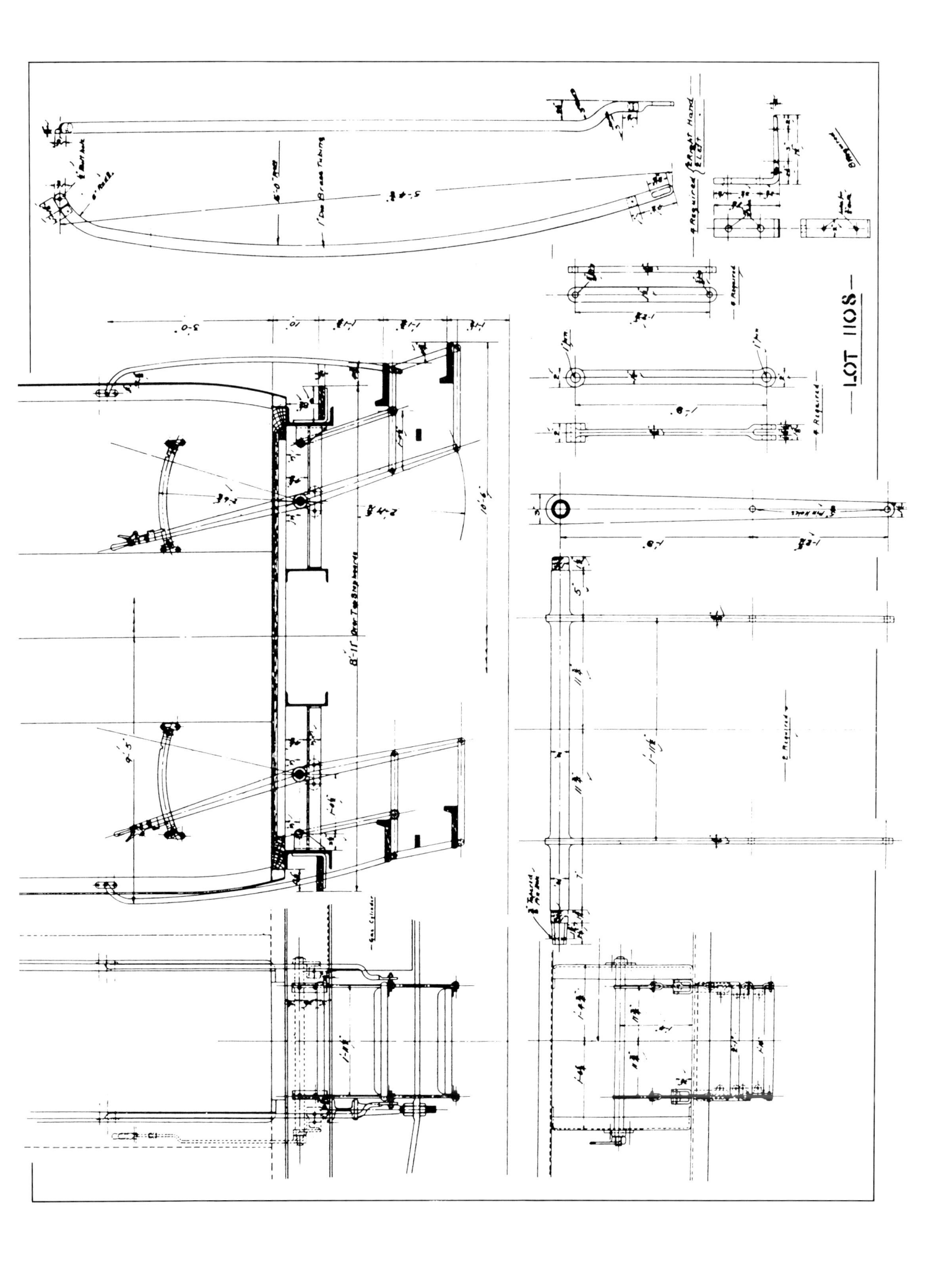

DOORS

There appear to have been several types of door fitted to trailers. The standard size for hauled stock with outwardly-opening doors had a width of 2 ft. Traditionally, these doors conformed to the bodyside profile and were fitted flush with the body side. On trailers, things were somewhat different; it was normal practice for trailer vestibule doors to open inwards because of the rectractable steps below them. These sometimes provided the only passenger access to the trailer, and were often wider than the hauled stock standard; on one design (Diagram S) the measurement is given as a 2 ft 7½ in wide door fitting into a 2 ft 8 in wide opening. An inward-opening door could usually be identified externally, because it had to clear the floor inside the coach and so the bottom of the door did not quite reach the bottom of the trailer bodyside. It was normal practice for inwardly-opening doors on trailers to be flat, and slightly recessed into the bodyside.

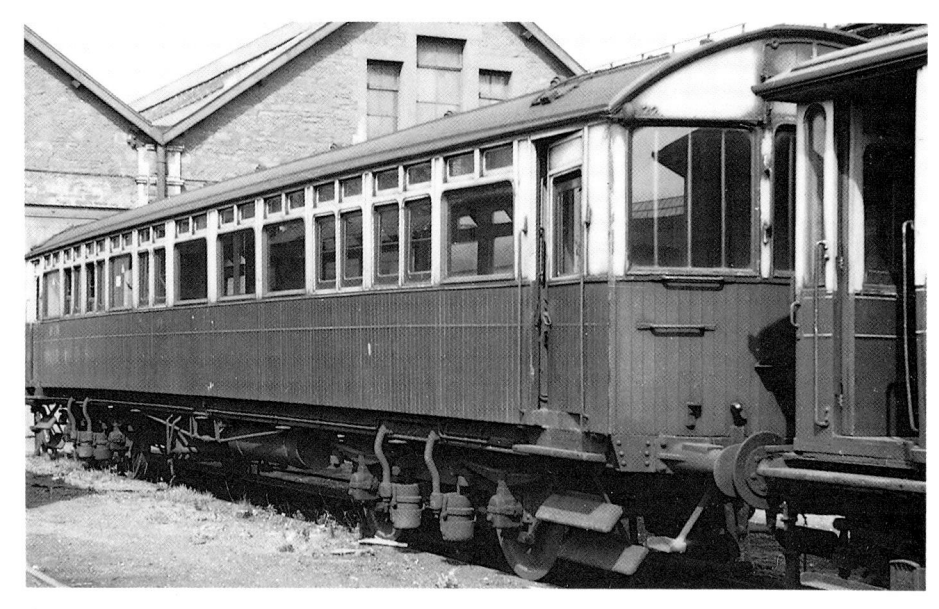

GWR Diagram A No. 1 at Caerphilly in the 1950s. This style of retractable steps was unique to No. 1 (on trailers). P. J. GARLAND

Passengers' vestibule showing 'pigeon-hole' and lever for the steps on the preserved No. 231 at Didcot. AUTHOR

Trailer steps in the extended position ready for use. Moving the lever inside the coach retracted the steps below the solebar and pulled the handles close to the body sides. AUTHOR

Historical Overview

Some trailers were equipped with end vestibules at either or both ends that were only about 3 ft 6 in deep from the partition to the coach end. In these cases, the distance from the corner pillar to the partition was only about 2 ft 3 in, and there was only room for a 2 ft wide door to be fitted. Other cases where 2 ft wide doors were fitted were the conversions from hauled stock, and each leaf of luggage doors. In the case of luggage compartment doors in trailers, these normally conformed to the body side profile, were fitted flush with the bodyside and both opened outwards. Matchboarded trailers, however, seem to have had luggage compartment doors where one opened outwards, the other inwards. There was a fill-in under the inward-opening luggage door so that it matched the other one. It is difficult to be certain from diagrams just what doors were fitted in all instances, and photographs are more reliable. However, doors should be taken to be of the wider standard (about 2 ft 7½ in) unless otherwise noted.

LAMP IRONS

A few trailers had side lamp irons on their ends, like those on hauled stock. In the early 1920s, the design of these side lamp irons was altered from the Victorian style, which was tucked tight against the coach end, to one which protruded diagonally from the end. This new design saved a forging operation (there was only one bend in the bracket). Some trailers are recorded as being fitted with lamp iron adaptors. Because the records for these seem sparse, the discussion on the individual trailers does not go into this detail.

DOOR LOCKS

From about 1934, in those trailers with a luggage compartment, 'a throwover catch' was fitted to the partition door between the luggage compartment and the passenger accommodation. This was to improve security 'for the conveyance of mails'. These are not discussed in the section on individual trailers.

Coaches allocated to the Severn and Wye Joint Railway had their door locks altered from the GWR standard to, it is believed, the LMS standard. (The S&WJR was a joint operation between the GWR and the Midland Railway, later the LMS, until nationalisation.) As this provides a useful insight into trailer allocations, this modification, where recorded, is discussed. It is understood that the alteration allowed the luggage compartment to be locked securely when a guard did not travel in it; some trains on this line apparently ran without a guard.

Destination boards and holder for guard's flag, etc. on No. 231 at Didcot. AUTHOR

Trailers carried destination boards next to the passengers' vestibule. Originally, they were also in the driving end. This is the Watlington branch board as carried in June 1951. The 1947/8 waist lining also shows. COLLECTION R. S. CARPENTER

LIVERIES

As far as external liveries were concerned, the GWR and BR(W) often treated trailers in the same way as their best main-line coaches.

It should be emphasised that, as far as can be ascertained, the dates quoted are those when the change took place for stock that was being built or that was routinely going through the paint shops. It would appear that there was normally no programme of premature repainting of rolling stock following livery changes, although following nationalisation in 1948, the introduction of the 'W' prefix to the running numbers and the obliteration of GWR crests seems to have been rapid.

In most cases, the ends of trailers were painted in the same fashion as the sides; this included the non-driving as well as the driving end. The practice seems to have been a continuation of that of the 1890s (and possibly earlier), when some hauled coaches with end observation windows had those ends painted in the same manner as the sides. In the case of trailers, the non-driving end was still painted like the sides even when its windows had been plated over, and the new British Railways Western Region trailers of the 1950s appeared with their non-driving ends painted in carmine and cream.

The main exceptions to the rule were the conversions from hauled coaches, and the Diagram C trailers. In the case of the converted coaches, the driving ends with their windows were treated in the same way as purpose-built trailers, and painted like the sides. The non-driving ends, and both ends of intermediate trailers, were painted in the same way as contemporary hauled coaches – unlined brown until 1912, and unlined black thereafter. Apart from the driving ends, the livery of converted coaches tended to follow that of hauled coaches, rather than that applied to the purpose-built trailers.

The Diagram C intermediate trailers had the luggage end constructed in wood panelling with vertical beading, like an ordinary contemporary hauled coach, and the other end (which would have been the driving end if driving apparatus had been fitted) equipped with windows like the driving end of other purpose-built trailers. These Diagram C trailers had the luggage end treated like a hauled coach (brown until 1912, black thereafter) and the other end painted like the sides.

The conversions from steam railmotors were painted in the same way as purpose-built trailers, a noteworthy feature being that a few of them retained the very deep waist panel at what had been the power unit end, and which was now the luggage end of the trailer. In this case, the windows at this end were correspondingly shorter than usual and the waist line, cream above and brown below, was continued round the luggage end of the

Diagram L No. 34 as built. NATIONAL RAILWAY MUSEUM

Diagram B1 trailer No. 4 as built. This picture pre-dates the addition of droplights. No. 4 was rebuilt several times and finished with a gangway connector at the driving end. It is thought to have been the first trailer numbered in the trailer series, 1–3 being initially in the SRM series.
NATIONAL RAILWAY MUSEUM

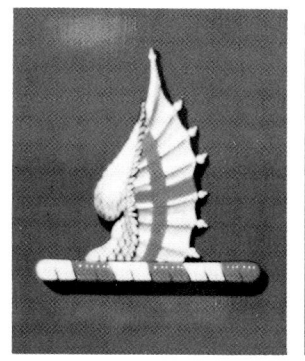

Historical Overview

trailer at the usual height, and so the boundary between the colours split the end waist panel horizontally.

1904–1908

Trailers up to No. 70 would have been painted in the fully lined brown and cream livery when built, with the mouldings picked out in black, and lined in gold, black, brown and cream. Initially, the rules followed were that third class coaches would carry the current monogram, and those with first class accommodation would carry the GWR's garter crest with its two supporters.

In this period, trailers had the running number (in relatively large characters) twice on the waist panel in the format 'Nº 33', with the entwined 'GWR' monogram in a central panel below. On some, this meant that the monogram was not central on the coach as there was a vertical moulding on the centre line, or a door. They also had Nº 33 (for example) on the driving end in the waist panel, with the Nº and the running number arranged either side of the central lamp bracket and the vacuum pipe.

In this livery, the window frames and bolection mouldings were venetian red or mahogany, the roofs were white with a 2 in black line across each end, and the underframes were painted black.

In 1906, the *Great Western Magazine* offered a prize for a design of monogram to be used in place of the 'entwined' GWR; the prize was given to a design that incorporated only the letters 'G' and 'W'. Some of the examples built in 1906 had this 'prize monogram', but vehicles built late in that year and in 1907–8 (such as No. 42) were given the garter crest with supporters.

As usual, there were exceptions. Trailer No. 1, the only one in the matchboarded style, would have had lining around the panels above the waist, but only around the edges of the matchboarded areas below the waist, if photographs of some of the early SRMs are anything to go by. It would have had the entwined 'GWR' monogram in the centre of the side below the waist level, with Nº 1 at the same height, probably towards each end nearer the doors. In addition, it would have carried the number more or less centrally on the driving end, at the same height, positioned to avoid the central lamp iron. However, contemporary matchboarded-style SRMs only had the number once on the sides.

In the absence of photographs of the clerestory and low-roof coach conversions, it is thought that these coaches probably retained the accommodation class designations on the doors (particularly the compartment stock), although the standard trailers did not have this. It is also thought that the low-roof conversions did not have the running numbers on the ends, but this remains an open question with regards to the clerestory conversions since they had two-digit trailer series numbers. Some hauled coaches had the areas on the roof below the lower rain strips painted brown. This may have applied to the trailer conversions, but not to the purpose built trailers which had the elliptical profile roofs.

The GWR's 'Garter' coat of arms and supporters. AUTHOR

The standard waist panels of hauled coaching stock were appreciably narrower than those on trailers, and these coaches are believed to have had the standard size coach numbering in the waist panels, possibly without the 'Nº', following contemporary hauled stock style. The clerestory trailers *may* have had the ends of their clerestory roofs painted cream; at least one example in the 1922 fully-lined livery did.

1908–1912

When new, Nos. 71–80 would have been painted in the all-brown lined livery of the period, and it is possible that some of Nos. 81–98 were also painted thus, together with any of the earlier ones that were repainted during 1908–12. Ordinary hauled coaches in this livery were noted for having 'G.W.R' *twice* in their waist panels, with the coach number at each end, also in the waist panel. They had the garter coat of arms with supporters as near as possible centrally in the panels below the waist. Trailers also followed these general principles. They no longer had

Diagram L trailers Nos. 42, 43, 46 and one other posed for an official photograph with 0–6–0T No. 2120 disguised as a coach. These trailers have the 'full' brown and cream and the garter coat of arms with supporters, officially for coaches with first class compartments at this time. These Diagram L trailers were never gangwayed together. NATIONAL RAILWAY MUSEUM

'Nº' preceding the running numbers. Trailers continued to have the running number on the ends, in the waist panel to the right of the central lamp bracket.

Roofs were still painted white, with a 2 inch black line across each end; underframes were black.

On the evidence of a photograph, which shows three out of four 'Clifton Downs' coaches with 'GWR' twice in the waist panel, it is quite possible that several of these low-roof coach conversions were painted in this livery. The running number was in the standard hauled stock (smaller) size. The 'Clifton Downs' conversions did not carry their running numbers on the front of the driving trailers. One coach that can be identified is No. 3332, which seems to have been converted in August 1913. Its accompanying intermediate trailer had 'G.W.R' only once in the waist panel, so it is possible that this represents a non-standard livery.

1912–1922

Trailers Nos. 81–98 would have been built, and Nos. 99–128 rebuilt from SRMs, in the 1912 crimson lake livery; older trailers would have been repainted in this livery in due course. Subject to the usual exceptions, and to the exigencies of the Great War (which left some coaches painted in khaki and even black), the sides and ends were painted in lined crimson lake; bolection mouldings and droplight frames were also painted lake. Roofs were white, with a 2 in black line along the ends. The underframes were black.

Drybrook Halt and a two-car auto train. The one nearest the camera is probably of Diagram L. The interesting thing about it is that it appears to be in brown livery, 1908-style. Unfortunately, the running numbers are out of the picture and behind the pagoda. LENS OF SUTTON

On trailers, the running numbers were painted towards the ends of the sides (inboard of any end doors) without any 'Nº'. They were also applied to the driving ends to the right of the central lamp bracket, again without the 'Nº'. The letters 'GWR' were placed in the waist panel, with the garter arms and supporters in the main panel below the waist, as centrally as possible; problems were caused by some trailers having doors or other obstructions in the centre of the sides. The ends of standard trailers in this period were lined crimson lake.

Matchboarded trailers (Nos. 1 and 99–124) did not have any waist panels, so lining out was confined to the waist line, the edges of the matchboarding areas, and the panels above the waist. The running number (twice) and 'G.W.R' were positioned just below the top of the matchboarding with the garter coat of arms below the 'W'. No. 99 had a central door, so the 'G.W.R' was off-centre, with one

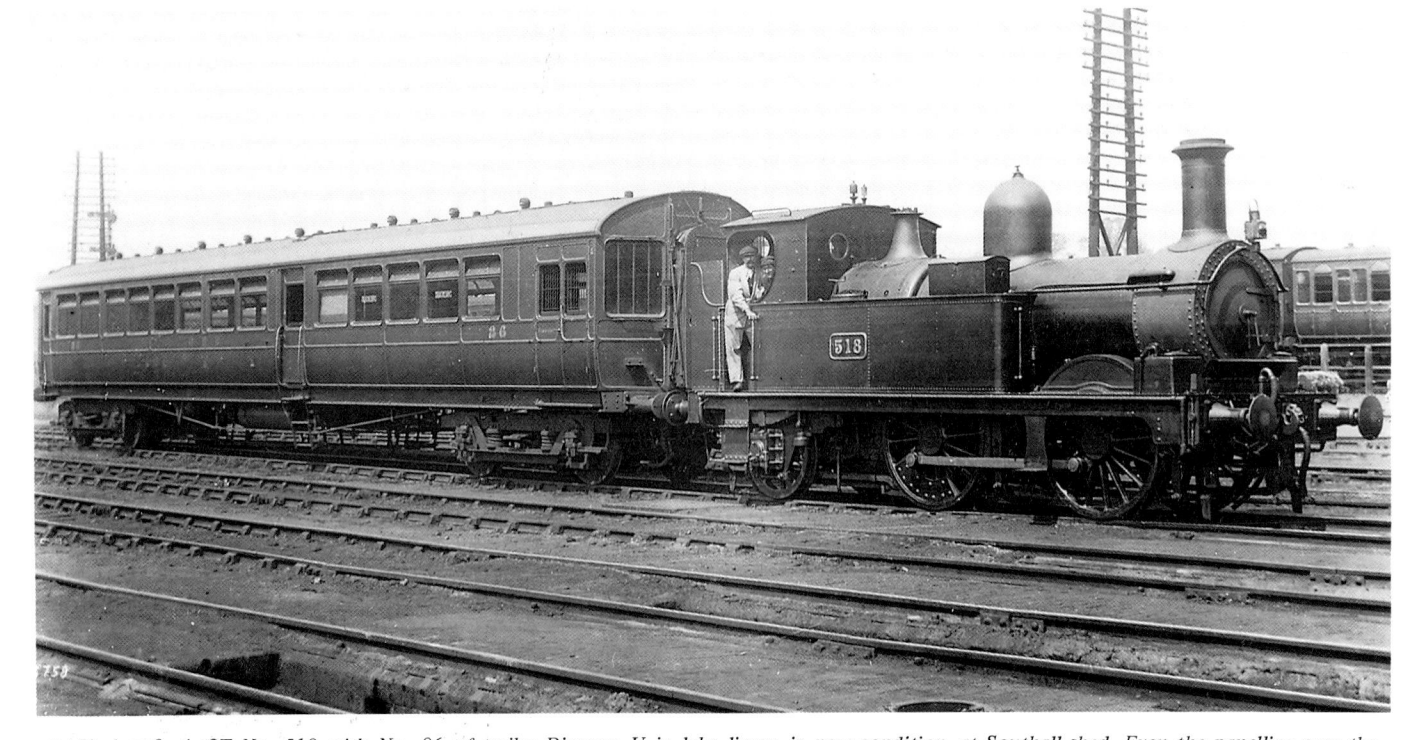

'517' class 0-4-2T No. 518 with No. 86 of trailer Diagram U in lake livery in new condition, at Southall shed. Even the panelling over the gangway connector appears lined out. If the trailer was as new as it looks, the date would have been August/September 1912 and No. 518 might well have been in brown or lake. No. 86 was built around the time the lake livery was introduced. It seems likely that if it had been brown, it would have had 'GWR' twice in the waist panel. COLLECTION J. E. KITE

The very impressive Diagram Q trailer No. 94, one of the last trailers to be built for many years. It is in lake livery and normally ran with a Diagram R trailer.
NATIONAL RAILWAY MUSEUM

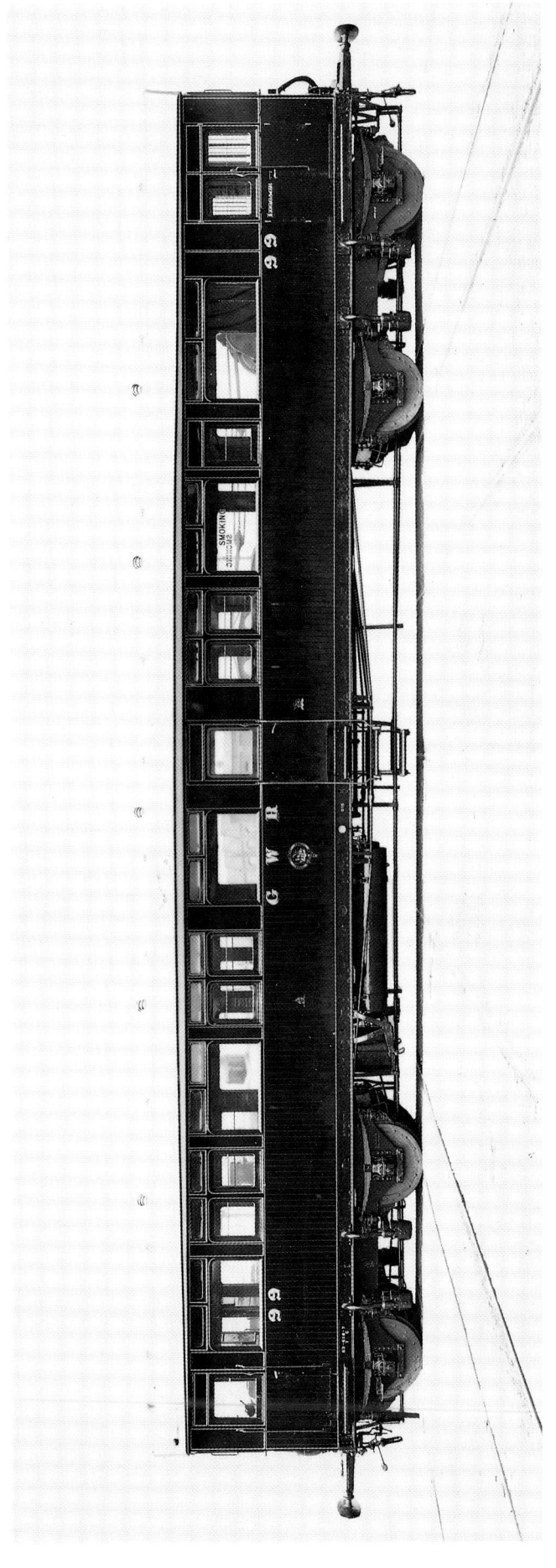

Trailer 99 of Diagram Z, converted from SRM No. 3 in June 1915, resplendent in its lined lake livery in spite of the Great War.
NATIONAL RAILWAY MUSEUM

This photo shows Diagram A7 trailer No. 108 in the 'full' 1924 brown and cream livery in which there was no lower waist line, and the vertical mouldings above the driver's windows were not picked out. No. 108 had not yet been fitted with a gong or sandboxes. The signalling cable is visible in a loop by the left-hand buffer. The trailer at the rear is of Diagram U. The location is Ruislip and Ickenham (later West Ruislip).
NATIONAL RAILWAY MUSEUM

Historical Overview 39

of the supporters by itself on the far side of the door to the garter device. The number was also repeated on the driving end as with wood-panelled stock.

Some of the 'Clifton Downs' trailers should have been initially painted in this livery, but as mentioned above, driving trailer No. 3332 had 'GWR' twice in the waist panels. This is shown in an official picture taken after its alteration to a trailer, apparently in August 1913.

1922

In the summer of 1922, the GWR reintroduced their fully-lined brown and cream livery. Seemingly, it was to have been the same as that abandoned in 1908, but there were a couple of differences.

The mouldings below the waist had largely disappeared, or were in the process of being removed, except for those along the bottom of the coach body and at its ends. These mouldings were the only ones below the waist that were lined out in the 1922 scheme, and they were now painted brown instead of black, as seems to have been the case before 1908.

The 'GWR' and 'GW' monograms in use were replaced by the GWR garter coat of arms device with its two supporters – the practice since 1908 in this respect continued.

The ends of trailers were in the lined livery, like the sides; the roofs were white and the underframes black. Window frames and bolection mouldings were mahogany again, whilst numbering followed the same rules as in the 1912 livery.

Nos. 128–140 (SRM conversions) and Nos. 141–3 and 145 (absorbed trailers) would have appeared in this version of the 1922 fully-lined brown and cream livery, together with all trailers repainted between mid-1922 and mid-1924.

1924

In 1924 there were some subtle changes in the livery, the most noticeable one being the introduction of a thin area of cream between the corner pillar and the end window, on trailers; previously, this area had been black. The other main change was in the black line below the gutter – this became narrower, and gave the impression that the eaves panels were slightly deeper than before.

No. 144 (ex-Cardiff Railway) probably appeared in this altered livery, together with any trailers given a full repaint before the Spring of 1927.

1927–1942

The simplified livery introduced in 1927 continued until the Second War, but was subject to a steady evolution. The relevant changes and the dates when they were introduced are indicated below.

0–4–2T No. 528 with No. 86 of Diagram U. The trailer is in the 1924 'full' brown and cream livery. Note the narrow cream panels either side of the corner pillar and the cream above the gangway connector. COLLECTION J. E. KITE

The trailer on the left is in the 'full' brown and cream livery of 1924–7. The black (?) area over the gangway connector is thought to be non-standard. LENS OF SUTTON

No. 99, Diagram Z, at Oxford in April 1927. No. 99 is in the 1924 'full' livery, and the presence of No. 1473 Fair Rosamund *indicates a probable Woodstock train.* H. C. CASSERLEY

No. 2102 with Diagram A7 trailer No. 111 and a clerestory trailer. No. 111 is in the 1927 'simple' brown and cream livery. The clerestory trailer is too far away for details to be clear, but appears to be either 16, 17, 18 or 35. COLLECTION GRAHAM BEARE

No. 170 of Diagram A27 as built in January 1929 and painted in the autumn 1927 livery with only a black line at the waist and the twin shields device. Note the blue tops to the axleboxes. The positions of the commode handles by the driver's door on these trailers were altered and the corner pillars cut back to improve clearances on the Eastern Valleys lines. NATIONAL RAILWAY MUSEUM

Historical Overview

Trailer 205 of Diagram A31, although converted in 1934 was painted in the 1929 livery with one gold/black waist line.
NATIONAL RAILWAY MUSEUM

SPRING 1927

From April 1927 (the date on the drawing), the GWR abandoned the fully-lined, two colour livery in favour of a plain, two colour scheme, with brown below the waist and cream above, separated by a $\frac{9}{16}$ in black line along the top of the waist panel (on those coaches that had this feature), just below the windows. It is possible that a few coaches were outshopped without this black line. The ends of trailers were painted the same as the sides, except those with ends panelled like hauled coaching stock, which were still painted unlined black. This now applied to absorbed stock as well as the GWR trailer conversions from hauled stock, and to the Diagram C trailers.

The roofs were still painted white with a black line across the ends, but the gutters were now painted brown, instead of white. Window frames and bolection mouldings were painted mahogany colour; underframes were black. The manner of lettering and numbering on the sides and driving ends was unchanged.

These changes should have only affected repainted trailers, as none were built new or rebuilt from SRMs during 1927.

AUTUMN 1927

In about September 1927, the GWR replaced their garter crest and its supporters with a coat of arms device combining the arms of the Cities of London and Bristol. This can be dated reasonably closely, as composite No. 6237 of Lot 1376 had the garter crest, and No. 6345 of the same Lot had the coat of arms. This Lot was of non-continuously numbered coaches, and was completed in October 1927. A system, whereby the axle box covers of modified units were painted blue, was introduced at this time.

Trailers Nos. 146–158 rebuilt from SRMs, and Nos. 159–170 built new to Diagram A27, were in this style.

The curious feature of this picture is that No. 119 seems to be in a hybrid livery; below the waist it has double gold/black lines and apparently the garter emblem with supporters. Above the waist the mouldings are not picked out at all. The photograph is post-August 1929 as the large saloon is 'Smoking'. To add to the complications, No. 119 is not officially recorded as having gold lines. It seems likely that it was repainted in the 'simple' brown and cream livery between 1927 and October 1929 – hence the garter crest. When it was decided to add the gold waist line(s) it was done without a repaint, so the garter etc. survived.
COLLECTION P. KARAU

OCTOBER/NOVEMBER 1929

In October 1929, the livery was revised again, and a $\frac{3}{8}$ in gold line was to be painted below the black line along the coach waist. Trailers Nos. 171–180 (Diagram A28, built new) and Nos. 181–2 (Rebuilt from SRMs) would have been produced in this livery. Main line 8-wheel coaches were to have the waist panels lined out in gold and black, giving double lines along the waist (circular 4974, Nov. 29, 1929).

MARCH 1930

On 10th March the GWR officially extended the double waist line to all 8-wheel coaches. However, in practice this was only applied to selected coaches. A few repainted trailers did receive the second line during 1930. Some of Nos. 171–186 did receive the second line as early as 1932. Nos. 187–196 (Diag. A30) and some subsequent trailers were built (or rebuilt) in this livery.

1931

Photographic evidence shows that, during 1931, the word THIRD was dropped from the doors of third class compartments as an economy measure, whilst FIRST, GUARD and LUGGAGE continued to be used. This change did not affect the GWR purpose-built trailers which never had the accommodation class written on them, but it did concern compartment stock trailers such as the Diagram A1 conversions, and possibly some of the

Diagram L trailer No. 69 at Stourbridge Junction in April 1939 in the 1934 livery, with one gold/black waist line and without the running number on the end of the coach. The end windows at the luggage end have been painted black at the top, and the whistle cord can be seen hanging down.
COLLECTION R. S. CARPENTER

clerestory conversions which had compartments. Some of the absorbed trailers which offered first class accommodation continued to have THIRD on them.

1934
In 1934, the GWR coat of arms was replaced by the 'shirtbutton' monogram on all new and repainted carriage stock. The centre of the monogram was placed 1 ft 5 in from the bottom of the coach body and on the coach centre line, subject to the position of doors or other obstructions. The running number was no longer painted on the trailer ends.

1942–1947
During and after the war years, the liveries carried by GWR coaches underwent a number of changes. The history is made more difficult by wartime economy measures which involved retouching paintwork rather than completely repainting, and which led to partial livery changes such as the new style numbers being used with the 'shirtbutton' monogram. The notes which follow set out the general principles.

1942
Coach repainting recommenced in 1942. As an economy measure, coaches that required complete repainting were coated brown, including the ends of trailers (with the usual exceptions). A single orange line was painted along the waist, just below the windows, but some coaches (non-corridor ones in particular) appeared without this line. The coat of arms replaced the 'shirtbutton' monogram. The roof was painted grey, the underframe black, and where appropriate, axleboxes continued to be painted blue. Trailers painted brown were recorded thus in the Register, some being 'brown' and some 'red-brown';

Trailer 107 of Diagram A7 at Cardiff on 1st July 1947 in all-brown livery and still with the GWR 'shirt-button' monogram, indicating a wartime repaint. P. J. GARLAND

the record of this is incomplete, and mostly applies only to 1942. It appears probable that coaches were recorded as being painted brown until this became standard practice, and recording then ceased.

1943
In 1943 two notable changes took place. A new style of lettering was introduced, with sans-serif characters in gold, outlined in black. The running numbers continued in a larger size for trailers and a smaller one for hauled stock.

In September of that year, a cream and brown livery appeared once more, at least for the more prestigious main line stock. The brown and cream were separated by a gold and black line at the waist, and the very best stock had two such lines. The livery was rather like that of 1934, but with the coat of arms replacing the 'shirtbutton' monogram, and the lettering 'G.W.R' above it in the waist panel (if present), or just below the windows otherwise. There were full stops *between* the letters (but not after the 'R'). Non-gangwayed, clerestory and absorbed coaches usually seem to have been painted in the brown livery until the end of 1947 at least, but some trailers received the two colour livery. A number of coaches appeared without the 'G.W.R'.

1947
In 1947, the livery was amended yet again. Instead of 'G.W.R' above the crest, the arrangement was:

GREAT (coat of arms) WESTERN

In general, when applying the 1947 livery, coaches built before 1937 had a single gold and black waist line, and those built subsequently had the double lines, but (as usual) some trailers got favourable treatment. Officially, the livery included a 7 in-deep brown band immediately below the roof, with

Historical Overview 43

GWR No. 1099, ex Rhymney No. 58, semi open third, similar to the Rhymney Railway coaches altered to intermediate trailers. This is a good example of a 1943 brown-liveried coach featuring the small 'GWR' above the shield. This picture was taken at Dowlais Cae Harris in 1947.
P. J. GARLAND

Diagram A28 No. 175 next to the loco is in the 1943 brown livery with a single waist line and 'GWR' just visible above the crest. The other coach in this picture taken at Brixham is A25 No. 148.
H. C. CASSERLEY

No. 169 of Diagram A27 at Merthyr on 20th September 1947. The end windows have not been plated over and the vehicle is in the 1943 brown livery with the revised style lettering. Although ATC is fitted, this is not recorded in the register.
J. H. RUSSELL

a gold and black line between it and the cream. However, as far as can be ascertained from photographs, this upper brown band was not usually applied to coaches with toplights, which included the vast majority of trailers. On one example (a compartment-type trailer) where the full livery *was* applied, the brown band, was *not* continued round the driving end of the coach, unlike with the BR standard carmine and cream livery. Examples have come to light of a very few trailers with toplights which seem to have a narrow dark-coloured band, which makes it very difficult to distinguish between brown and cream and the BR carmine and cream liveries in a black and white photograph. A number of trailers were still painted brown.

BRITISH RAILWAYS
1948
Initially under British Railways, the 1947 liveries continued, but without the Great Western insignia. Regional prefixes ('W ...') to the running numbers were introduced immediately. This rather simple statement covers a considerable number of variations to the basic brown and cream livery, which included:

1. There could be either one or two gold and black waist lines, or alternatively none at all
2. There could be one running number (at the left-hand end, here termed the '1949-style'; see below), or two (the GWR arrangement)
3. The brown band below the roof could be present (in one of two widths) or not.

Some coaches continued to be plain brown but it is not known if any were actually painted thus in 1948.

1949
In 1949, BR introduced three liveries:

1. Malachite green for multiple unit trains
2. Plain maroon (officially crimson lake) for non-gangwayed stock
3. Carmine and cream for gangwayed main-line express stock

Except for trailers and multiple units, the ends were to be black; in the case of trailers with hauled stock-type coach ends, the non-driving ends were painted black. In all other cases, the ends were painted like the coach sides (carmine and cream, or maroon). The two colour livery was even applied to the luggage ends of the BR(W)-built open trailers, which had always been steel-panelled. Roofs were grey and underframes black.

Lettering and numbers were in a Gill Sans lettering style in 4 inch gold characters with a thin black line surrounding them; the allocated region was indicated by a letter prefix

Ex-TVR trailer as GWR No. 6422 at Caerphilly Works in August 1951. It is in the 1947 livery with two waist lines, but has hauled-stock size running numbers at both ends. It is difficult to see whether the end is painted black or is merely dirty. Note 'FIRST' in the waist towards the left.
COLLECTION R. S. CARPENTER

No. 140 of Diagram A19 in the 1947 brown and cream livery with two waist lines.
J. H. RUSSELL

Historical Overview

No. 124 of Diagram A9 in Caerphilly Works yard. It is in brown and cream with 1949 style lettering and 9ft 'fish belly' bogies. No. 124 was originally the last of the matchboard style SRMs to be built (No. 28) but not the last of them to be converted to a trailer.
R. C. RILEY

Diagram Z No. 102 at Pontsticill in a variant of the 1948 brown and cream livery. There appears to be no waist lining and the running number (W102) appears at each end of the sides.
W. A. CAMWELL

(W ...). The carmine and cream were separated at the waist by a $\frac{3}{8}$ in gold line and a $\frac{3}{4}$ in black line; there was another broad carmine band below the roof, again separated by a similar line from the cream, with the gold against the carmine, as at the waist. The cream area was 3 ft $6\frac{1}{2}$ in deep.

The standard position of the running number was toward the left-hand end of the coach, officially below the window immediately on the right of the door nearest the left-hand end of the coach. This meant that if the coach had an arrangement: window 1/door/window 2 at the end of the coach, then the running number went under window 2. On BR standard stock, at least, the running number was to be positioned 5 in below the waist line. This was adopted in the case of the trailers built by BR(W), but most ex-GWR trailers had waist panels, and the running number was put into that panel. It was a tradition on the GWR for trailers to have rather larger-than-usual running numbers, and in general GWR practice was initially followed, so that trailers were given 6 in-high running numbers. The previous exceptions noted in the cases of compartment trailers continued.

In addition to the running number, non-gangwayed BR stock carried a coaching code in $1\frac{1}{2}$ in-high letters, about $1\frac{1}{2}$ in from the bottom of the coach side at the right-hand end of the coach. In the case of trailers, the code carried was TRAILER, although TRAILER D and TRAILER BT are known. This lettering was usually positioned next to and inboard of the end door, but if there was room beyond the door, it went next to the end.

This BR livery was applied to most ex-GWR trailers, but it did not suit them very well as their toplights were too close to the roof for the carmine band below the roof to be properly applied. The BR-built GWR-type trailers W220–W234 were turned out in the carmine and cream livery.

It can be quite difficult to differentiate in photographs between the GWR 1947 livery with one waist line and the brown band below the roof, and the BR carmine and cream livery as applied to ex-GWR coaches. On trailers, however, the BR livery can often be identified by the carmine band below the roof being extended round the trailer ends, following the roof contours.

In this period, a number of coaches (including a few trailers) that should have been painted plain maroon were turned out in maroon with lining. It is believed that this was an unofficial initiative by Swindon.

The lining was similar to that applied to carmine and cream trailers, ie a gold/black line above the windows, about 5 in below the roof and a black/gold line below the windows at the waist. Both lines were continued round

No. 1671 of Diagram A34, is believed to have spent its life on the Lydney Town–Berkeley Road service. It is seen here at Lydney in a 1948 livery with the brown band at the eaves, but it is not extended round the end of the coach (i.e. ex-1947 style). HMRS

Another puzzle picture from the Severn & Wye, this photo shows one of the A33 trailers, 4350 or 4364 in early BR days. Given its double waist lining, it ought to be in 1948 brown and cream, but the upper band of dark colour follows the roof line, which was BR maroon and cream practice. It is possible that the A33 is in brown and cream and the brown band under the roof has been extended round the ends in the new BR style. This coach looks as if it has 7ft Collett bogies. The lettering on the side next to the driver's door reads 'To work between Lydney Town and Berkeley Road', all written in upper case. HMRS

This is one of the A33 trailers Nos. 4350/64 altered from D117 brake thirds in 1937 for the Lydney Town–Berkeley Road service. It is unusual to find pictures of these coaches solo – this one has presumably just returned from being overhauled at Swindon. It is in the BR plain maroon style with the unofficial lining. Note the single yellow/gold line at the waist.
R. M. CASSERLEY

Historical Overview

the ends of trailers, the upper one following the roof contour. It is possible that cream, yellow or orange was used instead of gold.

A coach in this lining can be differentiated from one with the 1956/9 lining (see below) because the latter had gold/black/gold lining at the waist. It seems that this livery was only applied to compartment trailers and coaches with 1949-style numbering. Examples include 2646 (hauled Diagram C83), 3338 (ex-Clifton Downs driving trailer), 6820 (Diagram A32), either 4350 or 4364 of Diagram A33, and an intermediate trailer to Diagram A41 or A42. In the case of 6820, Mr R. C. Riley positively recorded that the colour was 'red'.

No. 108 of Diagram A7 in its later days at Llantrisant without toplights, but resplendent in BR carmine and cream, 1949 style. It now has sanding gear, gong and chain alarm. The absence of toplights meant the BR livery could be 'properly' applied.   R. M. CASSERLEY

W143 ex-Cardiff Railway trailer in 1949 BR carmine and cream with the wood panelled ends painted in two colours, not black.
P. J. GARLAND

The front of an A38 trailer in the Brixham bay platform at Churston in BR 1949 maroon and cream livery. Unfortunately, the driver is obscuring the running number, but 222 was used on the Brixham branch in 1952.
J. H. MOSS

1951

In late 1951, the running number was repositioned at the right-hand end of coaches, and 4 in lettering became standard for the running numbers, with the regional prefix and suffix 'W...W', for all trailers. As in 1949, the running number should have been positioned 5 in below the waist line, but on most ex-GWR trailers it was applied in the waist panel, or where one would have been if present.

A considerable number of variations within these standards can be noted from photographs, but in this book '1949-style' refers to the form which gave 'W123' in 6 in letters at the left-hand end of the trailer, and the '1951-style' as that giving 'W123W' in 4 in letters at the right-hand end. Although the trailers W220–W234 had appeared by August 1951 in the carmine and cream livery with 1949-style lettering, when two of them were rebuilt in February and March 1952, they reappeared in the same livery, but with lettering in the 1951-style as W220W and W221W.

1956

A new main-line livery was introduced in 1956, together with special regional liveries, including a chocolate and cream version of the carmine and cream style for certain Western Region express trains. The new standard livery was maroon body sides, but with a gold/black/gold line at the waist and a yellow/black line above the windows. With the introduction of these liveries, carmine and cream was no longer applied, and most trailers that were repainted during this period became plain maroon, with the running number in the 1951 style.

W109 of Diagram A7 appears to have been recently repainted in BR maroon livery, yet the luggage end windows have not been plated over. The running number is in the 1951 position at the right-hand end, but large characters are in use. They seem to have been the norm on matchboarded trailers in the 1951 maroon livery. This trailer was condemned in July 1953. 9ft bogies, ATC cable and sandpipes are visible.
H. C. CASSERLEY

No. 160 of Diagram A27 as W160W in BR plain maroon livery, exhibits the 'proper' positioning of the running number. If 160 had had a waist panel, this number would have come across the moulding.
D. LARKIN

A30 No. 193 being propelled onto the Coryton branch at Heath Junction by 45XX class 2–6–2T No. 5572 about 1955. No. 193 is in BR maroon and cream with 1951 style numbering. The top maroon band was rather thinner than usual to avoid the toplights.
S. RICKARD

Historical Overview

1959

In 1959, the use of main-line lined-maroon livery was officially extended to non-gangwayed stock, but only the last survivors of the GWR-type trailers received it, mostly the BR 1953-built examples; GWR purpose-built trailers were rapidly disappearing by then. In spite of the predilection for treating trailers as main-line stock, no examples have been found of them being given any of the BR crests! As applied to trailers, the lining was extended round the coach ends, the upper yellow line following the roof contours.

DEPARTMENTAL STOCK

A number of trailers entered Department stock after being officially condemned; with one exception, these were all in BR days. The BR examples were usually given running numbers in white towards the left-hand end of the coach, rather like the 1949 style, but with smaller numbers.

At least three series of running numbers were used: the GWR 'Pilot Van' series ('pilot van' was a Victorian euphemism for 'breakdown' or 'accident van', but the series was not confined to breakdown vehicles); the BR 'DW150xxx' series for 'movable' service stock, and the '079xxx' series for vehicles which were not normally allowed out on main lines. Some ex-trailers had additional information painted on them with regard to their allocation (such as OFFICE) painted in 6 in letters near the centre of the coach side below the windows.

The body colour of service stock is rather indeterminate; some examples were not repainted, and others were noted in maroon, salmon (faded maroon, perhaps) green, red and black.

TRAILER LIVERIES – SUMMARY

This is intended as a brief guide for recognition purposes. The dates given are those when the livery revisions were introduced, but in general, new liveries were not applied until coaches became due for repainting. During wartime, coaches were often only partially repainted, and during early BR days they could be renumbered with a 'W' prefix and suffix without being otherwise generally repainted.

1905 Fully-lined brown and cream livery. Crest: the 'entwined monogram'.

1906 Some trailers appeared in the fully-lined two colour livery, but with the 'prize' monogram.

Late 1906 The garter crest and supporters were used on trailers instead of a monogram.

1908 Lined brown livery. 'GWR' twice in the waist panels. Garter crest.

Diagram A44 No. 246 leading a Pyle–Porthcawl auto into Porthcawl station in July 1962. No. 256 and another A44 trailed together with 0–6–0T 6431 make up the remainder of the train. No. 246 is in lined BR maroon livery.
S. RICKARD

An example of British Railways service stock livery. The body colour is described as 'near maroon'. The regulator/TRG has been removed but the ATC plug remains. Originally this trailer was A27 No. 165. It entered service stock in December 1960.
COLLECTION R. S. CARPENTER

1912 Lined lake livery. 'GWR' once in the waist panels. Garter crest.

1922 Fully-lined brown and cream livery. The only mouldings below the lower waist moulding that were lined out were those round the sides and bottom edge of the coach body side. The garter crest with twin supporters were used.

1924 Slight changes to the full brown and cream livery, principally the introduction of cream above the waist between the door opening and the adjacent window frame.

Spring 1927 Simple brown and cream livery, with black line between the two colours. Crest: still the garter coat of arms with supporters.

Autumn 1927 As for Spring 1927, but with a gold line below the black at the waist.

October/November 1929 Simple brown and cream livery, with black and gold line between the brown and the cream. Twin shield crest without any supporters.

March 1930 Second black and gold waist line applied to some trailers; otherwise as for October 1929.

1931 THIRD dropped from coach doors. (Only affected compartment trailers.)

1934 'Shirtbutton' monogram introduced in place of the twin shield crest. Coaches could have one or two black and gold waist lines.

1942 Coaches painted in brown or red-brown, with grey roofs. Twin shield crest instead of monogram. Some coaches given single orange waist line.

1943 New lettering style introduced with sans serif characters. In Summer 1943, the brown and cream livery reintroduced for some coaches with one or two waist lines in gold and black. Crest: Twin shields, with 'G.W.R' above it in the waist panel (or in an equivalent position if no panel present). Brown coaches could have the revised crest arrangements.

1947 Brown and cream livery as in 1943, but with GREAT (twin shields device) WESTERN, instead of 'G.W.R' in the waist. Coaches without toplights had a 7 in brown band below the roof, edged at the bottom with a gold and black line. This brown band was not continued round the ends of trailers.

1948 GWR colours and lining as in 1947, but without any insignia, and with the 'W' prefix to the running number. The running number appeared once or twice at the waist.

1949 BR maroon and cream, and plain maroon liveries introduced. Running numbers at left-hand end of coach only. Trailer numbers usually in 6 in characters in the waist panelling, although standard position was 5 in below the waist line using 4 in characters – '1949-style'. Unofficial lined maroon appeared.

1951 Running numbers moved to right-hand end of the coach with 'W' suffix and in 4 in lettering. Positioning comments for 1949 apply here too.

1956 Lined maroon introduced for main-line stock. 1951-style lettering.

1959 Lined maroon livery extended to all stock. 1951-style lettering.

No. 1 in the London area, having just passed under the overbridge carrying the empty carriage stock lines over the main line near Old Oak Common. The loco was 0–6–0PT No. 5415.
PHOTOMATIC

CHAPTER TWO
PURPOSE-BUILT MATCHBOARDED TRAILER
59 ft 6 in Trailer No. 1: Diagram A

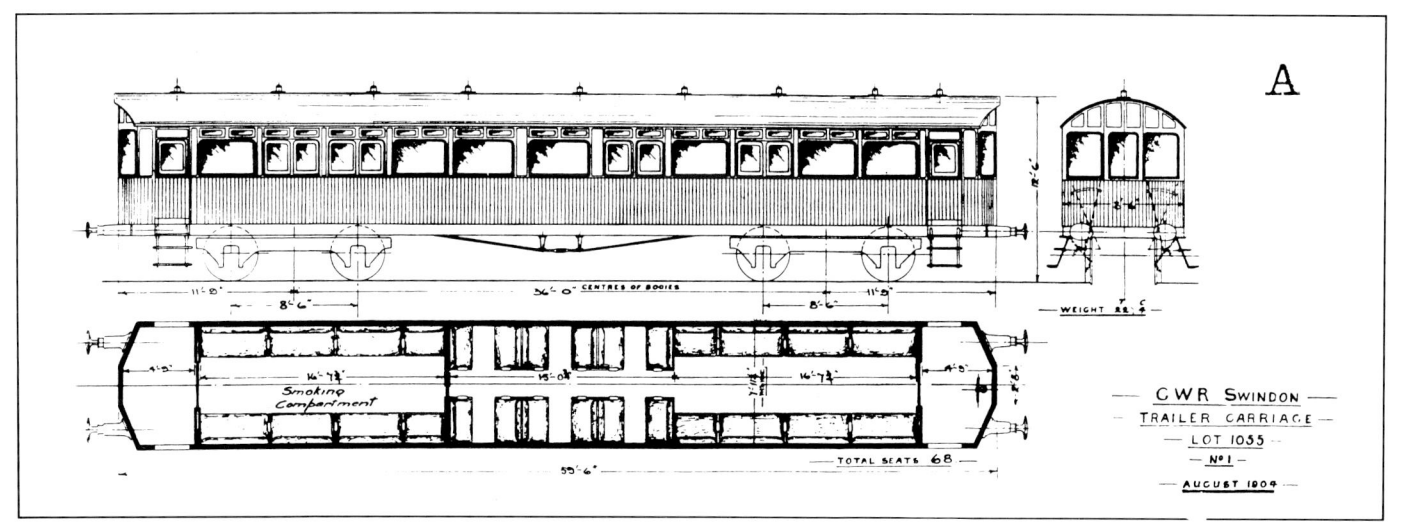

THE pioneer Great Western trailer was ordered in December 1903 on Lot 1055, together with No. 2 which will be dealt with later. The cost of the pair was £2,056, an average of £1,028 each; Nos. 3–6 cost £1,185 each so No. 1 may have cost as little as £871. No. 1 was presumably intended to accompany SRMs Nos. 3–14 which were ordered at the same time on Lot 1054, although the SRMs were delivered by July 1904, whilst trailer No. 1 did not appear until September 1904. Initially, it was numbered 53 in the SRM series, but became No. 1, probably early in 1905 and certainly by September that year when SRM No. 53 was built (see the next chapter under Diagram B trailers).

Trailer No. 1 was the only trailer to be built in the matchboarded style. It could be differentiated from later matchboarded SRM conversions in having the earlier type of retractable steps below the doors. When the steps were folded back on No. 1, their treads were no longer horizontal; in fact, they only assumed this angle when fully extended. Other trailers had the later type of steps where the treads were always horizontal. All other match boarded trailers had the steps below a central doorway on each side; on No. 1, they were below each of the end doors.

The vehicle was 59 ft 6 in long, 8 ft 6 in wide, and 12 ft 6 in high from rail to roof. Its wheelbase was 44 ft 6 in, and it had 'Dean' type bogies of 8 ft 6 in wheelbase. It had the automatic vacuum brake with Armstrong's moving vacuum cylinder.

The underframe was trussed for strength with cast queen posts – like the clerestory coaches built up to this date – and tie rods of round section. Like SRMs Nos. 3–14, it was bow-ended in what became the standard GWR style, with three large windows in each

Trailer No. 1, at Cardiff on 1st July 1948, still has its end windows intact at the luggage end, and they are not painted black. The alarm indicators are at this end. It is in the 1943 all-brown livery, although, curiously, above the waist looks darker than below in this picture.   P. J. GARLAND

Trailer No. 1, Diagram A, in wartime all-brown livery. No. 1 was the only trailer with this type of retractable steps. The Dean bogies and Armstrong vacuum cylinder are prominent in this photo together with the round-section truss rods with their cast queen-posts and the turnbuckle for adjusting tension in the truss rods between the queen-posts.   J. N. SLINN

end. The area between the end windows and the roof was divided into six panels – this was done only on the matchboarded vehicles. There were some matchboarded ex-SRM trailers that are shown with this arrangement on the Diagrams Z, A6, A7 and A9, but in many cases these panels were plated over in due course.

Trailer No. 1 had two vestibules (one at each end), one of which was used by the driver. It is believed that originally there may have been an expanding metal gate each side in each vestibule to give access to the trailer (instead of a door), as the contemporary matchboarded SRMs had this feature; but there is no record of these fittings. If these gates were provided, then they were replaced at an early date by inward-opening doors. Each vestibule was 4 ft 9 in between the coach end and the partition. Originally, the passenger accommodation comprised a single saloon, which had 11 large fixed windows each side, with a pair of opening toplights above each of them. The seats were arranged with lengths of inwards-facing bench seating along the coach at each end, and seating bays across the coach in the centre. The coach seated 68 passengers.

The coach seems to have been substantially altered twice; the first time is not recorded specifically (but is known from a diagram), the second was in 1917. In the first alteration, a partition with sliding door was inserted towards the guard's end of the trailer between the longitudinal seating and the transverse seating bays to form a saloon 16 ft 7¾ in long between partitions. This portion of the coach then became the smokers' compartment, with the large saloon the non-smoking area. Droplights replaced some of the fixed windows so that the coach looked like:

Guard's Door	FXD d d d d FXD	FXD FXD d d FXD d d FXD FXD	Driver's door
	<– Smoking –>	<– Non-Smoking –>	

(d = droplight)   (FXD = Fixed window)

It is possible that this was done in August 1905 when the trailer was equipped with steam heating. In May 1913 it was given incandescent gas lighting in place of the original system of flat flame burners.

In 1917 the layout of the trailer was altered further, and it re-emerged in May of that year with the small smoking saloon moved to the other end of the trailer. What the GWR seem to have done was to install a new partition with sliding door between the longitudinal and bench seats at the driver's end, and to remove the sliding door from the original partition (a photograph seems to indicate that this was left in place, although the diagram does not show it). Two more droplights were inserted in the new smoking compartments so the coach now appeared as:

Guard's Door	FXD d d d d FXD	FXD FXD d d	FXD d d d FXD	Driver's door
	<– Non-Smoking –>		<– Smoking –>	

(d = droplight)   (FXD = Fixed window)

At the same time, through regulator gear was also fitted, enabling the coach to be used as an intermediate trailer if necessary.

After this, the coach seems to have led a relatively uneventful life, the only other alterations noted in the records being the fitting of an 'alarm bell' (presumably a warning gong) in June 1927, and chain communication (the chain alarm) in May 1930. Also in May 1930, the large non-smoking area was allocated to smokers and the small saloon became non-smoking. The top 17 in of the end windows at the 'locomotive' end of the trailer were painted black in May 1935.

The coach was equipped with ATC 'dual bells' circuitry in September 1945, and a note dated June 1946 stated that it was provided with 'additional circuits and switches', but this may not be a further modification. The end windows were plated over after being painted black, from photographic evidence.

No. 1 went to Laira for a month when new, then to Croes Newydd (Wrexham). A photograph exists of it in plain 1942 wartime brown livery (which appears to show sand pipes), and it was also recorded near Old Oak Common in brown and cream livery with a 54xx 0–6–0T locomotive and another trailer.

The trailer was condemned in November 1953, but not broken up immediately. In July 1954 it was reinstated (and, one hopes, overhauled), being photographed during that month at Caerphilly Works by the late Eric Mountford, when it was still painted in GWR brown and cream with two waist lines, but without any GWR insignia. It was then numbered W1W in the waist panel, but in the 1949 style. It survived for just over a year until finally being condemned in December 1955 at Goodwick, having been used on the Trecwn branch.

No. 1 in early BR days, in 1948 livery (as W1) with double lining to the waist. The end still has the vertical beading above the window. ATC plug and wire are visible on the end above the buffer.   J. N. SLINN

Summary

No. (SRM series)	Lot	Built	Renumbered in trailer series	Trailer Series No.
53	1055	Sep. 04	by Sep. 05	1

Steam Heating	First Rebuild	Incand gas	TRG
Sep. 05	Sep. 05?	May 13	May 17

No.	Second rebuild	Sand boxes	Chain Comm.	Smoking Cpts Changed	Black End Windows
1	May 17	+	May 30	May 30	May 35

ATC	Out of stock	Reinstated	Cond.
Sep.45db	Nov. 53	July 54	Dec. 55

db = dual bell

CHAPTER THREE
PURPOSE-BUILT 70 ft TRAILERS
70 ft Trailers Nos. 2–6: Diagrams B1, B, V, W, X, A4

This photograph has caused much trouble in the past. It shows SRM No. 43 and a trailer numbered 55. However, the latter was shortly thereafter renumbered 3 in the trailer series. It is to Diagram B1 and is brand new in this photograph taken in January 1905. Trailer 55 was, in due course, to Diagram L and had a passengers' vestibule.
NATIONAL RAILWAY MUSEUM

TRAILERS Nos. 2–6 represented the GWR's first essay in building such vehicles in the style of contemporary wood-panelled conventional carriages, as distinct from the matchboarded SRMs. As the contemporary coaching stock were the famous 'Dreadnoughts', it might seem strange to refer to them as 'conventional' but there was a distinct external family resemblance between some of the Dreadnoughts and the 70 ft wood-panelled trailers.

Trailers 1–3 are thought to have been initially numbered in the SRM series as 53–5, but must have been given their new trailer numbers by September 1905 at the latest, when SRM 53 was built. The building (release to traffic) dates of the first four trailers were:

No. 1 (53)   September 1904
No. 2 (54)   December 1904
No. 3 (55)   January 1905
No. 4 (–) February 1905

An official photograph of No. 55 was taken in January 1905 (negative No. MT8) together with SRM No. 43 (which was released to traffic in February 1905). This is an exterior view which has caused considerable confusion in the past, being usually described as of trailer No. 55 of Diagram L. Trailer No. 55 of Diagram L, however, had a central passenger vestibule which is absent in this photograph, and in any event it was not built until January 1908. The photograph does show a new trailer looking like one conforming to Diagram B1.

Official photographs are also recorded of the interiors of trailers 53 and 54, taken in December 1904; these are presumably of

The interior of trailer No. 2 (No. 54) in December 1904. It has gas lighting, walkover seats and no droplights. (Diagram B1)
NATIONAL RAILWAY MUSEUM

Nos. 1 and 2 under their original numbers. The photograph of No. 54's interior does seem to correspond to a Diagram B1 trailer and not a Diagram L. Information from Mr J. N. Slinn suggests that in a register of gas-lit coaches at Swindon it was recorded that, in December 1904, trailers 53 and 54 were extant, and gas lit. To further confuse the record, there is also a photograph of the exterior of trailer No. 4, also said to have been taken in January 1905 (reference MT7). This shows the brand-new trailer by itself, and it is clearly numbered 4. The 1905 Locomotive Allocations Register has (deleted) references to trailers 53–55, and the Lot list at the NRM gives the running numbers of Lot 1055 as 53 and 54 corrected in red to 1 and 2.

However, in other places where references to trailers 1–3 under the identity of Nos. 53–5 might be expected, they are not to be found. The Lot list for Lot 1080 refers to trailers 3–6, and has no indication of the original numbers. The SRM Register in the NRM, York, shows no signs of an entry for these trailers under Nos. 53–5. Further, the Trailer

Trailer No. 2 at Clifton Bridge station, near Bristol, being hauled by a steam rail motor. No bell wire is visible at this end; this was before TRG was fitted to the driving end.

LENS OF SUTTON

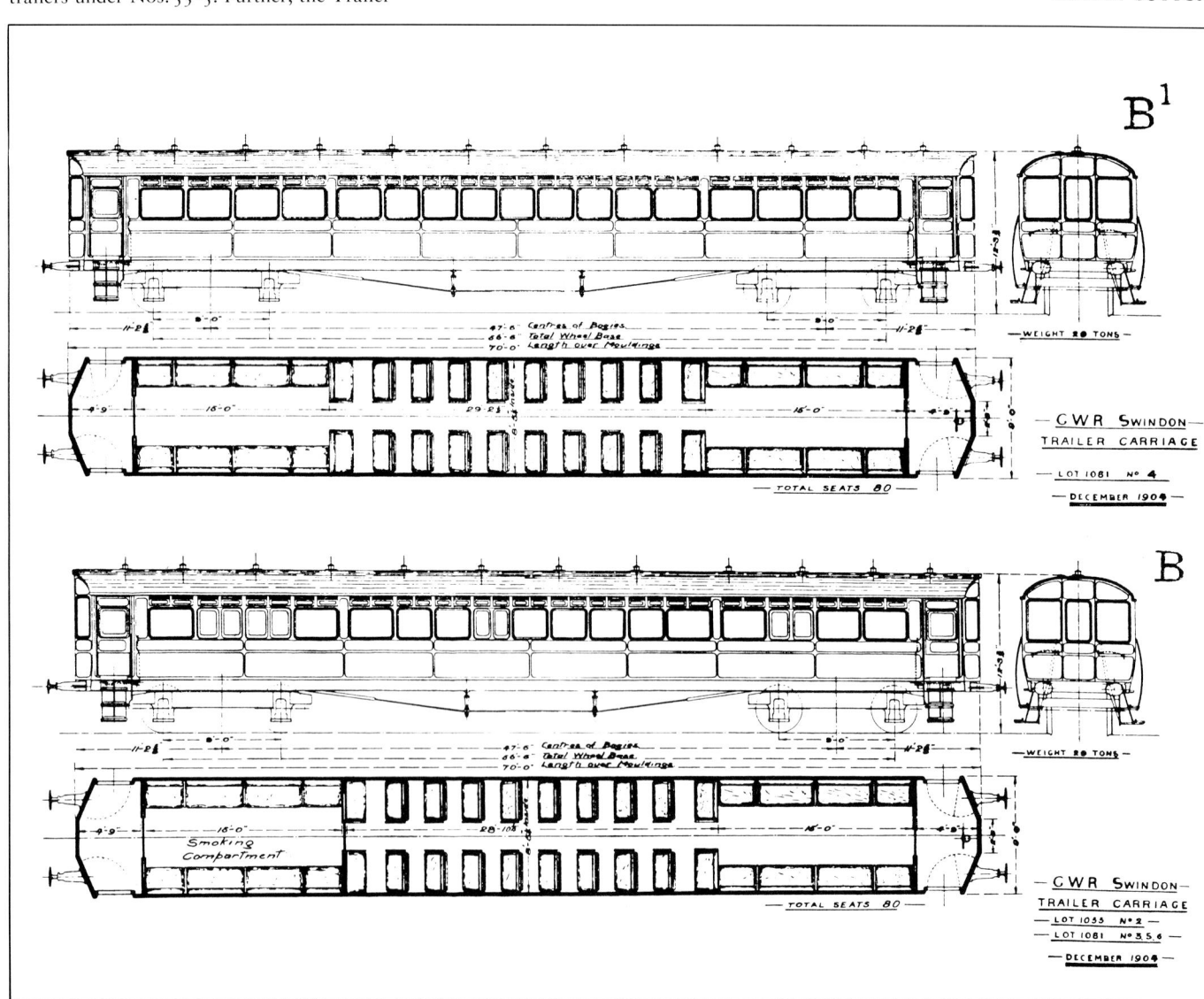

Purpose-built 70ft Trailers

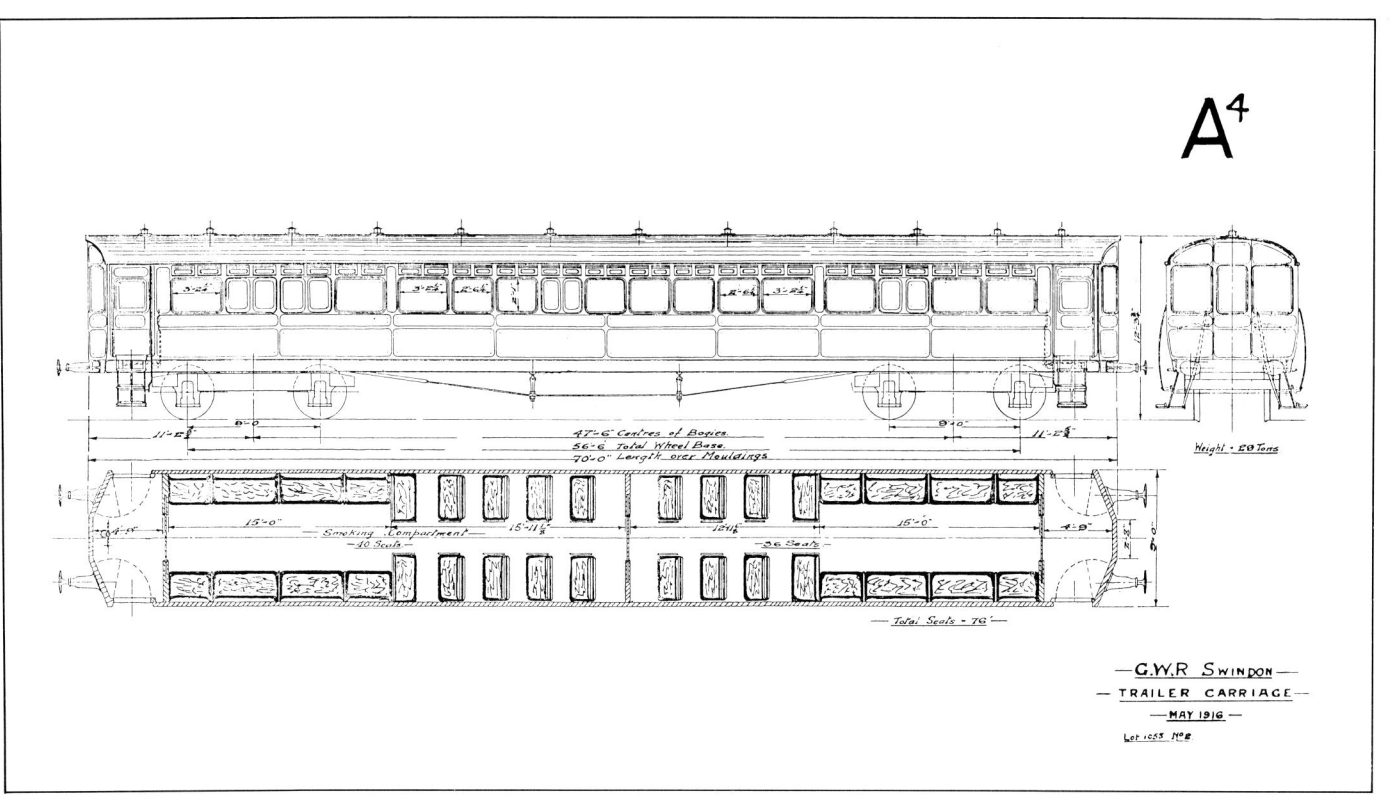

A^4

G.W.R SWINDON
TRAILER CARRIAGE
MAY 1916
Lot 1055 No 2

Register itself makes no reference to their having been numbered 53–5, or to their having been renumbered (it was normal practice to note the original number of any renumbered rolling stock).

The conclusion must be that trailers Nos. 1–3 almost certainly ran as 53–5 until early in 1905, and were then renumbered in the trailer series. No. 4 seems to have always run carrying the number 4, and is an indication that the trailer numbering series was introduced by the end of January 1905. However, this does raise questions as to when the Registers and Lot list were written up, and there was more than one copy of the Lot list.

To avoid confusion, Nos. 2–3 will be referred to by their trailer series numbers (only) subsequently in this account.

The first of them to be built was No. 2 which appeared in December 1904, having been ordered in December 1903 on Lot 1055 together with trailer No. 1 (which was completed in September 1904). No. 2 was closely followed by trailers 3–6, which were ordered in September 1904 on Lot 1081, and built between January and April 1905 at an average cost of £1,185 for each vehicle.

These trailers were 70 ft long, 9 ft wide, and 12 ft 3¾ in high from rail to roof. They had a wheelbase of 56 ft 6 in (only 3 ft less than the body length of trailer No. 1) and ran on 9 ft volute bogies. The underframe was of steel, and was braced by four queenpost trusses. The queenposts themselves were of round section with adjustable nuts on the bottom ends; the trussing was of flat section.

As built, the bodies were bow-ended with a 4 ft 9 in vestibule at each end, one for the driver, the other for the guard. Both vestibules had flat, slightly recessed access doors on each side, opening inwards. They were separated from the passenger saloon by partitions with sliding doors. Passenger access to the coach was via these vestibules, and there were the usual retractable steps below the doors.

Nos. 2, 3 and 4 of these coaches were lit by flat flame gas lighting, but 5 and 6 appear to have been built with incandescent lighting. As built, they were shown on a Diagram that was given the index number B1.

The seats were arranged into three areas: longitudinal benches at each end (15 ft long) and transverse walkover seating in the centre occupying 29 ft 2½ in. eighty passengers could be seated.

The windows in the sides consisted of large fixed lights, with a pair of hinged toplights above each to give ventilation. There were four fixed lights on each side in the longitudinal seating sections, and two pairs of fixed lights flanking five smaller lights in each side of the transverse seating section in the centre. There were two widths of the fixed lights on these trailers, the wider being 3 ft 2¼ in × 2 ft 1 in, the others about 2 ft 6¾ in × 2 ft 1 in. Unlike No. 1, the area between the end windows and the roof was only divided into three panels, with the vertical mouldings corresponding to the angles of the bow ends.

These trailers did not remain long in this condition. In October and November 1906, Nos. 6 and 2 respectively were altered by the fitting of partitions with sliding doors between the longitudinal seats and the transverse seats, towards the guard's end of the coach. The area partitioned-off at the guard's end became the smoking saloon; two of the fixed windows on each side were removed, and twin droplights fitted in place of each. The hinged toplights must have proved generally inadequate as a means of ventilation, because the centre fixed light and one in the non-smoking longitudinal seating area each side were also replaced by pairs of droplights. These droplights all worked in the window framing, whereas the fixed lights were kept in place by bolection mouldings as usual. In this revised condition, they were shown on Diagram B. In addition to Nos. 2 and 6, trailers 3 and 5, and possibly even 4, were altered in this fashion around the same period, but no dates are known.

From 1907, the history of No. 2 differed significantly from that of the other four (which were paired together, and sent to the Plymouth area). It was fitted with incandescent gas lighting and through regulator gear (TRG) in March 1913, in 1916, it was altered internally again. This time, a partition with sliding door separating the smoking and non-smoking sections was located near the centre of the coach. This meant the removal of two double walkover seats, and reduced the seating capacity by four. In this form, the non-smoking area had five pairs of walkover seats in addition to the longitudinal seats at the guard's end, whilst the smoking area had four pairs of walkover seats and the remainder of the longitudinal seating. It was now shown on Diagram A4. By 1930 it had two

The Newbury–Lambourn service employed 'ordinary' i.e. non-auto locomotives. Here 0–6–0 Dean Goods No. 2532 is hauling Diagram A4 trailer No. 2. For many years trailer 58 of Diagram L was the regular coach on this line. This picture was taken near East Garston on 21st July 1951.
J. F. RUSSELL-SMITH

Purpose-built 70ft Trailers

Perivale Halt looking towards Paddington on 30th May 1937, long before the London Transport Central line arrived on the scene. Perivale is on the direct line from Greenford to Old Oak Common. The nearest trailer is No. 2, the second oldest in the fleet and the pioneer 70ft trailer. By this time it was to Diagram A4. Note how the droplights do not have bolection mouldings like the adjacent fixed lights. It has 9ft 'fish-belly' bogies and is in 1934 livery with the 'shirtbutton' monogram, but only a single line at the waist. The second coach is probably a Diagram L trailer, and the front one an A23, A26 or A29, with small luggage end windows and a deep waist panel.
G. N. SOUTHERDEN

No. 5405 propelling two trailers on the 3.34 p.m. Reading–Newbury train near Reading West in 1946, apparently in substitution for a diesel railcar. Both trailers appear to be in 1942 or 1943 brown. The leading trailer is No. 2 of Diagram A4, the other is one of Diagrams L or P.
M. W. EARLEY

0–6–0PT No. 1570 and trailers 4 (nearest the camera) and 3 at Tavistock. At this time No. 4 was shown on Diagram W and 3 on Diagram V. The period of the photograph is September 1930–March 1932 as No. 4 is gas-lit and appears to be fitted with the chain apparatus. No. 4 has 'Smoking' signs visible on several windows. No. 3 was for non-smokers. The livery of No. 4 appears to be late 1927 – plain brown and cream with the GWR twin shield device.
DR. IAN C. ALLEN

more droplights than are shown on Diagram A4.

Later changes include the fitting of 98 ft 'fish belly' heavy duty bogies at a date not recorded, but probably in the late 1920s or early 1930s. It was fitted with sanding apparatus in August 1927, and in August 1931 it was awarded a livery of cream and brown, with gold lines. In October of that year, it was fitted with the chain alarm. In November 1932, the smoking/non-smoking areas were changed round so that the smoking was the larger compartment, whilst in November 1935, the end windows at the guard's end had the top 17 inches painted black; they were not plated over at a later date.

No. 2 was photographed at an early date in the Bristol area, and at Perivale in the London area in 1937. It was fitted with ATC equipment in September 1944, and was condemned in September 1953.

To return to Nos. 3–6. The volute-spring bogies with which these trailers were fitted seem generally to have proven unsatisfactory for passenger-carrying stock, and were quickly changed. In the case of No. 3, this took place in July 1907, whilst No. 4 was changed in June 1906, when the coach was only 16 months old. The dates of the bogie changes on Nos. 5 and 6 are not recorded.

In 1907, Nos. 3 and 4 were given incandescent gas lighting, and Nos. 3–6 were rebuilt to run in pairs, 3 with 4, and 5 with 6; additionally, they were all fitted with TRG at this time. The work involved removing the central window in the non-driving ends of 3 and 6, and in the driving ends of 4 and 5, and cutting a gap in the end walls of the trailers. There is evidence (Diagram X) that an unusual coupling arrangement was used involving a central buffer, or a solid sprung drawbar (rather like that on the later 'B Set' close-coupled coaches), but how this was arranged is not shown. It is not at all clear how the guard and/or passengers transferred from one trailer to the other; it is possible that there was simply a gap in the ends of the coaches (hopefully protected by chains), and the guard simply stepped from one coach to the other. They were close-coupled, and there appears to have been a plate above the buffing gear heading towards the partnering coach.

Trailers Nos. 4 and 5 had the guard's vestibule enlarged to 7 ft 9 in between the end wall of the coach and the partition. Double doors were fitted each side to give a guard's compartment with luggage space; these doors were flat and slightly recessed, despite the fact that they opened outwards. They appear to have been the usual width of 2 ft. The creation of the luggage compartment reduced the seating of the trailer by four.

At the same time, the arrangement of droplights was changed on No. 5, with additional units being fitted. In addition, the retractable steps below what had become the luggage compartment doors were removed. All these alterations had been completed by July 1907. It should be noted that Nos. 4 and 5 normally ran with the luggage compartment next to the locomotive. In spite of being principally used as intermediate trailers, it would

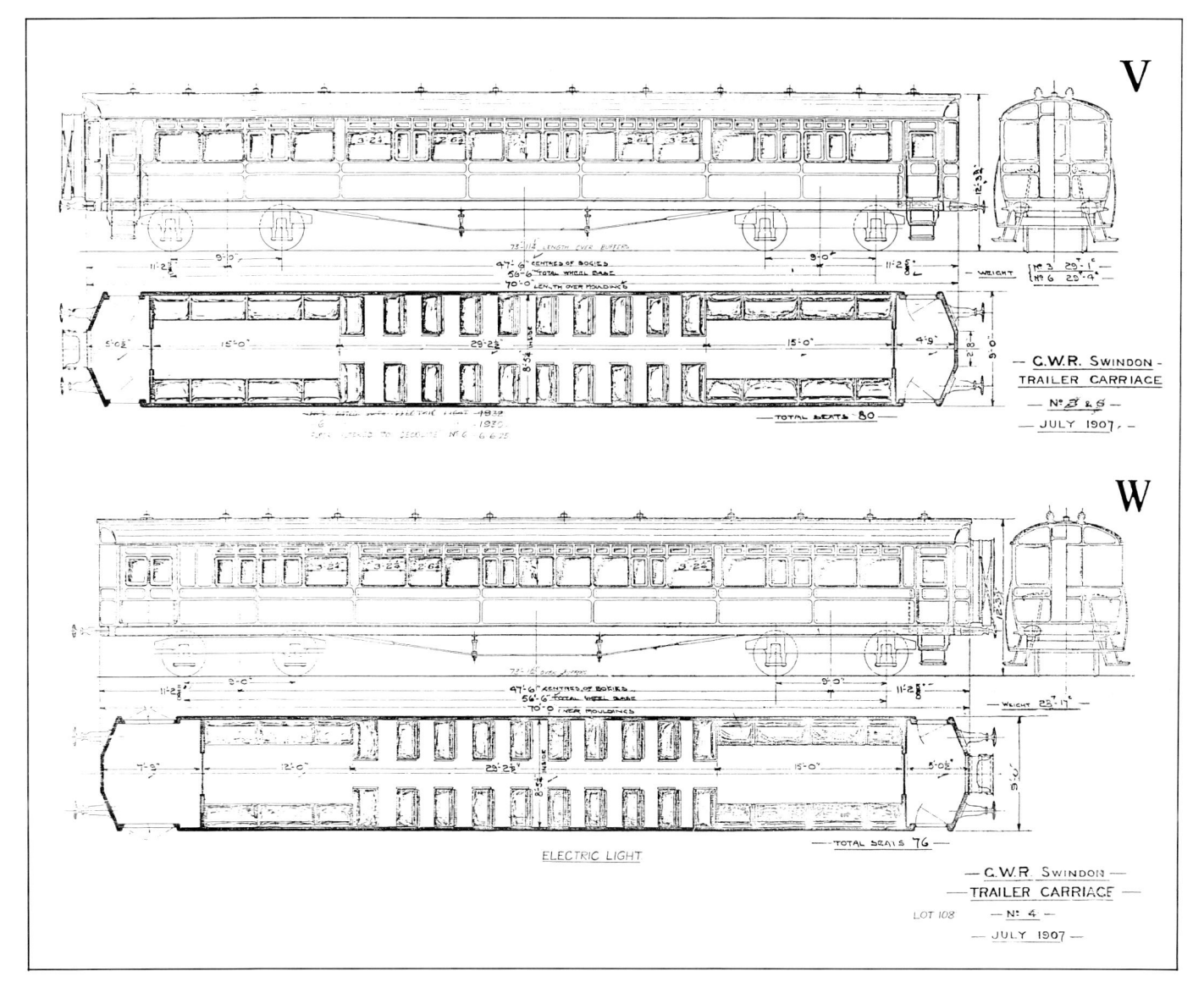

The leading coach of this pair of trailers is No. 3 of Diagram V as it has 9ft American bogies. Its partner, No. 4, also has these bogies. The locomotive in this scene at Tavistock is 2–6–2T No. 4409 which was not fitted for auto working and had to run round the train. Other photos of auto trains at this location show the trailers with the luggage ends facing this way, but, given the triangular junctions at Plymouth, trailers easily got turned round. The photograph was probably in the period September 1930 to March 1932 as chain communication apparatus has been fitted, but No. 3 appears to be gas-lit. There seems to be a lamp in the driver's vestibule towards the side of the roof. 'No smoking' signs are visible on several of the windows of No. 3. LENS OF SUTTON

appear that Nos. 4 and 5 both kept their driving apparatus (regulator handle, etc.) in the leading cab, and No. 4 (at least) received a warning gong at this end. However, both 4 (1907) and 5 (1947!) lost their screw handbrakes.

There is a reference to these trailers in a report by Mr T. Hurry-Riches, the Locomotive Engineer of the Taff Vale Railway, to his General Manager, Mr Amon Beesley, dated 14th February 1910. Mr Hurry-Riches was a strong advocate of steam rail motors, and the Taff Vale had a sizeable fleet of them. Mr Hurry-Riches and a colleague from the TVR (whose signature is unfortunately indecipherable!) went on an official tour of the GWR. They were briefed at Paddington, then went to Plymouth where they observed SRM and auto train working in the area. With regards to their findings, it was reported in part:

> 'A multiple train is also in use consisting of an engine type 0–6–0T and two close-coupled trailer cars at either end, the train can be driven from either of the end compartments or from the engine footplate.
> 'The cars are 70 ft long, the first and last are non-smoking. Smoking and luggage accommodation is provided in the others. Communication between the smoking and non-smoking compartments is established by means of a gangway...'

By 'gangway' an 'open gangway' is presumably meant. The expression 'multiple' train is also interesting; it is getting close to the modern 'multiple unit'!

In June 1911, Nos. 3 and 4 were 'short coupled together' and fitted with standard gangways. They are shown thus as Diagrams

No. 4 at Saltash with toplights plated over, in BR maroon livery. The vehicle is on 9ft American bogies and the gong is below the driver's window. The white line can also be seen on the driver's droplight. HMRS

No. 4, now of Diagram W, at Plymouth North Road in August 1954 in BR plain maroon with 1951-style running numbers. All toplights have been sheeted over. H. C. CASSERLEY

Purpose-built 70ft Trailers

No. 5, Diagram X, at Plymouth with 7ft bogies and electric light. HMRS

V and W respectively, which indicate that the trailers were by then fitted with side buffers. No 'over-buffers' measurement is given on these diagrams, so it is not possible to discover the length of buffer fitted at the gangway end. Nos. 5 and 6 were similarly dealt with in March 1913. Trailers 3 and 6 were shown on Diagram V, No. 4 by Diagram W and No. 5 by Diagram X. Apart from the central buffing arrangement shown on Diagram X, and the lack of a gangway connector, the differences between Diagrams W and X seem to be the number of droplights fitted. Diagram X is also drawn the opposite way round to W, so it presumably ran at the other end of the train. None of these three diagrams show any internal partitions separating the smoking and non-smoking areas, and in view of the report above, it is possible that they had been removed from Nos. 3 and 4.

Trailers Nos. 5 and 6 had their coil spring 9ft bogies changed to Collett heavy duty types (7ft wheelbase), possibly in July 1927 when No. 5 was given sandboxes. Nos. 3 and 4 had their bogies changed to 9ft 'American' at an unknown date, but possibly about this time.

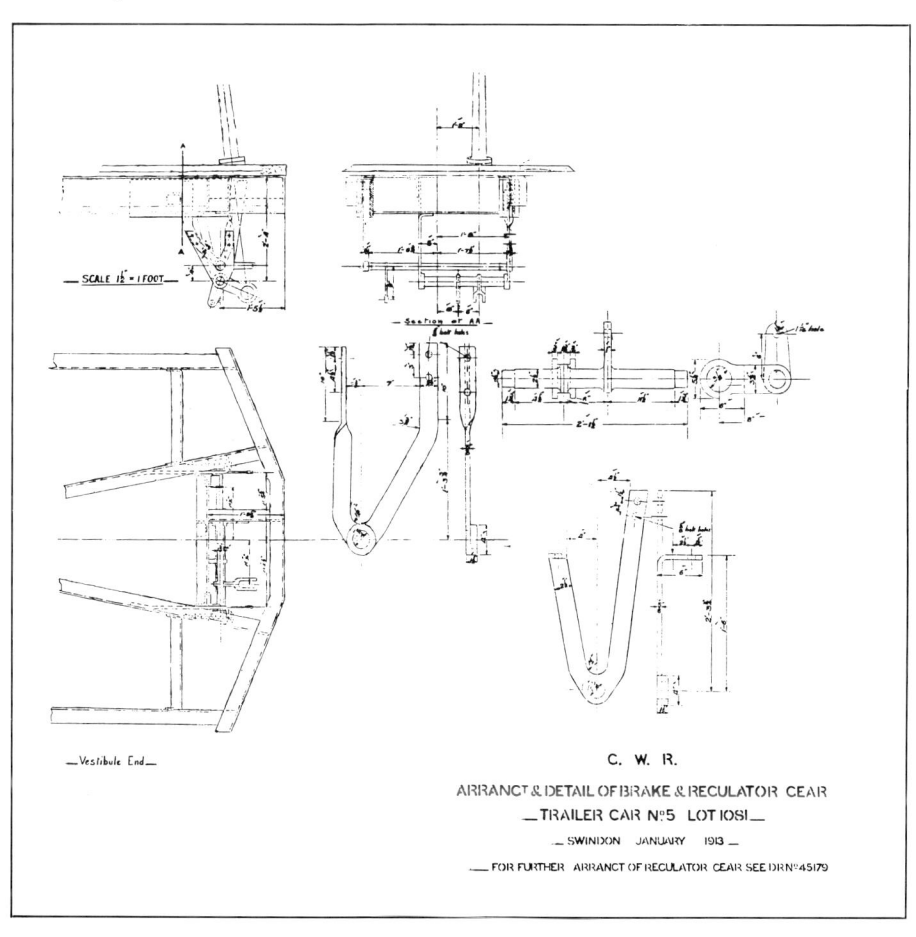

Chain communication is recorded as being fitted to No. 5 in July 1929, and to the other three in September 1930. In July 1930, Nos. 3 and 4 are recorded as having the larger compartment designated for smoking, so the partition should have been present on these coaches. However, notes in the Register say that 'these coaches are probably running in pairs, one a smoker and the other a non-smoker'. These notes are dated September 1930 for Nos. 5 and 6 (5 the non-smoker), and December 1931 for the other pair.

These vehicles were equipped with Lucas-Leitner electric lighting in 1930/32.

In 1935, the non-driving end windows were reported as being painted black; this time Nos. 4 & 5 were dealt with in February, and 3 & 6 in October, so it is possible that they were paired thus at this time. It was normal practice for the blackened windows to be plated over in due course. However, photographs of No. 6 taken in BR days show it with windows at both ends, whilst No. 5, to which it is coupled, has the luggage end plated over and windows present at the other end.

They were fitted with ATC in January (3 and 4) and July 1942 (5 and 6).

Trailer No. 3 (as No. 55) was officially photographed in the company of SRM No. 43 when new. Both the SRM and the trailer were in the full brown and cream livery of the period with the 'entwined' GWR monogram. The monogram was placed in a body panel nearer the 'loco' end when compared to No. 4.

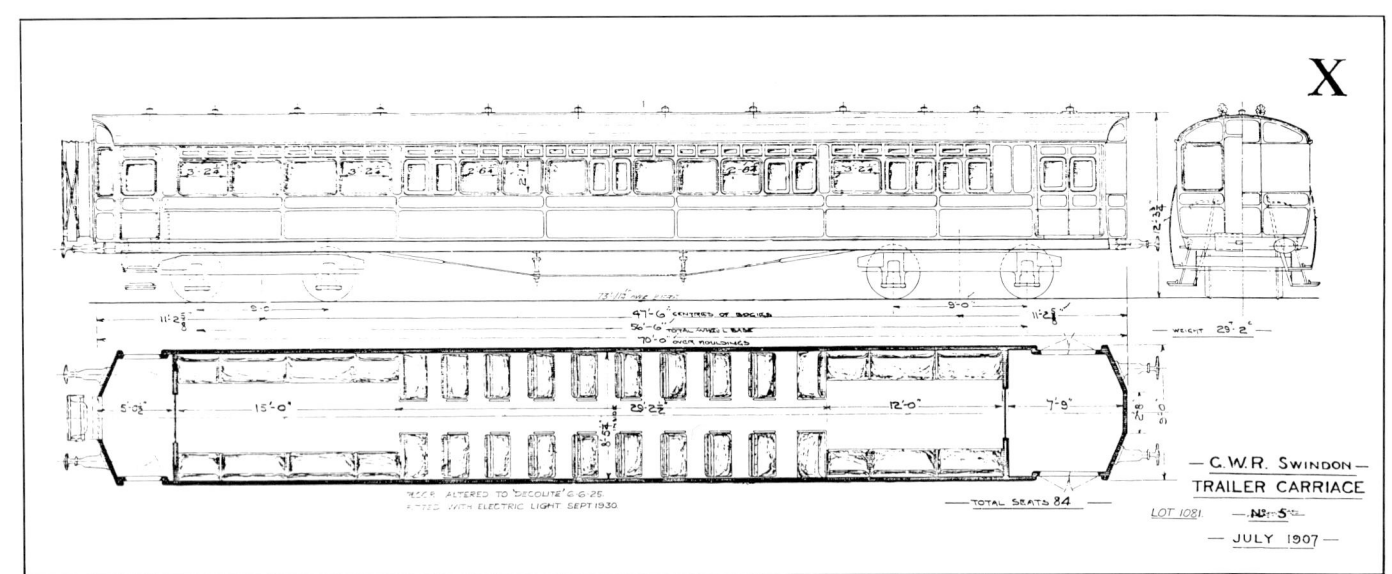

W6 Diagram V at Plymouth in brown and cream livery, with 7ft bogies and ATC, coupled to No. 5.

Purpose-built 70ft Trailers 63

Nos. 5 and 6 (nearest camera) awaiting departure for Yealmpton from Plymouth Fiary in August 1945. Both coaches are in 1942 all-brown livery.
H. C. CASSERLEY

Trailers Nos. 6 (Diag. V) and 5 (Diag. X) near Plymouth after the toplights had all been plated over. The bearing springs on the leading bogie seem to have rather more camber than usual, perhaps because the trailer was empty. Both trailers are in the 1951 plain maroon livery. R. P. WALFORD

No. 4 was officially photographed as No. 4, apparently in January 1905, just before entering service. It was also photographed on the first auto train at Southall, accompanied by class '517' 0-4-2T No. 1160 which was in a matching, gleaming, chocolate and cream livery! By this time, No. 4 had a dirty roof. In 1905, No. 4 was photographed on the Brentford service. In all these instances it had the full livery with the 'entwined' GWR monogram. No. 4 was photographed at Tavistock in 1931 on a Plymouth auto train, presumably with trailer No. 3.

Trailers Nos. 3 and 4 both acquired the 1947 brown and cream livery with one waist line in that year, whilst Nos. 5 and 6 ran in brown and cream as W5 and W6 with 1949-style numbering. In BR days, No. 4 ran as W4W with no stoplights, and with a gong at the leading end next to the gangway connector. It was in a maroon livery with 1951-style numbering.

Nos. 3–6 were photographed on a number of occasions on Plymouth suburban services – at Plymouth Friary, Laira, Saltash, and on a Yealmpton train. For additional information see the section below on Plymouth services.

Trailer No. 3 was condemned in March 1956, No. 5 in October 1957, Nos. 4 and 6 in October 1958.

No	Lot	Built	Altered to Diag B	Altered to run in pairs	Coil Spring Bogie	End Door fitted	Luggage Cmpt fitted	TRG	Close cpld.
2	1055	Dec.04	Nov.06	–	?	–	–	Mar.13	–
3	1080	Jan.05	+	Jul.07	Jul.07	Jul.07	–	Jul.07	Jun.11
4	1080	Feb.05	?	Jul.07	Jun.07	Jul.07	Jul.07	Jul.07	Jun.11
5	1080	Apr.05	+	Jul.07	+	Jul.07	Jul.07	Jul.07	Mar.13
6	1080	Feb.05	Oct.06	Jul.07	+	Jul.07	–	Jul.07	Mar.13

No.	Incand gas light	Further altered to Diag	Date	Bogie Changed to	Date	Blue A/boxes	Sand boxes	Chain comm
2	Mar.13	A4	May.16	9ft F/B	Nr	Nr	Aug.27	Oct.31
3	Jul.07	V	Jun.11	9 ft American	Nr	Nr	+	Sep.30
4	Feb.07	W	Jun.11	9 ft American	Nr	Nr	Nr	Sep.30
5	Built	X	Mar.13	7 ft Collett	Jul.27?	Nov.28	Jul.27	Jul.29
6	Built	V	Mar.13	7 ft Collett	Jul.27?	Nov.28?	Jul.27	Sep.30

No.	Smoking Compts rearranged	Elec. light	Cream brown & gold	End windows black	Red-brown/ brown	ATC	Cond
2	Nov.32	–	Aug.31	Nov.35	Nr	Sep.44	Sep.53
3	See text	May.32	Mar.32	Oct.35	Nr	Jan.43	Mar.56
4	See text	May.32	Mar.32	Feb.35	Nr	Jan.43	Oct.58
5	See text	Aug.30	Aug.30?	Feb.35	*Jul.42	Jul.42	Oct.57
6	See text	Sep.30	Jul.30	Oct.35	Jul.42	Jul.42	Oct.58

* = brown

No. Notes
2
3 Usually coupled to N⁰ 4, from Jun.11.
4 Screw brake removed, Jun.07. Usually coupled to N⁰ 3 from Jun.11 until 1956.
5 Usually coupled to N⁰ 6 from Mar.13. Screw brake removed Jun.47
6 Usually coupled to N⁰ 5 from Mar.13 until 1956.

D

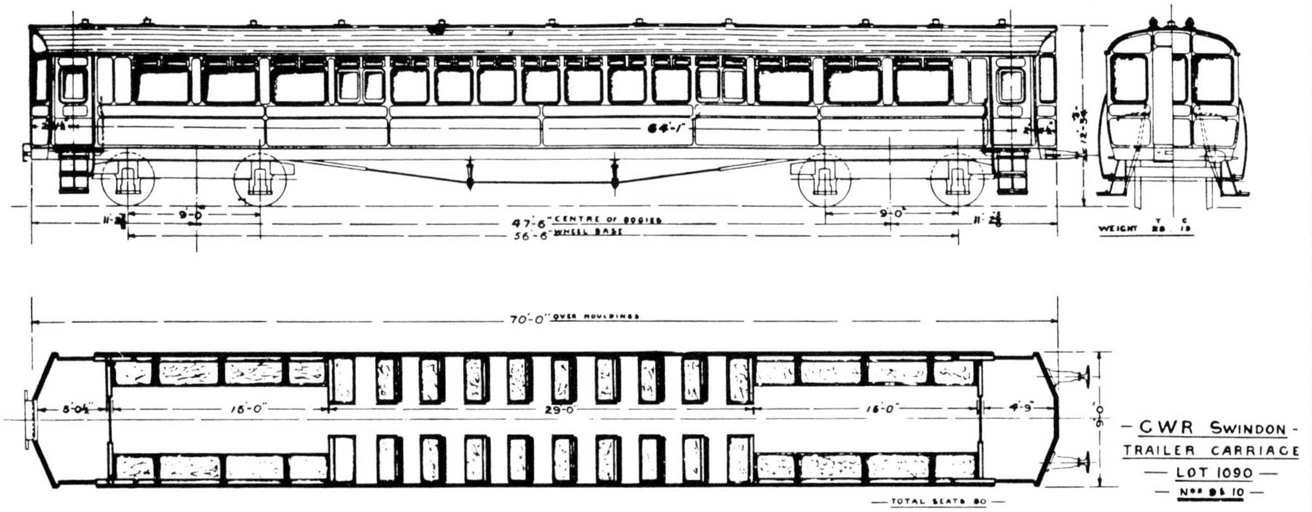

47'-6" CENTRE OF BOGIES
56'-6" WHEEL BASE
9'-0"
WEIGHT T 28 C 13
70'-0" OVER MOULDINGS
15'-0"
29'-0"
16'-0"
4'-9"
9'-0"
TOTAL SEATS 80
– G W R SWINDON –
TRAILER CARRIAGE
– LOT 1090 –
– Nos 9 & 10 –

A11

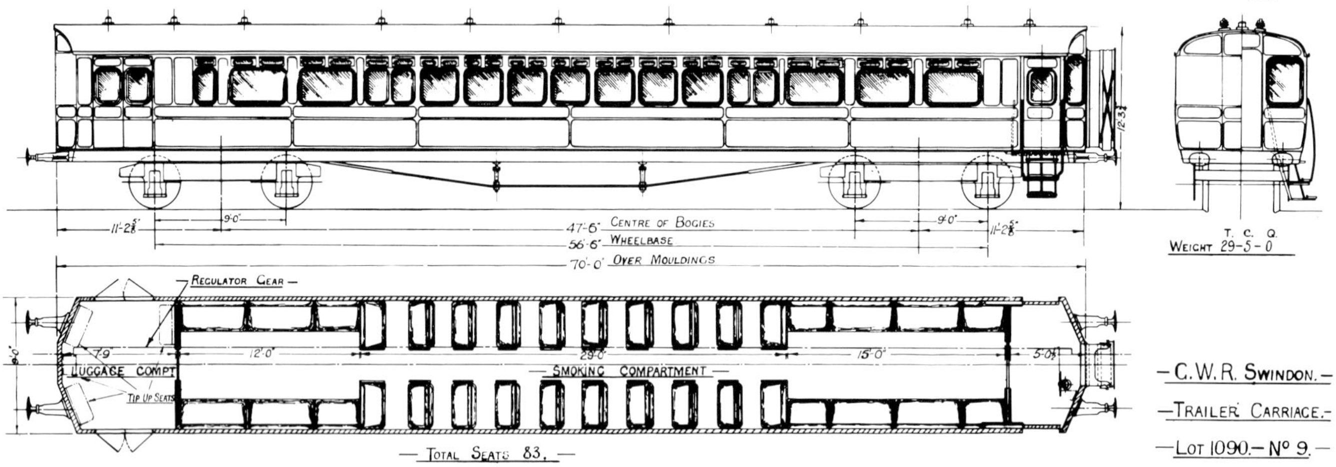

9'-0"
11'-2⅝"
47'-6" CENTRE OF BOGIES
56'-6" WHEELBASE
70'-0" OVER MOULDINGS
WEIGHT T. C. Q. 29-5-0
REGULATOR GEAR
LUGGAGE COMPT
TIP UP SEATS
7'-9"
12'-0"
29'-0"
15'-0"
SMOKING COMPARTMENT
TOTAL SEATS 83.
– G.W.R. SWINDON. –
– TRAILER CARRIAGE. –
– LOT 1090. – No 9. –

A12

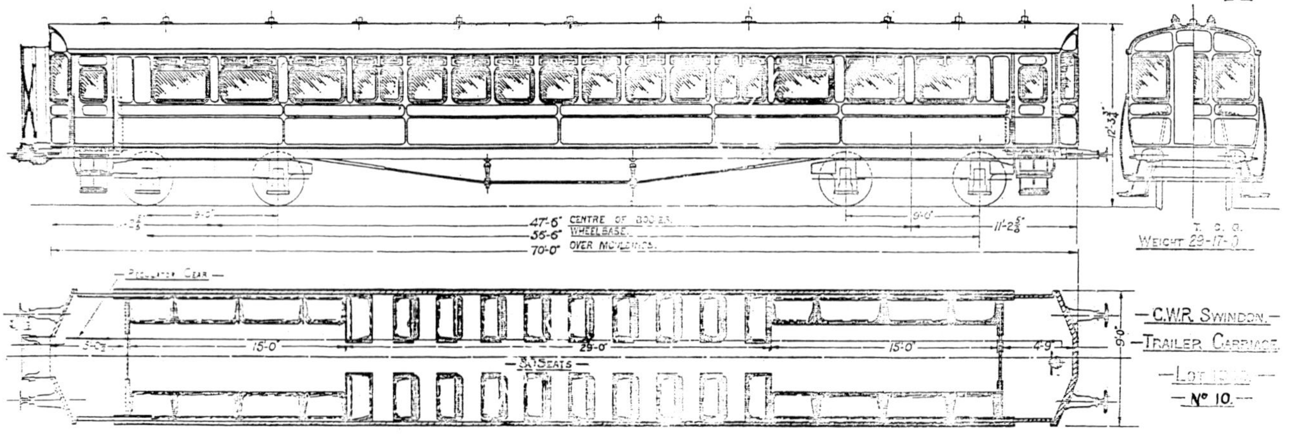

9'-0"
47'-6" CENTRE OF BOGIES
56'-6" WHEELBASE
70'-0" OVER MOULDINGS
WEIGHT T. C. Q. 29-17-0
REGULATOR GEAR
15'-0"
29'-0"
4'-9"
9'-0"
– G.W.R. SWINDON. –
– TRAILER CARRIAGE. –
– No 10. –

70 ft Trailers Nos. 9 & 10: Diagrams D, A11 & A12

This photograph shows SRM No. 59 coupled to trailer No. 9 of Diagram D. Unfortunately, it is not possible to see quite how the two were coupled and if there were gangway connectors. However, they are close coupled and neither trailer nor SRM have buffers visible at their adjacent ends. Both trailer and SRM appear to be as built and are in the 'full' brown and cream livery, but neither carries a monogram, initials or the GWR's garter device. The photograph is not dated but is before 1910 when they were altered (gangway standard connectors fitted) and probably were repainted in the then current brown livery.   COLLECTION R. C. RILEY

The next two 70 ft trailers appeared in October and November 1905, and were numbered 9 and 10 respectively; they had been ordered in March 1905 on Lot 1090. These two coaches cost an average of £1,211 each, and according to the Lot list they were built for the Plymouth area.

They were built with an end doorway (but without a gangway) at the non-driving end, similar to the modified trailers Nos. 3–6, Nos. 9 and 10 were built with this feature so that they could work with SRMs 59 and 60, which had a similar provision. Trailers Nos. 9 and 10 were very similar in appearance to Nos. 2–6, and had similar histories.

Like Nos. 3–6, they are (by implication) mentioned in Mr Hurry-Riches' report of February 1910:

> 'Some of the motors and trailers are fitted with close couplings and were designed to run in pairs, each pair consisting of a 74 ft motor and a 70 ft trailer, an open gangway being provided between the cars.
> 'Two sets may be coupled together to form a four vehicle train. When this is done the motor cars are placed at the ends of the trains.'

Later, he reports that the train could be split into its two constituent halves, which could then be operated independently. He travelled in this train, noting that it ran very smoothly, without any jerking.

This is the only written reference found suggesting that this was an accepted practice, and it is open to speculation as to how control of the train was achieved. The problem was that no normal provision existed for the driving end of one trailer to be attached to the driving end of another with the regulator gear connected between the two trailers.

Either there was an unknown special fitting on these trailers, or the trailing SRM was 'driven' by its fireman in response to bell signals from the driver in the leading SRM. The latter appears to be the more likely – the power/weight ratio would have been too low for the leading SRM to have hauled both trailers and the trailing SRM. Incidentally, the reference to 'a 74 ft motor' relates to a 70 ft SRM; they were 74 ft long over the buffers.

Trailers 9 and 10 were 70 ft long, 9 ft wide, and 12 ft $3\frac{3}{4}$ inches in height. The wheelbase was 56 ft 6 in, and they started life with 9 ft volute spring bogies. These were changed to coil spring units, probably at an early date. They had the standard queen post truss underframe, with round section queenposts and flat section truss rods.

As built, the bodies had 4 ft 9 in vestibules at each end, with sliding doors to the outside and retractable steps under each. These vestibules also had sliding doors in the partitions to the interior of the trailer. Internally, the coaches had a 15 ft length of longitudinal seating at each end, and 9 walkover seats in between (29 ft long).

It is thought that as built they had only fixed lights to the passenger accommodation, but pairs of droplights were inserted in place of the fourth fixed light from each end at an early date.

These two trailers had an opening at the non-driving end and appear to have been coupled to SRMs 59 and 60 via a centre-buffing arrangement. There seems to have been a short platform over the buffer to facilitate transfer from one coach to the other, and this is how they appear as Diagram D. In this state, they could not be coupled together to run as a pair of trailers with their end openings together, because the regulator apparatus would not be compatible (assuming the standard regulator couplers were fitted).

Between October and December 1911, both coaches had standard gangways fitted at the non-driving ends. At this overhaul, No. 9 had its drawgear and buffers changed to the volute-sprung type, and No. 10 had 'long buffers' (ie, standard items) fitted at one end to go with the similar pair already installed at the other (driving) end. Both Nos. 9 and 10 were equipped with TRG in November 1913.

It appears that in 1920, they both came in for some more attention at Swindon. No. 9 was, in effect, turned round; it had the non-driving end vestibule enlarged to 7 ft between the end wall and the partition, the end wall being made solid with a middle window fitted in place of the gangway, and the sliding side doors to the exterior were replaced with double leaves, which opened outwards. Three tip-up seats were fitted here, for passengers' use when the rest of the train was full. The driving compartment had an opening made in it, and a GWR standard (scissors) gangway connector was fitted. As such, No. 9 is shown as Diagram A11; at the same time, No. 10 was shown as Diagram A12. These alterations meant that they could be used together as a pair with their gangways connected, and it is believed that this is how they ran. SRMs Nos. 59 and 60 were converted to trailers Nos. 127 and 127 in June 1920 and ran as a gangwayed pair themselves (see under Diagrams A13 and A14 in Chapter 8.)

No. 10 is recorded as having been fitted with dry sand boxes in January 1927. Both coaches had their gas lighting changed to elec-

Steam rail motor, possibly No. 60, and Diagram D trailer, probably No. 10. AUTHOR'S COLLECTION

tric, both were fitted with the chain alarm apparatus, and each had their axleboxes painted blue; this work was carried out in March 1930 and it is recorded that the larger compartment in No. 9 was made into the 'smoking' saloon at the same time (No. 10 had been dealt with in September 1928). There is no note of the reason why there was this difference in dates, or why the examples of other pairs was not followed, in having one coach designated smoking, the other non-smoking. The A11 Diagram shows No. 9 as being 'Smoking'!

Both trailers were given cream and brown livery with gold lines in September 1932. The top 17 inches of their non-driving windows were painted black in February 1935, and both were fitted with ATC in October 1940. In the early 1950s, No. 10 was photographed at Exeter St Davids in brown and cream livery, numbered W10, 1949-style. It then had Collett 7 ft bogies, although there is no record of their being fitted in the register.

These two trailers were condemned together, in April 1955.

0–6–0PT No. 1570 at Yealmpton with what appear to be trailers Nos. 9 and 10, in September 1931. DR. IAN C. ALLEN

Summary

No.	Lot	Blt	Coil spring bogies	Std gangways	TRG fitted	To Diag A11	To Diag A12	Sand boxes	Chain Comm
9	1090	Nov.05	+	Oct.11	Dec.13	Jan.20	–	–	Mar.30
10	1090	Oct.05	+	Dec.11	Nov.13	–	1920	Jan.27	Mar.30

No.	Smoking cmpts altered	Blue a/boxes	Electric lighting	Cream, Brown & gold	End windows black	ATC	Cond
9	Mar.30?	Mar.30	Mar.30	Sep.32	Feb.35	Oct.40	Apr.55
10	Sep.28?	Mar.30	Mar.30	Sep.32	Feb.35	Oct.40	Apr.55

70 ft Trailers Nos. 11–13: Diagrams E & F

No. 13 Diagram F as built with 9ft volute spring bogies and 'prize' monogram. Note the side lamp on the far end of the trailer. This is a good illustration of the pre-Great War 'full' livery. The destination board reads 'Calne'. NATIONAL RAILWAY MUSEUM

Three more 70 ft trailers appeared hot on the heels of Nos. 9 and 10; these were Nos. 11–13, which were built in November and December 1905 on Lot 1097.

These trailers were built with an off-centre vestibule for passengers to enter the coach; this vestibule was 4 ft 2 in between partitions, and became a fairly standard feature thereafter. There was still a vestibule at the front of the trailer for the driver, with a 4 ft 9 in maximum between the coach end and the partition. The driver's doors opened inwards, being flat, and slightly recessed into the body. Instead of a similar vestibule for the guard, there was a luggage compartment with a maximum length of 7 ft 7½ in between the coach end and the partition. This luggage compartment had double doors on each side, opening outwards. The 'passengers' vestibule' (author's term) enabled travellers to board and alight from the trailer without having to go through either the driver's compartment or the guard's luggage area. Instead of retractable steps below the doors at each corner of the coach, these were now only provided below the doors of the passenger vestibule, thus saving two sets.

By having a single passenger entrance to the coach, it made the guard's task of controlling the passengers and issuing fares much simpler. The doors to the passenger's vestibule were slightly recessed, flat, and opened inwards, so that opening the doors would not knock anyone off the steps! The presence of this vestibule arrangement also meant that the coach could easily be divided into 'Smoking' and 'No smoking' areas. Nos. 11–13 were apparently built with droplights (the first purpose-built trailers with this feature).

These trailers were the standard 70 ft long, 9 ft wide and 12 ft 3¾ in high. However, they had a wheelbase of 61 ft, longer than was possible on earlier trailers, because they did not have retractable steps at the ends. They were initially fitted with 9 ft volute spring bogies; these may have been changed to coil spring units soon after building, although eventually Collett 7 ft heavy duty types were fitted. The underframe was the standard queenpost truss, with round section queenposts and flat section truss rods. Incandescent gas lighting was fitted from new.

Internally, these coaches were a little unusual in that some provision was apparently made for first class accommodation. The 11 ft 11½ in compartment between the luggage area and the passengers' vestibule had two seating bays each side of the central aisle, which meant that they were almost 6 ft between seat backs, instead of the more usual 4 ft 11 in elsewhere in the coach. Between the passengers' vestibule and the driver's there were (in order) a 12 ft length of longitudinal benches, a 14 ft 9 in area with three seating bays each side of the aisle and, next to the driver's compartment, a further 12 ft (or 12 ft 3 in) length of longitudinal benches.

There is some evidence that No. 13 did have the appropriate compartment upholstered to first class standards, although officially designated third class. It was used on the Calne service, the area in which the Marquess of Lansdowne had his country seat (he was Foreign Secretary between 1903 and 1905, and returned to the Government 1915–16 as Minister without portfolio). No. 13 appears in an official photograph when new with CALNE on its destination board. 'Auto Car No. 13' is shown as working on the Chippenham–Calne branch in the *Bristol & Westbury Divisions Working of Coaches* programme for April 1918 ('and until further notice'). This is one of the very few specific allocations of a coach to a given service shown in these books:

Working No. 263

6.20 am Chippenham to Calne and back
8.00 am Chippenham to Box and back (SX)
8.50 am Chippenham to Calne and back
11.35 am Chippenham to Calne and back
6.10 pm Chippenham to Calne and back
8.30 pm Chippenham to Calne and back

No. 13 was shown as Diagram F, whereas the other two appear on Diagram E. The only difference between the two diagrams is that there is an additional partition with sliding door between the longitudinal bench seats at the driver's end, and the adjacent seating bays. This would have enabled these bench seats to be used as the smoking compartment.

The subsequent history of these trailers is as follows. TRG was fitted in 1912/13, and sand boxes in 1927. The axle boxes of Nos. 11 and 13 were painted blue in 1928 and 1931 respectively; this may well have been when the 7 ft bogies were fitted. The 'larger compartment' became 'smoking' in 1928; this apparently referred to the area between the passengers' vestibule and the driver's compartment. In 1935, the end windows were painted black, and ATC was fitted in the 1940s.

During the late 1940s, No. 11 was based at Banbury, and was in the 1947 livery with twin gold lines at the waist panels.

In 1935, No. 13 was based at Taunton. After the Second War it appeared in the Bristol Division, on occasions being used on the Yatton–Clevedon service (where it was seen in 1947 carrying the brown and cream livery, but without waist lines).

These trailers were condemned in 1954 and 1955.

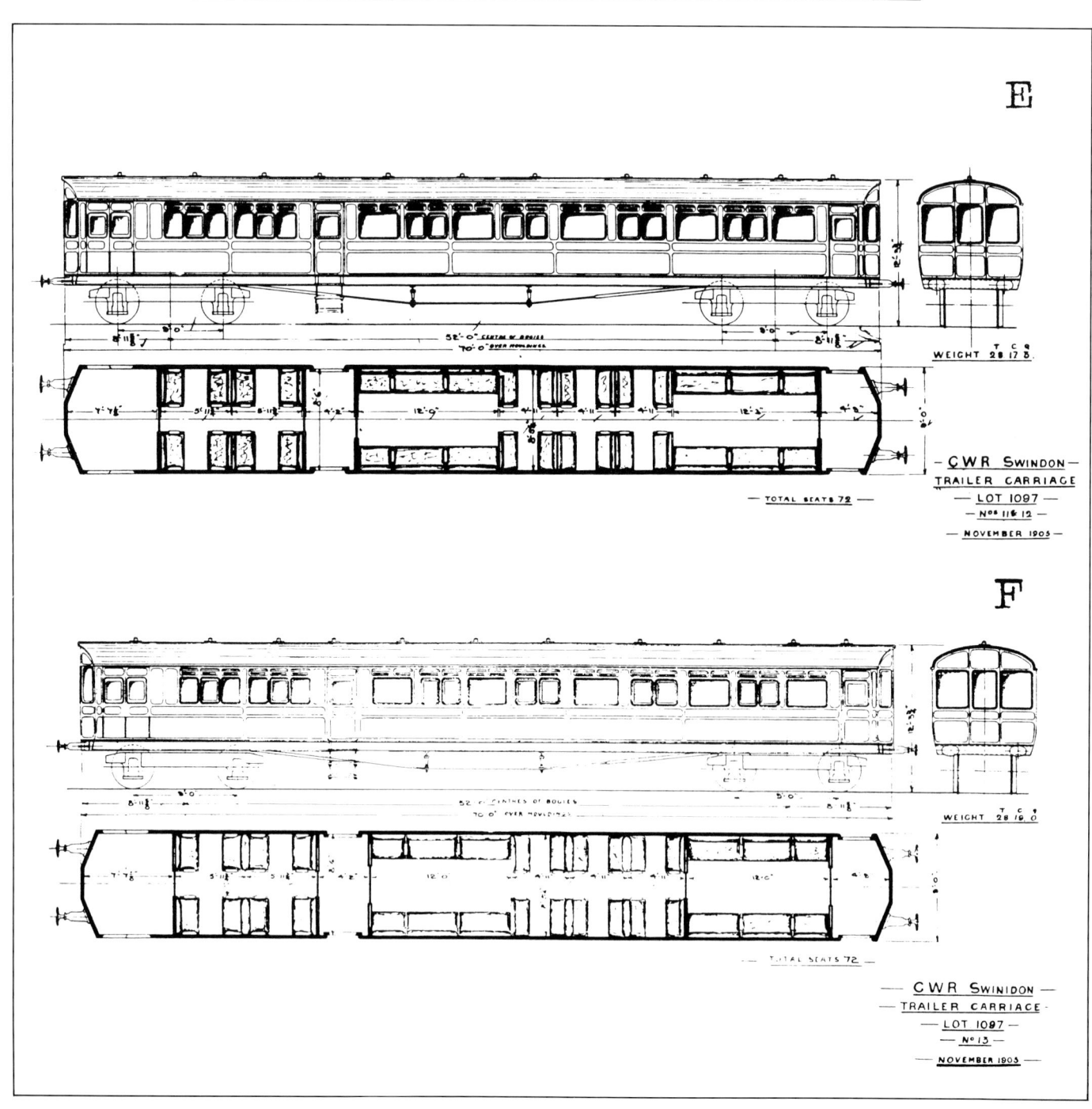

No.	Lot	Built	Diag	Coil Spring Bogies	TRG	Sand boxes	7 ft Collet bogies
11	1097	Nov.05	E	+?	Feb.13	Jan.27	Aug.28
12	1097	Nov.05	E	+?	+	Nr	Nr
13	1097	Dec.05	F	+?	Sep.12	Jul.27	Mar.31?

Blue A/Boxes	Smoking Cpts rearranged	Chain comm	Cream brown & gold	End windows black	Brown	ATC	Cond
Aug.28	Sep.28	Jul.29	Sep.32	Feb.35	–	Sep.40	Oct.54
Nr	Sep.28	Aug.31	Aug.31	Nov.35	–	Mar.45	Dec.55
Mar.31	Nov.28	Nov.29	Mar.31	Mar.35	Jun.42	+	Jan.54

Purpose-built 70ft Trailers

Diagram E No. 11 at Banbury with 7ft bogies and the 1947 livery.   J. H. RUSSELL

No. 13, Diagram F, at Clevedon in March 1947 with 7ft Collett bogies. The bolection mouldings around the droplight were an original feature. Compare the droplights on 1–6 which were later additions without bolection mouldings.   L & GRP, CTY. DAVID & CHARLES

K

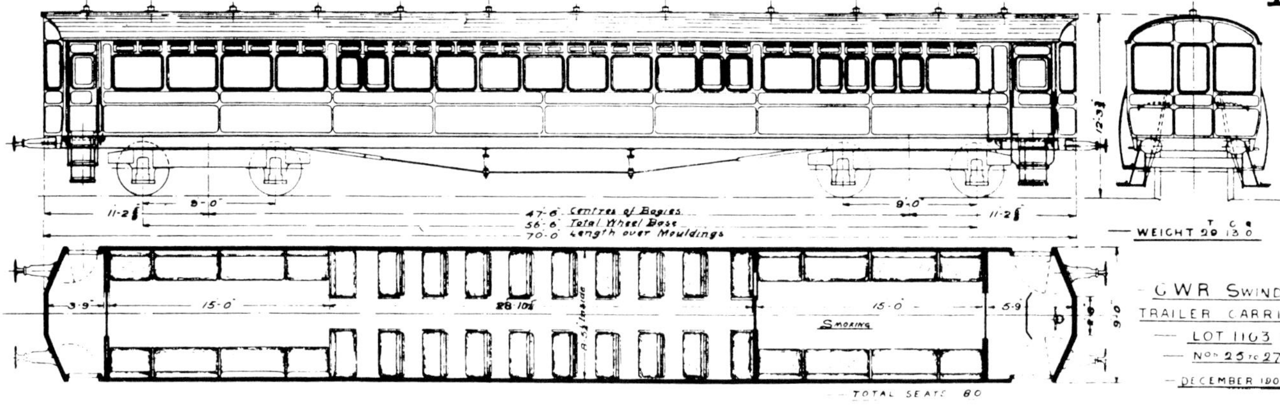

GWR SWINDON
TRAILER CARRIAGE
LOT 1103
Nos 25 to 27
DECEMBER 1905

K[1]

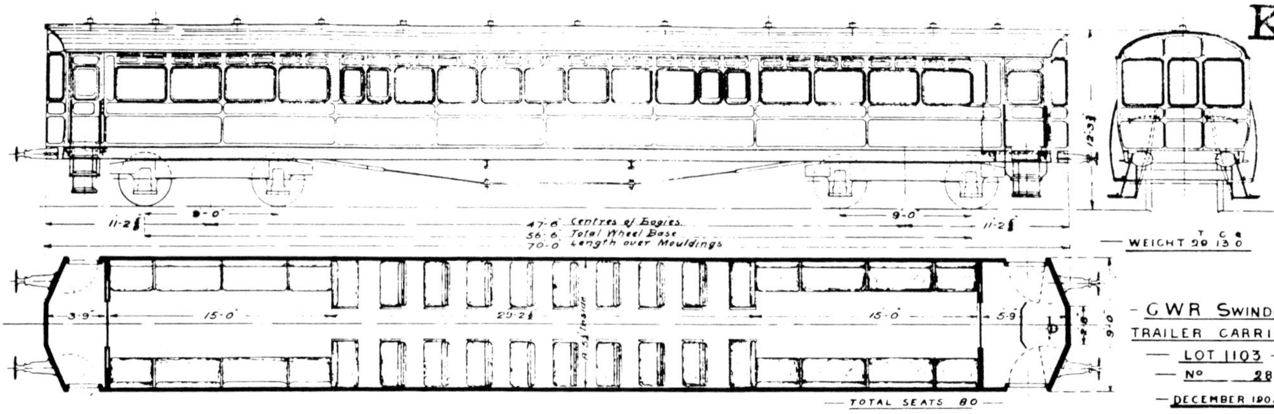

GWR SWINDON
TRAILER CARRIAGE
LOT 1103
No 28
DECEMBER 1905

Y

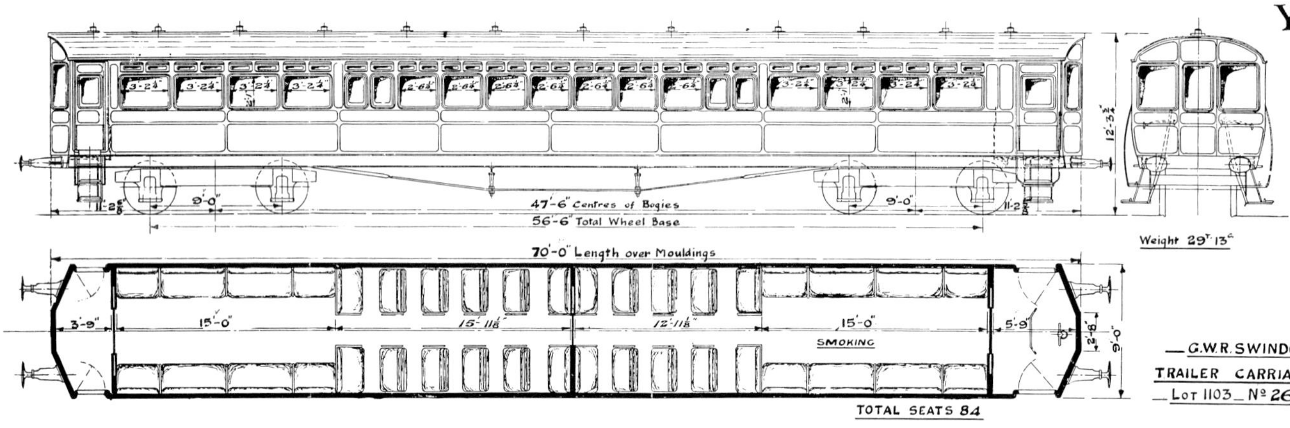

G.W.R. SWINDON
TRAILER CARRIAGE
Lot 1103 No 26

A[5]

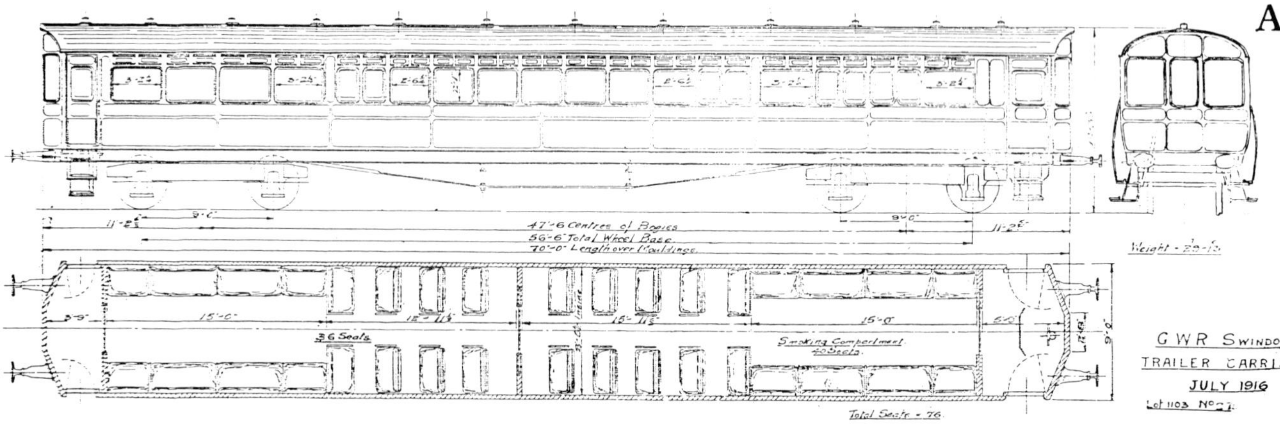

GWR SWINDON
TRAILER CARRIAGE
JULY 1916
Lot 1103 No 27

Purpose-built 70ft Trailers

70ft Trailers Nos. 25–8: Diagrams K1, K, Y & A5

No. 27 at Drayton Green Halt c.1930 is in the two-colour livery with one gold/black line. This vehicle was originally Diagram K1, then K and, as shown here, A5.
LENS OF SUTTON

The rate of building trailers was quite rapid in the latter months of 1905, and four more 70ft wood panelled ones, Nos. 25–8, appeared in December of that year; these had been ordered on Lot 1103 in July 1905, and cost an average of £1,226 each.

They were the usual 70ft × 9ft, and 12ft 3¾in high from rail to roof. They had 9ft-wheelbase volute spring bogies on completion, with a total wheelbase of 56ft 6in. The underframe was the standard trussed design of the period. They were all gas lit, with incandescent gas lamps.

These did not follow trailers 11–13 in having a passengers' vestibule near the centre of the coach, an alternative approach being tried. There was a wide vestibule for the driver, having a maximum length of 5ft 9in between the partition and the end wall of the trailer. Access to this vestibule was by two doors in the body sides, each being flat, slightly recessed, and opening inwards, with the door hinges towards the front of the trailer. In order to prevent the driver from being distracted by passengers entering at this point, there was a screen with angled ends across the coach, so that when the door was opened, the passengers were directed into the cross vestibule, leaving the driver protected by the screen and the open door. Access to the interior of the trailer from the vestibule was via a sliding door.

At the other end, there was the usual arrangement of a vestibule for the guard; this one was rather narrow, only 3ft 9in maximum between the partition and the end wall. The external doors at this end were of the narrow variety (2ft), flat, slightly recessed, and opening inwards. Again, there was a central sliding door leading from the vestibule into the saloon.

Internally, the coach was divided into the usual three areas; at each end there were longitudinal benches occupying 15ft, whilst in the middle there were ten walkover seats, the backs of those at the end being fixed against the ends of the benches. The coaches were not partitioned between the end vestibules. The window arrangement adopted had four fixed lights along the areas of the longitudinal benches, whilst the transverse seating was served by double droplights each end, and between them seven fixed lights, rather narrower than the end ones. Finally, there was a double panel between the windows and the driver's door, corresponding to the cross vestibule. In this condition they were shown as Diagram K1.

It was quickly realised that the coaches would be better if partitioned into smoking and non-smoking areas, with additional droplights in the former. A partition (with sliding door) was therefore inserted between the bench seating and the transverse seats at the driver's end, and the smoking compartment thus formed had the two central (of the four) fixed lights on each side changed for pairs of droplights. This was done at an early date (not recorded) in the case of Nos. 25–7, but No. 28 seems to have escaped this modification. This condition is represented by Diagram K. In both K and K1 forms, the trailers seated 80 passengers.

In May 1912, No. 26 had the partition between the smoking and non-smoking compartments moved nearer to the centre of the coach (to a position 12ft 11½in from the longitudinal benches at the driver's end), and somehow an additional pair of walkover-type seats were 'shoehorned' in, so that the trailer now seated 84. There were six pairs of transverse seats in the non-smoking compartment and five in the smoking. This arrangement is shown as Diagram Y. To complicate matters somewhat, this diagram is based on Diagram K1 instead of K, so it does not show the additional droplights in the smoking compartment which 26 possessed. The reason for this is perhaps found in a note on the diagram that No. 28 had no partition and 80 seats.

Also in May 1912, No. 28 was fitted with a partition 15ft 11½in from the driver's end bench seating. However, this time a pair of walkover seats were removed, so that there were now only 76 seats remaining. In this condition it is not shown on any surviving

71

No. 26 in BR days with its toplights plated over.

Below: *Rather a grim picture of No. 27 in BR maroon and cream with the running numbers in the 1951 position. Although the coach has lost its toplights, its luggage end windows are still intact.*
HMRS

diagram. In July 1916, No. 27 also had its partition moved to this position, with a loss of 4 seats; it is shown as Diagram A5, with seating for 40 smokers and 36 non-smokers. In August 1916, No. 28 appeared from Swindon works with additional droplights fitted, so it too corresponded to Diagram A5.

There is no record of these coaches being equipped with sandboxes, although a photograph of No. 27 appears to show them. The known dates for the fitting of chain communication apparatus and the reorganisation of the smoking compartments are shown in the summary table. As No. 27 already had the larger compartment designated for smoking, it was left unaltered when the compartments were being changed around.

The bogies on Nos. 25, 26 and 27 were changed to the 9 ft 'American' type in November 1931, June 1930, and a date unrecorded; No. 28 had received the Collett 7 ft heavy duty type in August 1929. No. 26 is the only one not recorded as having the gold lines livery. The end windows were painted black in 1935.

All were fitted with ATC in the 1940s, Nos. 26 and 28 having the dual bells arrangement. No. 28 received improved door handles to the vestibule in April 1951, covered by New Works Order 8375.

No. 26 ran in brown and cream livery in early BR days as W26 (in 1949-style), but by then it had lost its toplights.

No. 27 ran in the revised 1943 brown and cream livery with G.W.R above the crest. It also had horizontal bars across the droplights to stop passengers putting their heads out of the windows. The trailer had 9 ft 'American' bogies and sanding apparatus. In BR days, it ran as W27W in the BR carmine and cream livery, having lost its toplights, but still retaining its end windows at the luggage end.

The vehicles were condemned in December 1954, October 1953, June 1958 and November 1954 respectively.

Summary

No.	Lot	Built	Diag.	To Diag. K	To Diag. Y	To Diag. A5	TRG	Bogies changed to	Date
25	1103	Dec.05	K1	+	–	–	+	9 ft American	Nov.31
26	1103	Dec.05	K1	+	May 12	–	+	9 ft American	Jun.30
27	1103	Dec.05	K1	+	–	Jul.16	+	9 ft American	+
28	1103	Dec.05	K1	–	–	May 12	Jul.14	7 ft Collett	Aug.29

No.	Chain Comm.	Smoking compts rearranged	Cream brown & gold	End windows black	ATC	Cond
25	Nov.31	Aug.29	Oct.31	Apr.35	Oct.44	Dec.54
26	Jun.30	Jun.30	–	Apr.35	Feb.45db	Oct.53
27	Mar.30	Jan.16	Apr.32	Jun.35	+	Jun.58
28	Aug.29	Sep.29	Mar.32	?	Feb.45db	Nov.54

db = dual bells

70 ft Trailers Nos. 29–34, 42–7 & 53–70: Diagram L

Trailer 34 as built with 9 ft coil spring bogies and shown here coupled to SRM 61.

NATIONAL RAILWAY MUSEUM

The 30 trailers illustrated in Diagram L are probably the nearest the GWR got to having a standard trailer design. They were built on four Lots between January 1906 and February 1908.

Lot	Ordered	Completed	Running Nos.	Average Cost
1108	Aug.05	Jan.06	29–34	£1,194
1127	Jun.06	Dec.06	42–47	£1,208
1141	Jun.07	Jan.08	53–58	£1,280
1143	Aug.07	Feb.08	59–70	£1,252

The last two Lots illustrate the problems of reading too much significance into railway company building costs; these two Lots are believed to have been identical. They employed the 9 ft 'American' bogie from new, so some cost differential between them and earlier Lots can be expected.

These trailers were 70 ft long, 9 ft wide, 12 ft 3¾ in high, and had a wheelbase of 61 ft. The first to be built (Nos. 29–34, 42–7) were equipped with 9 ft coil spring bogies, which were eventually changed mostly either for 9 ft 'American' or to Collett 7 ft Heavy Duty bogies. The remainder were given 9 ft 'American' bogies when built which, it is believed, they retained throughout their existence.

The trailers built on the last two Lots (No. 53–70) had underframe trusses without a twist in the flat truss rods, and so were to the then new standard. The queenposts were the adjustable round-section design under a transverse 'I' section beam, as normal. Armstrong moving vacuum cylinders were fitted. The vehicles were all gas lit, with incandescent burners, and remained so throughout their lives.

Diagram L trailers incorporated an intermediate passengers' vestibule near the middle of the coach. This had slightly-recessed flat profile doors that opened inwards, with the retractable steps below them. The driver had a vestibule 3 ft 9 in (maximum), also with recessed flat doors, opening inwards. At the other end, there was a luggage compartment 7 ft 10¾ in (maximum) between the end wall of the carriage and the partition, which had the usual sliding door arrangement to gain access to the interior of the trailer. It had double doors that followed the profile of the coach side, and opened outwards.

Between the luggage compartment and the passengers' vestibule, there was a 10 ft-length of saloon with two seating bays each side of the central aisle, and a 9 ft length of longitudinal seats. The passengers' vestibule was 3 ft 9 in between partitions, and had sliding doors to the passenger saloons. Between the passengers' and the driver's vestibules, there were 9 ft-lengths of longitudinal benches at each end flanking a 15 ft-length containing three transverse seating bays.

The window arrangement in the small saloon was a single, large fixed light and a pair of droplights by the bench seats, with another pair of fixed lights by the seating bays. The large saloon had two fixed lights by each of the longitudinal benches, and two pairs of droplights either side of a single fixed light by the seating bays. There were the usual toplights above all these windows.

For once, these coaches were not immediately rebuilt or partitioned. However, No. 32 received a standard scissors-type gangway at the luggage compartment end in January 1910. When it was fitted with chain communication in 1929, the tell-tales and associated rodding were placed at the driving end; all the others are believed to have had this apparatus at the luggage end.

All the Diagram L trailers are believed to have been fitted with TRG between 1912 and 1916, but only a few dates are recorded. The same goes for sandboxes (recorded examples are circa 1927–9) and blue axleboxes (1927 onwards). So far as is known, all had the larger compartment designated 'smoking' in 1928–31, and received chain communication in 1929–30. No. 61 was given replacement second-hand gas cylinders in April 1929.

The end windows were all painted black in 1935, and plated over thereafter at unrecorded dates. ATC is believed to have been fitted to all Diagram L trailers in the 1940s. They were condemned in the 1950s; No. 43 became classroom DW079021 after it was condemned in June 1955, and Nos. 29 and 45 were temporarily used by the CM & EE department at Highbridge from November 1957. No. 29 was officially withdrawn in April 1955, although the CM & EE's 'temporary' use continued for some years, and it was still at Highbridge in August 1962 in BR carmine and cream livery, and numbered W29W in the 1949-style.

No. 31 was used on the Ashburton-Totnes service in BR days.

No. 32 was photographed in the London area on suburban working 'E' between 1925 and 1929. It carried the full (1924) livery, and a gangway connector at the luggage end; the trailer was still fitted with 9 ft coil spring bogies, and the small saloon can be seen to have 'Smoking' signs. It was photographed again in May 1936 at Gloucester, having been just repainted in the 1934 livery; by now, it had Collett 7 ft bogies, and the large saloon had become 'Smoking'. In the picture, the effect of painting the top 17 in of the luggage end windows black can be seen.

No. 33 ran in the BR carmine and cream livery as W33 (in the 1949-style). It was photographed at Slough running on 9 ft heavy bogies, and was condemned at Southall in 1955.

No. 34 was photographed in February 1908 in the company of SRM No. 61. Both were in the 'full' brown and cream livery, and both carried the 1906 'prize' monogram.

No. 40 was used on the Banbury–Kingham service in the late 1940s (it was seen on this run in 1948), sporting the 1943 brown and cream livery with a single gold waist line. By this time, ATC had been fitted, and sandboxes were carried at the leading end.

Nos. 42, 43, 46 (and one other) were photographed when new as a four-coach auto train, with a tank engine 'in disguise' as a coach, in the middle. These trailers were in the full brown and cream livery, and carried the garter coat of arms with supporters. Although No. 43 became officially DW079021 after withdrawal in June 1955, it was still identifiable as W43W in peeling BR carmine and cream livery at Carmarthen in July 1959.

No. 45 was photographed in the 1948 brown and cream livery with two waist lines, and was equipped with ATC. In 1954 it was used on the Cardiff–Coryton service as W45W, in plain maroon livery.

No. 53 ran for a time in brown and cream livery as W53, with lettering in the 1949-style. It was repainted in carmine and cream with 1949-style lettering, and was photographed in this condition at Bourne End. Eventually, it had its toplights plated over, and ran as W53W (with 1951-style lettering) in plain maroon.

No. 54 was operated in the London area in the late '40s/early '50s. It was photographed on London area suburban working 'A' at Ealing Broadway on a Greenford train, accompanied by 0-6-0T No. 5410; No. 54

'517' class 0–4–2T No. 847 with auto trailer No. 32. Built in January 1906, it is seen here with a gangway connector which was fitted at the locomotive end in January 1910. This photo was taken some time between 1924 and 1929.
AUTHOR'S COLLECTION

Trailer 32 at Gloucester in 1936, showing the gangway connector, 7ft bogies with blue tops to the axleboxes, and the communication tell-tale, etc., at the driver's end. Most trailers had it at the luggage end.
L. E. COPELAND

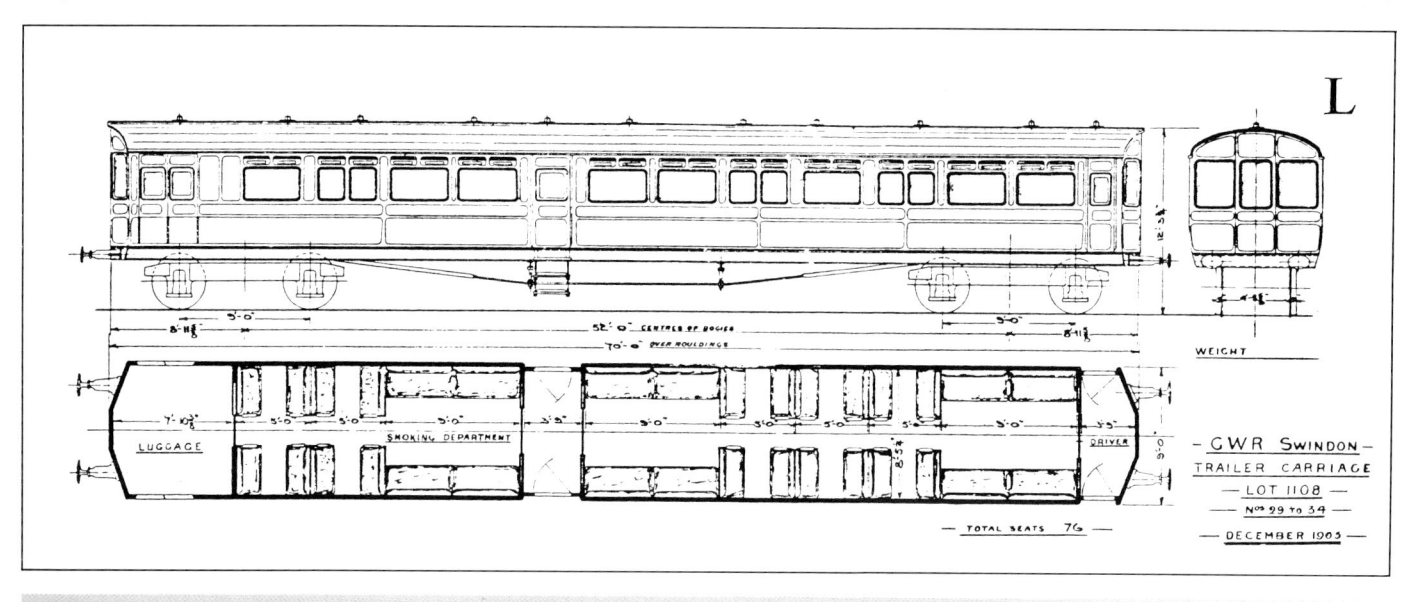

Purpose-built 70ft Trailers

Another view of No. 32 on 28th May 1936. L. E. COPELAND

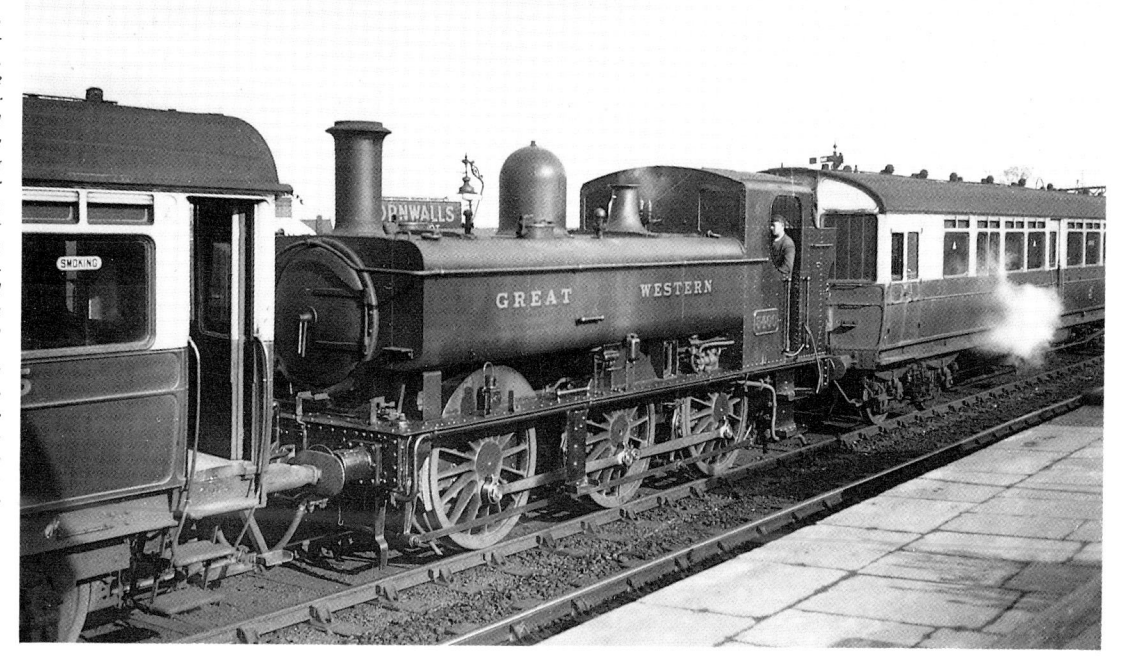

No. 5400 with two trailers, probably No. 25 of Diagram K on the left. If so, the photo was taken some time after November 1931 when it was fitted with 9ft American bogies and given the double lining at the waist. The other trailer is No. 32 of Diagram L in the 1930 single waist line, brown and cream livery. The gangway connector is just visible behind the loco's cab and the area above the connector is either black or dirty. No. 32 is said to have received gold lines in November 1931, but only the upper waist line is in evidence. As No. 5400 looks in new condition, the picture may have been taken in June or July 1932. Note the narrow, flat door at the non-driving end of No. 25, a characteristic of these and the J trailers.
M. D. ENGLAND

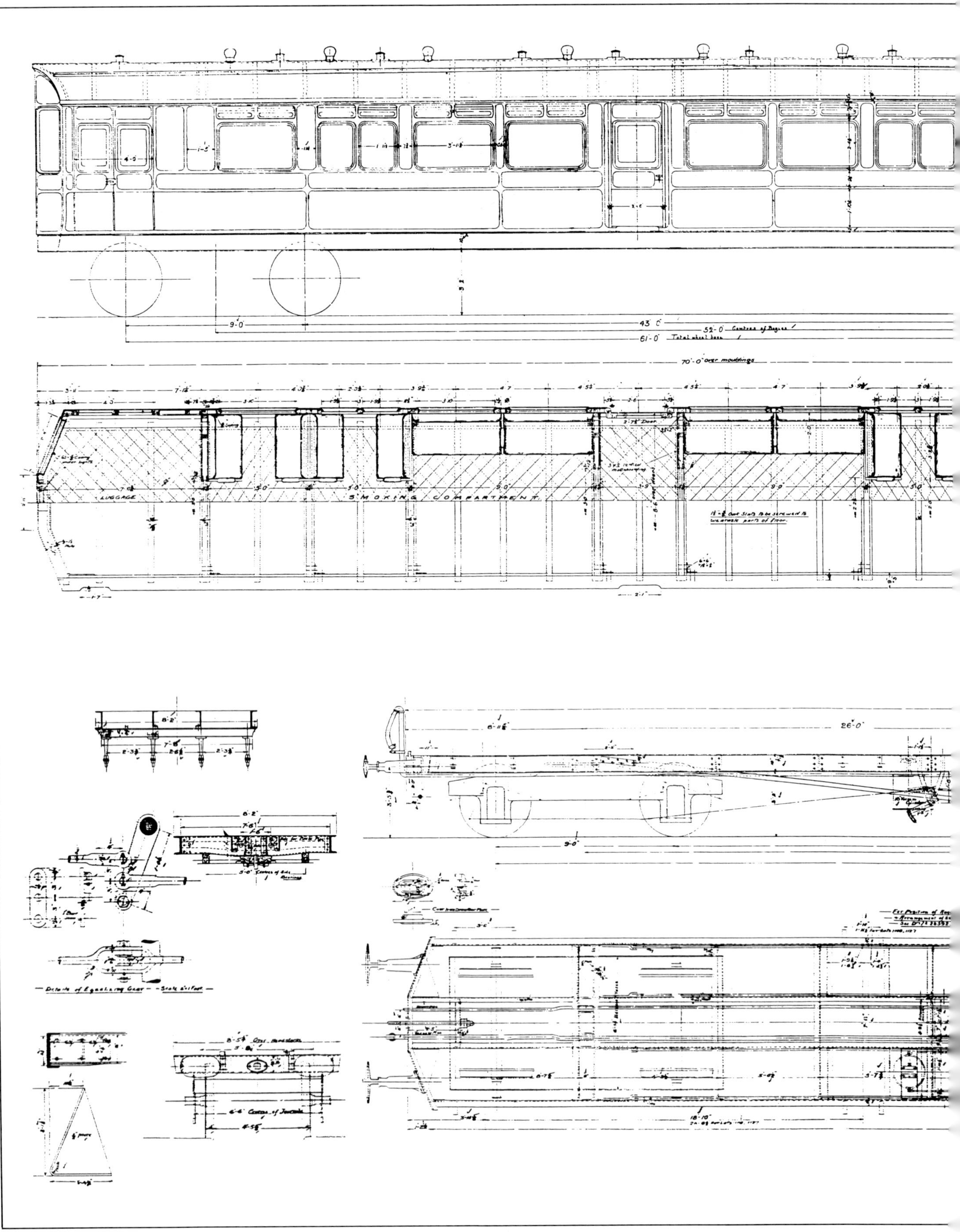
43'0"
52-0 Centres of Bogies
61-0 Total wheel base
70'-0" over mouldings
2-7½" Door
LUGGAGE
SMOKING COMPARTMENT
26'-0"
Details of Equalising Gear - Scale 1" Foot -
6-6" Centres of Journals

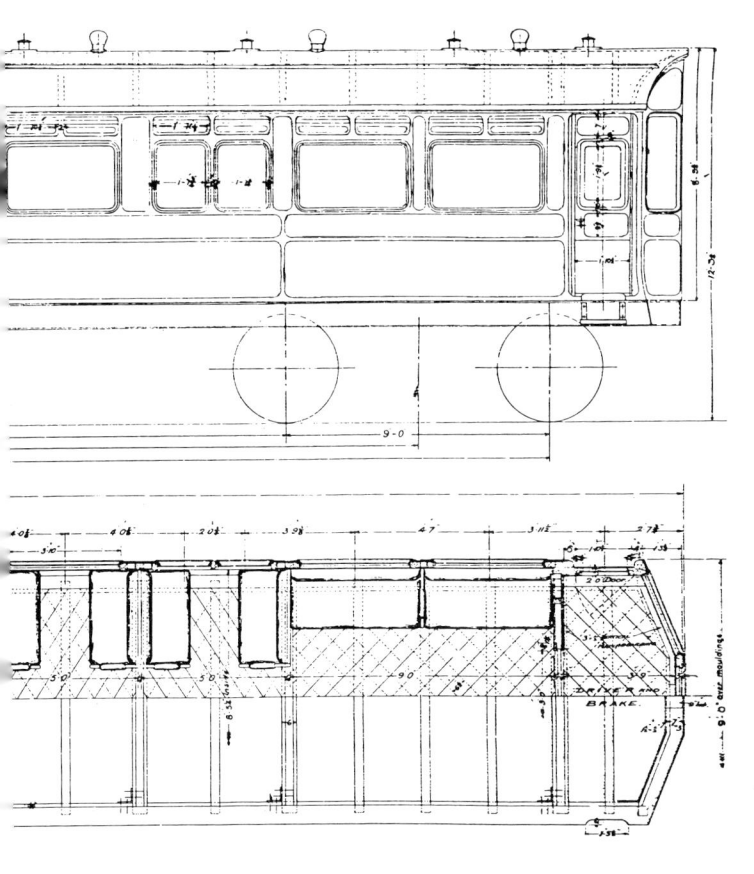

Purpose-built 70ft Trailers

Gangway end of No. 32 showing the internal 'wicket gate'.
L. E. COPELAND

— G.W.R SWINDON —
— 70' 0" STEAM MOTOR TRAILER BODY —
— AUGUST 1905 —

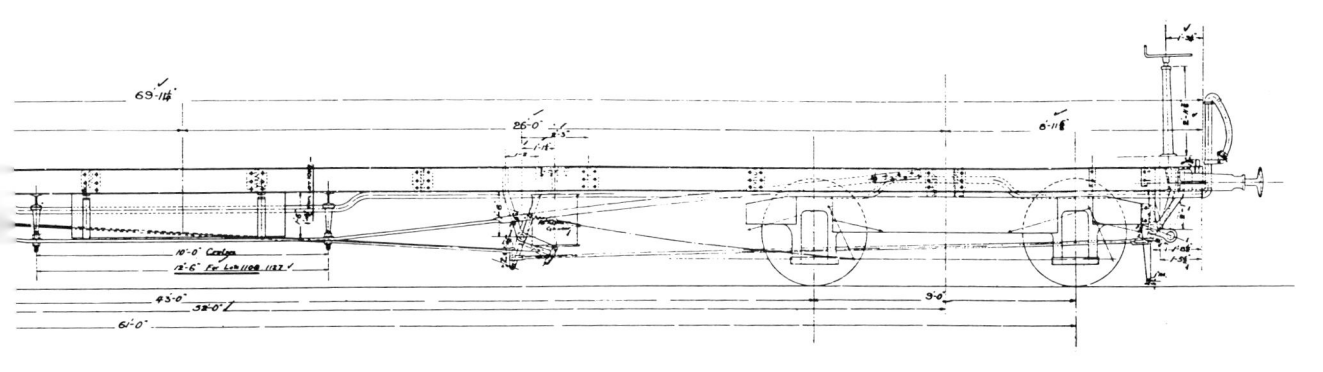

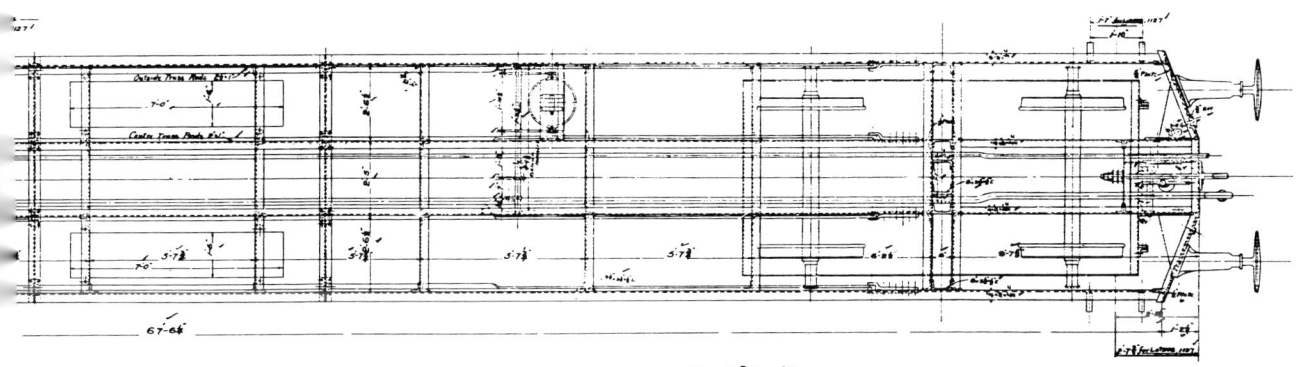

— G.W.R SWINDON —
— 69'-11¾" UNDERFRAME —
— AUGUST 1905 —

No.	Lot	Built	Initial bogies	U/frame truss rods	TRG	Replacement bogies	Date
29	1108	Jan.06	9ft coil spring	Twist	Oct.16	9ft American	?
30	1108	Jan.06	9ft coil spring	Twist	+	7ft Collett	Oct.29
31	1108	Jan.06	9ft coil spring	Twist	+	9ft fishbelly	?
32	1108	Jan.06	9ft coil spring	Twist	+	7ft Collett	by Jun.29
33	1108	Jan.06	9ft coil spring	Twist	May 15	7ft Collett	?
34	1108	Jan.06	9ft coil spring	Twist	+	9ft American	Oct.27
42	1127	Dec.06	9ft coil spring	Twist	Built?	7ft Collett	Sep.28
43	1127	Dec.06	9ft coil spring	Twist	Built?	7ft Collett	?
44	1127	Dec.06	9ft coil spring	Twist	Dec.12	7ft Collett	?
45	1127	Dec.06	9ft coil spring	Twist	+	9ft American	?
46	1127	Dec.06	9ft coil spring	Twist	Nov.13	Not recorded	?
47	1127	Dec.06	9ft coil spring	Twist	+	Not recorded	?
53	1141	Dec.07	9ft American	Flat	+	–	–
54	1141	Dec.07	9ft American	Flat	+	–	–
55	1141	Dec.07	9ft American	Flat	+	–	–
56	1141	Dec.07	9ft American	Flat	+	–	–
57	1141	Dec.07	9ft American	Flat	+	–	–
58	1141	Dec.07	9ft American	Flat	+	–	–
59	1143	Dec.07	9ft American	Flat	Jul.13	–	–
60	1143	Dec.07	9ft American	Flat	+	–	–
61	1143	Dec.07	9ft American	Flat	+	–	–
62	1143	Jan.08	9ft American	Flat	+	–	–
63	1143	Jan.08	9ft American	Flat	+	–	–
64	1143	Jan.08	9ft American	Flat	+	–	–
65	1143	Feb.08	9ft American	Flat	+	–	–
66	1143	Feb.08	9ft American	Flat	+	–	–
67	1143	Feb.08	9ft American	Flat	+	–	–
68	1143	Feb.08	9ft American	Flat	+	–	–
69	1143	Feb.08	9ft American	Flat	+	–	–
70	1143	Feb.08	9ft American	Flat	+	–	–

No.	Sand boxes	Chain comm.	Blue a/boxes	Smoking cmpt. rearranged	Cream brown & gold	End windows black	ATC	Cond
29	+	May 30	.	Jun.30	–	Feb.35	+	Apr.55
30	Jan.27	Oct.29	Apr.32	Oct.29	Apr.32	Feb.35	May 40	Jan.55
31	Jul.27	Jul.29	Jul.29	Jul.28	Mar.31	Feb.35	Feb.45db	Jul.56
32	+	Jun.29	Jun.29	Jun.29	Oct.31	Feb.35	Sep.40	Jul.55
33	Sep.27	Aug.29	Aug.29	Sep.29	Nov.34	Feb.35	Feb.45db	Jul.55
34	+	Jun.29	.	+	Sep.31	Oct.35	Oct.40	Dec.56
42	+	May 31	Sep.28	Oct.28	–	Feb.35	Apr.46	Jan.55
43	+	Apl.31	May.28	Jun.28	Mar.31	Mar.35	May 41	Jun.55
44	+	Feb.28	Jan.28	Jan.29	Sep.31	Feb.35	Jul.40	Nov.57
45	+	Oct.29	.	Oct.29	May 32	Feb.35	+	Nov.57
46	+	Jun.29	Aug.31	May.29	Aug.31	Feb.35	Apr.43	Jan.56
47	+	Feb.32	.	Jun.28	+	Feb.35	Mar.45db	Oct.54
53	May.27	Oct.29	Aug.27	Sep.29	Sep.31	Apr.35	May 40	Apr.58
54	Sep.27	Oct.29	.	Sep.29	Jan.32	Feb.35	Jul.45	Jun.51
55	+	Oct.30	.	Oct.28	–	Feb.35	Jul.40	May 56
56	+	Sep.30	.	Aug.28	–	Jun.35	Jun.40	Apr.58
57	+	Aug.30	.	Aug.30	Aug.30	Mar.35	+?	Jul.57
58	May 29	Dec.28	.	Jan.29	Feb.31	Apr.35	+?	Jun.56
59	+	Jan.29	.	Feb.29	Aug.31	Feb.35	+?	May 56
60	May.27	Sep.29	.	+	May 32	Oct.35	Dec.46	Mar.58
61	+	Apl.29	.	May.29	Aug.31	Oct.35	Dec.49	Sep.57
62	+	Sep.28	.	Oct.28	Mar.32	Feb.35	Jan.45	Oct.56
63	+	Sep.29	Nov.38	Oct.29	Nov.31	Feb.35	+?	Sep.57
64	+	Sep.30	.	Nov.28	Apr.31	Feb.35	Jun.52	Nov.57
65	+	Aug.29	.	Sep.29	Apr.32	Feb.35	+	Nov.57
66	+	Mar.30	.	Mar.30	–	Apr.35	+?	Dec.56
67	Jul.28	May 30	.	Aug.28	–	Oct.35	Jun.45	Nov.56
68	Jul.28	May 30	Sep.28	Oct.28	–	?	Nov.40	Dep.57
69	+	May.29	.	Sep.28	May 31	Oct.35	Nov.41	Mar.58
70	Apr.27	Aug.30	.	Sep.30	Aug.30	Feb.35	Jul.40	Oct.56

No. Notes

29 Painted brown Jul.42. Temp. use CMEE Highbridge
32 Gangwayed Jan.10
42 Painted red-brown May.42. To DW 079021 Feb.57 for Carmarthen MPD Mutual Improvement classes. Cond. Feb.60.

61 Second-hand gas cylinders Apr.26.
70 To DW079018 Nov.56. Mobile office for Industrial Consultants

was in brown and cream livery, with 1949-style lettering.

In BR days, No. 56 had lost its toplights, and was running as W56W in a monochrome livery, probably BR maroon, with the running number in 1951-style lettering.

For many years, No. 58 was the usual trailer used on the Lambourn branch. On this service, it was not used as an auto trailer, and was often used with other hauled coaching stock (at one period, a clerestory brake third). When diesel railcar Nº 18 was used on the Lambourn service, it was often accompanied by trailer Nº 58. In 1949, it was used on the Woodstock branch, as W58 (in brown and cream, with 1949-style numbering). In due course its toplights were plated over, and it appeared on the Marlow branch as W58W, painted in carmine and cream (with 1949-style lettering).

By the time No. 60 was condemned (in 1958), it had been painted in the BR plain maroon livery and was numbered W60W in the 1951-style.

No. 61 ran in BR plain maroon livery as W61W (in 1951-style lettering). By this time, its toplights had been panelled over.

No. 62 was specified in the winter 1937/8 *Bristol Division Local Coach Working Programme* as working with No. 201 (Diagram A29) on the Yatton–Clevedon service.

No. 66 was used between Leamington Spa and Banbury in BR days, running in the carmine and cream livery as W66, with 1949-style lettering.

No. 67 was operating in the Birmingham area in September 1937. It was painted in the 1934 livery, but had only one gold line at the waist.

Other services on which Diagram L trailer are known to have been used are:

Southall & Brentford (from about 1905 onwards)
Newnham & Cinderford (circa 1910) – two Diagram L trailers
Banbury & Kingham (in 1912–22 livery)
Staines & West Drayton (1929)
Bourne End & Marlow (1955) in plain maroon without toplights. Number in 1951-style

Purpose-built 70ft Trailers

No. 5401 and a Diagram L trailer, possibly No. 34, approaching Princes Risborough from the down direction in November 1932. The trailer appears to be in the 1930 brown and cream livery with two waist lines.
DR. IAN C. ALLEN

No. 34 at Banbury, probably in 1948.
J. H. RUSSELL

No. 34 at Banbury, showing the driver's end.

J. H. RUSSELL

'517' class 0—4—2T No. 544 with a Birmingham–Bearley auto train near Wood End in the 1920s. The leading trailer is Diagram L or Diagram P. No. 43 still has coil spring bogies whilst the rear one has 9ft American bogies with full length steps. The further one is either another of Diagram L or Diagram L No. 43.

L & GRP, CTY. DAVID & CHARLES

Purpose-built 70ft Trailers 81

0–4–2T No. 1408 and Diagram L trailer No. 43 at Stratford-upon-Avon in August 1952. The trailer has 7ft Collett bogies and may be in the 1948 brown and cream livery. T. E. WILLIAMS

No. 43 at Carmarthen in July 1959. It had been condemned in June 1955 and remained here as a classroom until 1962, still in BR maroon and cream livery. J. M. HODGETTS

No. 45 of Lot 1127, Diagram L, in 1948 brown and cream with 9ft American bogies. Unlike the later examples, the truss rods of this Lot incorporated 90° twists. H. C. CASSERLEY

0–4–2T No. 1455 and a Diagram L trailer at Tenbury Wells. W. A. CAMWELL

'850' class 0–6–0ST No. 2007 with No. 58 of Diagram L and a clerestory brake third on the Lambourn branch. No. 58 was the resident coach for many years on this service.
LENS OF SUTTON

No. 1448 taking water on the shed siding at Marlow in June 1952. The trailers are 58 (nearest camera) and 33, and both are to Diagram L. The absence of toplights makes 58 look quite different to 33.
R. C. RILEY

No. 53 of Diagram L, the first of the Lot 1141 trailers, is shown here in 1948 brown and cream with two gold lines.
COLLECTION
R. C. RILEY

No. 1446 and trailer 53 leaving West Ealing for Greenford on 31st July 1955. No. 53 was the first trailer of the second Lot (1141) of Diagram L. The 9ft 'American' bogies were original fittings on this Lot and the underframe truss no longer had twists. In this photograph it has lost its toplights and is in 1948 brown and cream with 1949-style numbers.
COLLECTION R. C. RILEY

No. 5401 and Diagram L trailer No. 56 (plus another trailer) near Ealing Broadway in August 1948. No. 56 is in the 1947 brown and cream livery with two waist lines.
S. W. BAKER

No. 56, Diagram L, Lot 1141. This Lot was built with 9ft American bogies. In this view it is in BR maroon livery with 1951-style running number and plated-over toplights. Again the underframe truss rods are flat without twists. AUTHOR'S COLLECTION

Diagram L trailer No. 60 after being condemned. It is in BR plain maroon with 1951-style running numbers. For a coach in this position (a crane was used?) it seems remarkably complete; ATC circuits, gong and sanding apparatus at least are still present. R. C. RILEY

The interior of No. 48 as built, the inset showing the handle used to wind the doors open or closed. It is just visible at the far left-hand end of the side, just below the ceiling. What appear to be panels with square corners above the large fixed windows seem here to be hinged toplights with frosted glass. One is 'open' near the winding handle.
NATIONAL RAILWAY MUSEUM

70 ft Trailer No. 48: Diagrams O & S

No. 48 as built with its twelve doors in the closed position. The ventilators in the doors were inadequate and the coach was extensively modified. Eventually, it was rebuilt to Diagram S and the sliding doors removed.
NATIONAL RAILWAY MUSEUM

This coach was an experimental design, aimed at producing a high-capacity trailer suitable for suburban services, with provision for quick boarding and alighting. It was ordered in July 1906, and was completed in March 1907 on Lot 1128 at a cost of £1,319, which made it the most expensive 70 ft trailer, and the most expensive trailer built by the GWR before the Great War (the Diagram J short trailers built by the Bristol Carriage & Wagon Co. for the GWR in 1906 cost no less than £1,530 each!).

It was the usual 70 ft long × 9 ft wide, but was marginally taller than normal at 12 ft $5\frac{1}{4}$ in. It had a 61 ft-wheelbase with 9 ft coil spring bogies. The underframe was the standard queenpost truss with flat section truss roads (without a twist) and round section adjustable queenposts. It was gas lit, with incandescent burners. No retractable steps were fitted.

The body was unique. It had the normal bow ends, with a vestibule at each extremity; these were a length of 3 ft 6 in (maximum) between the coach end and the partition. The external doors to the vestibules were all slightly recessed, flat, and opened inwards. They appeared to be of the standard hauled coaching stock door width of 2 ft. There were two sliding doors in each vestibule partition, giving access to aisles in the passenger saloons.

Passenger accommodation was in the form of a single open saloon with transverse seating. The seats appear to have been of wood, and were not upholstered. They were not the full internal width of the trailer, but were arranged back-to-back to give a narrow aisle along each side of the coach. The seats were 5 ft 4 in long and seated 4 passengers, with 1 ft 4 in aisles on each side. In this form, the coach seated no less than 96 passengers, about 12 more than other 70 ft trailers.

Each seating bay was provided with an external sliding door, which was mechanically controlled by the guard. From a photograph of the interior, it appears that the guard opened and closed the doors by winding a crank handle set in the wall at window height. One of the official photographs of the exterior of the coach (as built) shows a window-height panel at the left-hand end of the coach, which seems to have concealed the winding mechanism. These panels were diagonally across the coach from each other, so that they were always at the left-hand end of the coach.

As built, the coach had twelve sliding doors each side at 5 ft centres. The doors appear to be of a slightly substandard width, perhaps 1 ft 10 in. Between each pair of sliding doors there was a fixed window, practically square in shape, with opening toplights above each which were, unusually, hinged at the top. The doors had slatted ventilators above their windows, and these windows were fixed, not droplights. Externally, with the doors closed, it looked somewhat like the contemporary 'concertina' main-line coaches.

There were a few other unusual features of this coach. Instead of the central panel with a window in the bow end of the guard's vestibule, the diagram shows a pair of doors that opened inwards, and which appear to have incorporated a window in each so that the pair of them were approximately equivalent to the normal central window of a trailer end. These doors were as high as the top of the other end windows. There was no gangway connector, so it is not known how passengers were to get safely to the next coach. In this respect, it was similar to the design of Nos. 3–6 at this period. According to a note at the front of the Trailer Register, No. 48 did not have a regulator handle in the 'driver's' vestibule, so it could be used only as an intermediate trailer, and would have had TRG from new. This note may not be 100% reliable, for the register contains no record of the regulator handle being fitted, although the vehicle certainly had a regulator in BR days. Unfortunately, the diagram does not show which end was designated for the guard, even after rebuilding.

It was soon realised that the ventilation was inadequate, and in August 1907, No. 48 was partially rebuilt. Each of the square fixed windows between the doors were replaced by a fixed window and a droplight; the doors slid behind the fixed window. In addition, the window-height panel at the left-hand end of the coach and its associated quarterlight next to the end door were reproduced at the right-hand end, with the loss of one of the sliding doors each side. It is shown thus as Diagram O. The door-operating mechanism was also modified so that control of the doors on both sides was effected from apparatus at the driver's end only. The end doors were fastened shut in August 1910.

There were still problems with the coach in use; passengers, from time to time, were trapped in the sliding doors! It must be remembered that the coach employed a simple mechanical system of opening and closing, and given the number of doors to be operated, the system must have been given

88 GWR Auto Trailers

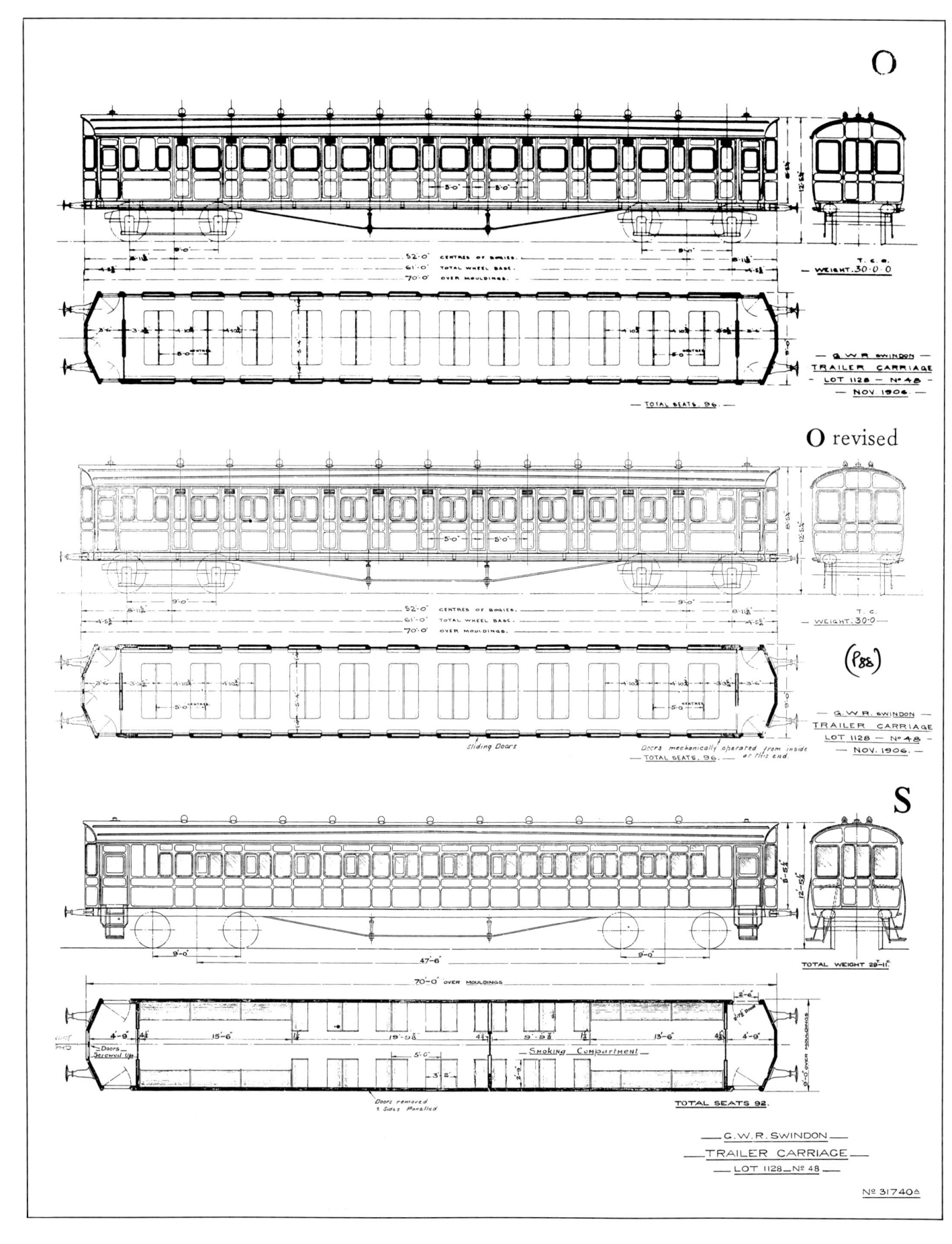

Purpose-built 70ft Trailers

an appreciable mechanical advantage. There would have been no automatic detection system which prevented the doors from squeezing trapped passengers, and the results of being caught by the doors could have been rather unpleasant!

In March 1912, No. 48 was rebuilt to a more conventional design of trailer, and it is significant that shortly thereafter, the GWR altered a number of conventional compartment coaches to trailers.

In this second rebuild, there was no change in window layout, although the intermediate doors were replaced by fixed panelling with non-opening windows. Internally, it had a vestibule at each end, as before, but these were now 4 ft 9 in deep and had 2 ft 7½ in wide doors which were flat, opened inwards and were slightly recessed into the body side. These now provided the only passenger access, and retractable steps were provided under each.

The vestibule partitions were rebuilt with a single opening door to the passenger accommodation. The seating was now in three areas: a 15 ft 6 in length with longitudinal benches at the guard's end, a 30 ft long area of six seating bays in the middle, and a further 13 ft 6 in length of longitudinal bench seats at the driver's end. According to the diagram and the register, in this form it could still seat 92 passengers, but this may well be a transcription error; 82 is a more likely figure, made up of 48 passengers in the seating bays, 9 each side in the 15 ft 6 in longitudinal seats and 8 each side in the 13 ft 6 in length.

The end doors in the guard's vestibule seem to have been restored to working order again. In order to allow the fitting of the retractable steps at each end, the wheelbase was reduced to 56 ft 6 in. If it had not already been equipped with regulator handles to the TRG, then this would appear to be the most likely time it was done. In this condition, it is shown as Diagram S.

The trailer was partitioned into smoking and non smoking areas in February 1913, and the end doors were permanently fastened shut again in February 1915.

In September 1928, it was fitted with 7 ft Collett heavy duty bogies and blue-painted axleboxes. In October of that year, the larger compartment was made 'smoking'. Sanding gear may well have been fitted at this time, too. Chain communication apparatus was fitted in October 1931. The windows in the non-driving end were painted black in February 1935 and in July 1941 it was given ATC apparatus.

Before rebuilding, No. 48 is said to have been used in Plymouth and afterwards in the Swansea area.

In 1953, No. 48 was photographed at Swansea High Street in BR carmine and cream livery, with 1949-style lettering, as W48W. It was the leading coach in the train, and had been fitted with a warning gong.

The trailer was condemned in January 1956, its survival to this date being largely due to the extent of its rebuilding in 1912.

This is how trailer No. 48 of Diagram S looked after rebuilding to more or less conventional form, although the multitude of side windows survive. This photograph was taken on 3rd June 1953 at Swansea High Street by which time the body panelling had been sheeted over, and Collett 7ft bogies and ATC fitted. It is painted in BR maroon and cream livery. Behind No. 48 is 1670 of Diagram A34 which appears to be in the 'unofficial' lined livery of the early 1950s. The locomotive is 0-6-0PT No. 6431.   R. C. RILEY

No.	Lot	Built	Altered Droplights	End doors fastened shut	Rebuilt	Diag.	Partitioned
48	1128	Mar.07	Aug.07	Aug.10	Mar.12	S	Feb.13

No.	End doors fastened shut	7ft Collett bogies	Blue A/boxes	Smoking cmpt. rearranged	Cream, brown & gold
48	Feb.15	Sep.28	Sep.28	Oct.28	Sep.31

No.	Chain comm.	End windows black	ATC	Cond	Notes
48	Oct.31	Feb.35	Jul.41	Jan.56	Experimental design until rebuilt in 1912.

Diagram P trailer No. 51 at Lampeter c.1911. The coaches are all in brown livery; behind the loco is a four-wheel all-third built for London suburban services, now exiled to West Wales, and a four-wheel three-compartment brake third. This was presumably the Aberayron branch train as the trailer has a destination board reading 'Lampeter'. If so, the engine and trailer would have to run round the two four-wheel coaches for the whole train to return to Aberayron.
NATIONAL RAILWAY MUSEUM

Purpose-built 70ft Trailers

70 ft Trailers Nos. 49–52: Diagram P

These four trailers were ordered in November 1906, constructed in May 1907, and were very similar to their contemporaries shown on Diagram L.

Trailers Nos. 49 to 52 were built on Lot 1130 at an average cost of £1,219, exactly £100 less than the experimental No. 48. They were 70 ft long, 9 ft wide and 12 ft 3¾ in high from rail to roof. They had the standard queenpost underframe of the period, without a twist in the truss rods (like the last two Lots on Diagram L). They had a 61 ft wheelbase and 9 ft plate frame bogies, which are believed to have been of the coil spring type. Externally, they were identical to the Diagram L trailers, which makes identification from photographs particularly difficult. At the non-driving end, there was a luggage compartment with double outwards-opening doors; at the driver's end, there were flat inward-opening doors, slightly recessed. Towards the centre of the coach, there was a passengers' vestibule, again with flat, slightly recessed, inwardly-opening doors, having retractable steps below.

The luggage compartment was 7 ft 10¾ in long between end wall and partition, whilst the other two vestibules were 3 ft 9 in. Between the luggage compartment and the passengers vestibule there were five pairs of walkover seats (14 ft 7¼ in) with the end seats fixed, as usual, and a 4 ft 6 in length of longitudinal seating. This seating was the main difference between the Diagram L trailers and those to Diagram P. Between the passengers' and driver's vestibules, there was a 9 ft length of longitudinal seating either side of another five pairs of walkover seats (15 ft 2½ in); the walkover seats were not quite evenly spaced along the coach.

The small saloon had a single large fixed window, a pair of droplights, and another pair of fixed lights. The large saloon had two fixed lights by each of the longitudinal benches, and two pairs of droplights either side of a single fixed light by the walkover seats. There were the usual toplights above all these windows.

TRG apparatus was fitted to all four coaches, but the dates are not recorded. Two of the four (Nos. 50 and 52) received 9 ft 'American' bogies in 1919 and two of these coaches had the other Collett 7 ft heavy duty bogies before the Second War.

Although No. 49 was not condemned until 1960, it was still in the BR carmine and cream livery as W49W, but in the 1949 lettering style. It was at Old Oak Common 'on loan' to the Motive Power Department, but marked 'COND'.

No. 51 was photographed at Lampeter circa 1910 in brown livery, with a newly-painted white roof. The remainder of the train consisted of a '517' class 0–4–2T loco, and two non-auto four-wheel coaches which

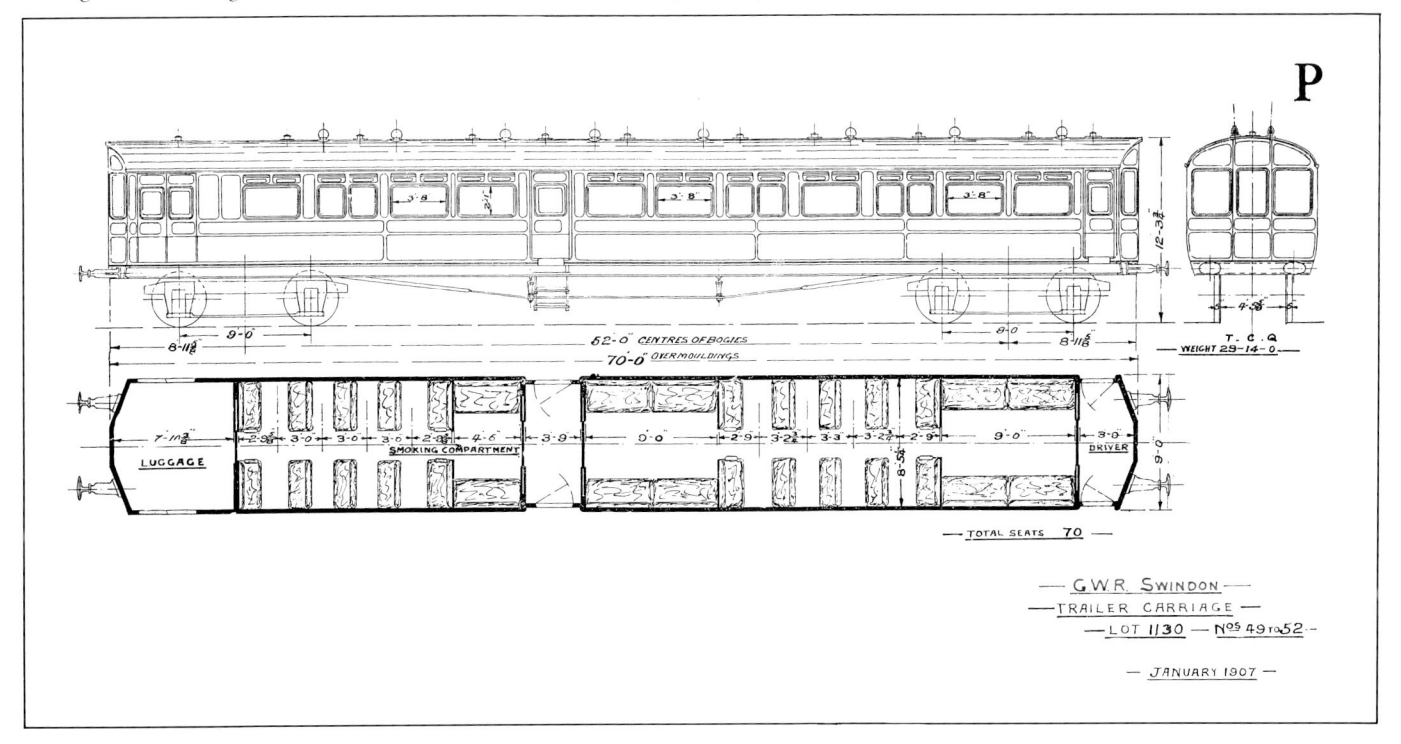

Diagram P trailer No. 49 at Ruislip & Ickenham in the 1934 livery but without its end windows painted black.
C. R. L. COLES

were being hauled, whilst No. 51 was being propelled. In due course, it was photographed again in the 1934 livery, but with only one gold waist line visible.

No. 52 was slightly damaged in a collision at Old Oak Common on 2nd November 1927.

Diagram P trailers were externally identical to some of the Diagram L coaches, so it is possible that some of the services where unidentified Diagram L trailers are said to have been used were in fact operated using Diagram P vehicles.

They lasted until 1956–60. When it was condemned in February 1960, No. 49 was probably the oldest ex-GWR trailer (theoretically) in passenger service.

Notes
No. 50 was taken into service internal user stock in November 1956 as DW 079019. Known allocations thereafter are:

Tavistock Junction	Apr.61
Bristol Temple Meads	Jan.65
Plymouth Friary	Jan.66

No.	Lot	Built	Diag.	Replacement Bogies	Date	Sand Boxes	Blue A/boxes
49	1130	May 07	P	7ft Collett	?	Jan.28	Jun.29
50	1130	May 07	P	9ft American	Aug.19	.	.
51	1130	May 07	P	9ft heavy	?	.	Aug.29
52	1130	May 07	P	9ft American	Apr.19	.	.

No.	Smoking cmpts. rearranged	Chain comm.	Cream, brown & gold	End windows black	ATC	Cond
49	Jun.31	Sep.30	May 31	Nov.35	Feb.45	Feb.60
50	+	Aug.29	Apr.30	Mar.35	+	May.56
51	Sep.29	Aug.29	Nov.31	Nov.35	Aug.49	Nov.57
52	Apr.30	Apr.30	Jan.32	Feb.35	Aug.41	Sep.57

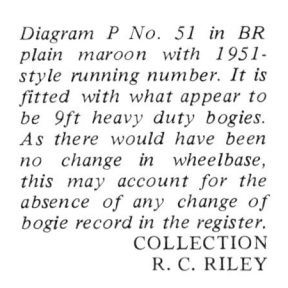

Diagram P No. 51 in BR plain maroon with 1951-style running number. It is fitted with what appear to be 9ft heavy duty bogies. As there would have been no change in wheelbase, this may account for the absence of any change of bogie record in the register.
COLLECTION R. C. RILEY

Diagram P No. 49 with 7ft Collett bogies at Old Oak Common after being condemned.   COLLECTION R. C. RILEY

70 ft Trailers Nos. 71–4 & 93–8: Diagrams Q & R

These ten trailers are best dealt with together, as they seem to have run in pairs (a Diagram R trailer with one from Diagram Q) for much or all of their lives; Nos. 71, 72, and 93–5 were driving trailers to Diagram Q, whilst Nos. 73, 74 and 96–8 were used as intermediate trailers with a luggage compartment (Diagram R). They were built in two batches on four lots:

Lot	Ordered	Completed	Running nos.	Diagram	Average cost
1160	Feb.08	May 09	71–72	Q	£1,127
1161	Feb.08	May 09	73–74	R	£1,172
1224	Nov.12	Oct.13	93–95	Q	£1,202
1225	Nov.12	Sep.13	96–98	R	Not recorded

All were 70 ft long, 9 ft wide and 12 ft 3¾ in high, with a 56 ft 6 in wheelbase; 9 ft wheelbase American bogies were fitted from new. The underframe was the normal queenpost truss type with adjustable, round section queenposts and flat section truss rods, without any twist between the queenposts and the solebars. The 1913 Lots were fitted with Churchward-type vacuum cylinders with moving pistons. All were built with incandescent burner gas lighting.

These coaches did not have intermediate passenger vestibules; passenger access was via the end vestibules, but not through the luggage compartment. The vestibules had retractable steps under them, hence the 56 ft 6 in wheelbase. As far as the passenger accommodation was concerned, the main difference between the two types was that the Diagram Q vehicles did not have the luggage compartment, and consequently had correspondingly longer longitudinal bench seating areas. The Diagram R coaches were built as smoking accommodation, and the Diagram Q coaches for non-smoking.

The drivers' vestibules were 5 ft 0½ in deep, whilst the trailing vestibules (as opposed to the luggage compartment) were 4 ft 9 in (maximum) between the end wall and the partition. The vestibules had flat, slightly recessed doors, opening inwards. The luggage compartment in the Diagram R trailers was 7 ft 9¼ in (maximum) between end wall partition, and had double doors each side which opened outwards. These double doors had tumblehome, and did not have retractable steps below them.

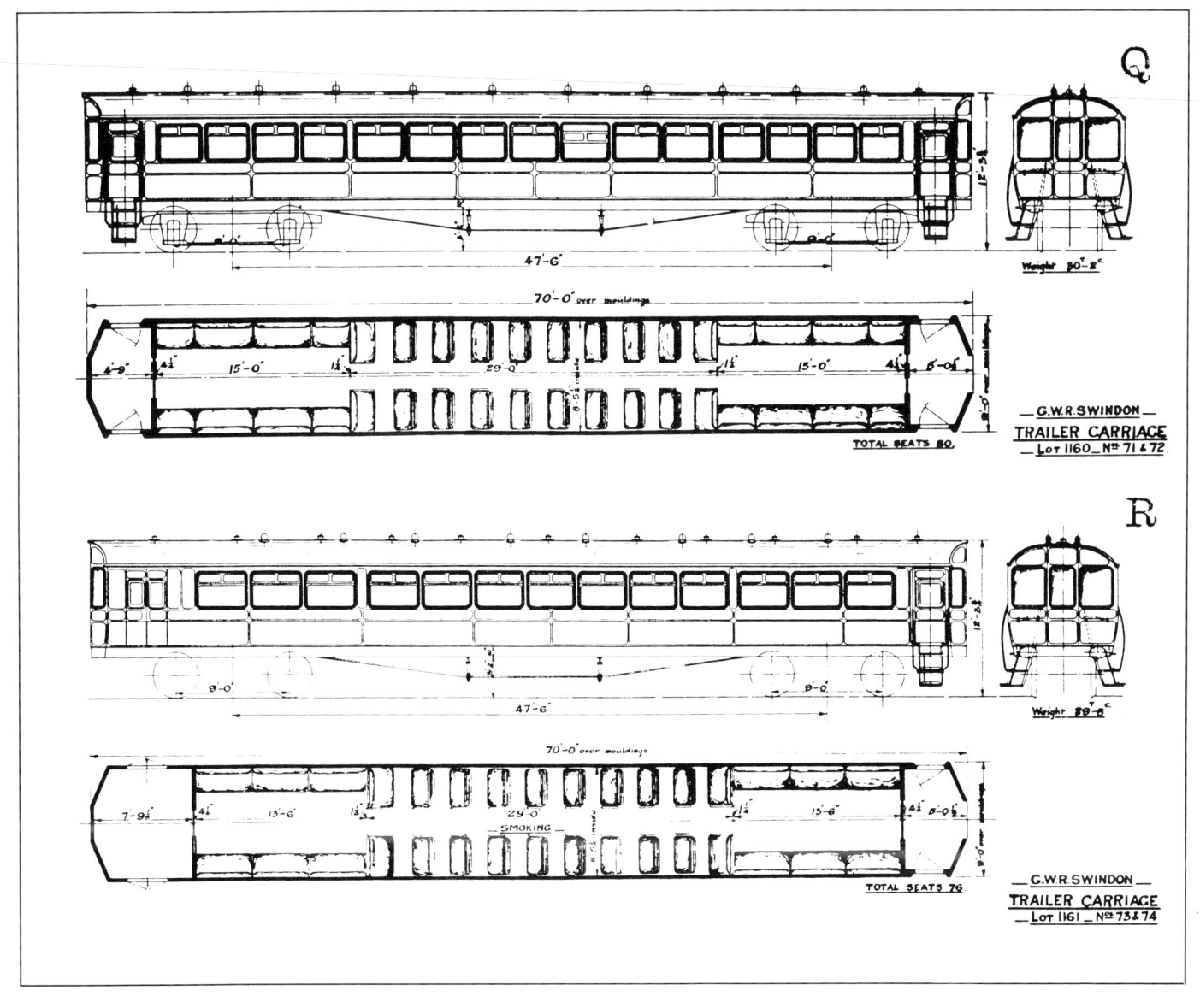

Adjacent to the non-driving vestibule on the Diagram Q trailers was a 15 ft length of longitudinal seating; on the Diagram R trailers with the luggage compartment, this length was only 13 ft 6 in. Next came a 29 ft length occupied by ten pairs of walkover seats, and finally another length of longitudinal benches, the same length as that at the other end of the coach – that is, shorter on the Diagram R vehicles. These coaches seated 80 passengers (Diagram Q) and 76, later 84 (Diagram R), because the latter had additional (emergency) seats fitted in the luggage compartment.

The windows marked a new departure for 70 ft trailers. Instead of the large fixed lights being held in place by bolection mouldings, with the toplights separate, the window frames (including the toplights) seem to have been made as a single unit, and the whole retained in place by a single bolection moulding. This window arrangement can be identified by the corners to the windows being rounded instead of right-angled, by the whole of the window area of each unit being slightly recessed, and by the toplights opening as a pair.

The longitudinal seating areas had four fixed lights in the Diagram Q coaches, and three in the case of the Diagram R trailers. The walkover seating had 7 fixed lights, with toplights above in all cases. The luggage com-

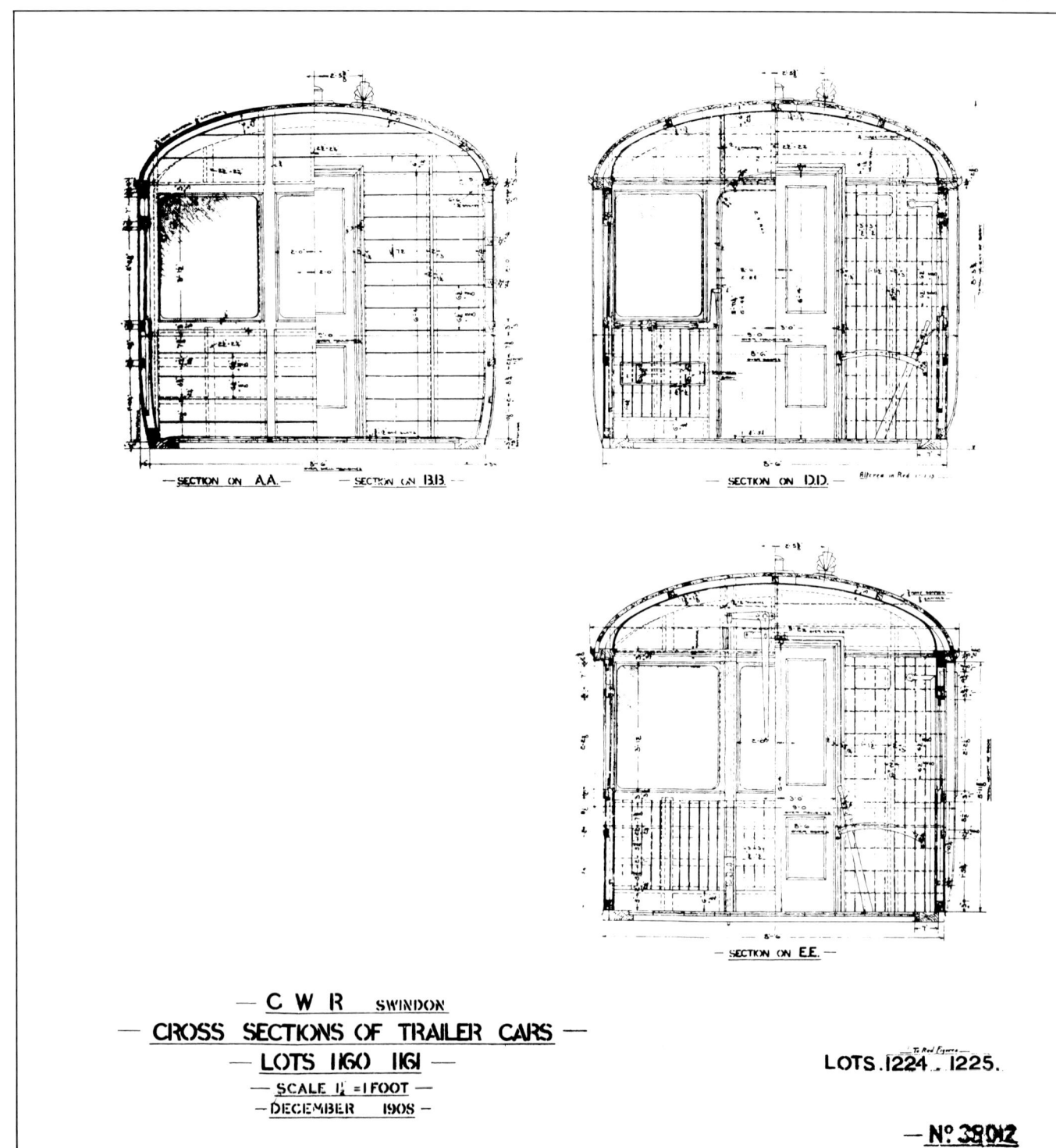

Purpose-built 70ft Trailers

Tiverton Junction in May 1933. The main line auto train comprises (from the back) No. 93 of Diagram Q, No. 98 of Diagram R, (loco), ex-SRM trailer. Although it cannot be seen, Nos. 93 and 98 are gangwayed together. Both are in the 1930 livery with two gold waist lines. The leading coach is probably an A19, either 138 or 139.
G. N. SOUTHERDEN

partment doors all had droplights. There were two window-height panels next to the luggage doors on Diagram R, otherwise there was a single panel next to the doors, and a narrow panel corresponding to the boundary between the longitudinal benches and the walkover seats.

The 1909 trailers (No. 71–4) were given end gangways in 1912, whilst the 1913 batch had them from new. Nos. 71 and 72 probably received the TRG at the same time, and 73, 74, and 93–8 are believed to have been built with it. From the register, it would appear that originally Nos. 73 and 74 did not have regulator handles in the leading vestibule, although they must have been fitted with TRG rodding. Regulator handles were fitted later, and these two trailers were not included in the list of trailers in the front of the register as being intermediate types without regulator handles. A photograph of No. 74 taken in BR days shows it to have been equipped with a warning gong at the driver's end. New pattern tail lamp brackets are recorded as being fitted to Nos. 94 and 97 in December 1922, and to No. 95 in September 1933.

One date is recorded for the fitting of a trailer with a warning gong: No. 72 was so equipped in September 1925. Nos. 71–4 all received sand apparatus in 1927, and No. 94 was similarly fitted in October 1928. No. 94's axleboxes were painted blue in December 1928.

Chain communication was fitted between 1929 and 1931 and, curiously, there are dates within that period when it is noted that the larger compartments became 'smoking'. As all of these vehicles were then of open design, there is an apparent contradiction here! At this time, the gas lighting was replaced by electric.

Most of the trailers were painted cream and brown with gold lining in the early 1930s, and had their non-driving/luggage-end windows painted black in 1935. It is possible that those on Nos. 93–95 were not done, as there is a note in the register against these trailers to the effect that they had 'no luggage compartment'! All received ATC in the 1940s. No. 93 was partitioned into two compartments in January 1943, under New Works Order 9558. All these trailers lasted until the mid/late 1950s.

A Plymouth area auto train with Diagrams Q and R trailers.
H. C. CASSERLEY

The 1909 trailers were intended for the Plymouth area, and it is possible that the others were, too. It would appear that No. 71 ran with 74, and No. 72 with 73. In 1932, Nos. 71–74 had 'Plymouth' written on them. Things are not so clear with regards to Nos. 93–8, but 94 may have run with 97, 95 with 96 and 93 with 98. It is, of course, possible that these coaches ran at times with other gangwayed trailers. In 1935, Nos. 93, 95, 96 and 98 were allocated to Exeter.

The 1913-built trailers were the last 70ft trailers to be constructed, and the last wood panelled trailers built by the GWR.

GWR Auto Trailers

Nos. 71 and 74 were photographed together in the Plymouth area. Both were in the 1948 brown and cream livery, with only one waist line. Unusually for a trailer with toplights, they appear to have a thin brown band below the roof with the gold/black dividing line.

Nos. 93 and 98 seem to have run together in the Exeter area, and were photographed at Exeter in August 1930, and at Tiverton Junction on an Exeter service in May 1933.

No. 96 was photographed with an unidentified trailer at Dulverton in BR carmine and cream livery, and numbered W96W in the 1949 style of lettering.

No. 98 ran in brown and cream as W98, curiously with the running number in large characters towards the right-hand end of the coach. It later ran in BR maroon as W98W in the 'proper' 1951 style with small characters, in which form it was seen at Exeter St Davids.

Top left: No. 74 Diagram R coupled to No. 71 at Laira Junction, Plymouth. Note both toplights open as one. These vehicles were electrically lit, hence the absence of gas piping and lamps on the roofs of these Plymouth area trailers. Left: No. 71 Diagram Q coupled to No. 74 at Laira Junction, on the same occasion. It is electrically lit and shown in brown and cream livery with 1949-style numbering. H. C. CASSERLEY

Summary

No.	Lot	Built	Diag	Gangway one end	Warning gong	Sand boxes	Blue A/boxes
71	1160	May 09	Q	May 12	+	Mar. 27	–
72	1160	May 09	Q	Feb. 12	Sep. 25	Aug. 27	–
73	1161	May 09	R	Feb. 12	+	Aug. 27	–
74	1161	May 09	R	Feb. 12	+	Mar. 27	–
93	1224	Sep. 13	Q	Blt	+	–	–
94	1224	Aug. 13	Q	Blt	+	Oct. 28	Dec. 28
95	1224	Oct. 13	Q	Blt	+	–	–
96	1225	Sep. 13	R	Blt	+	–	–
97	1225	Aug. 13	R	Blt	+	–	Dec. 28
98	1225	Aug. 13	R	Blt	+	–	–

No.	Smoking cmpts rearranged	Chain comm.	Electric lighting	Cream, brown & gold	Seats in luggage cmpt	End windows black
71	May 30	May 30	May 30	May 30	N/a	Oct. 35
72	Nov. 29	Nov. 29	Nov. 29	–	N/a	Oct. 35
73	Nov. 29	Nov. 29	Nov. 29	Oct. 31	Oct. 31	Feb. 35
74	May 30	May 30	–?	–	Mar. 31	Feb. 35
93	–	–	Nov. 29	Jul. 32	N/a	–
94	Jan. 29	Jul. 29	Jul. 31	–	N/a	–
95	Mar. 31	Feb. 31	Feb. 31	Jan. 31	N/a	–
96	Feb. 29	Feb. 29	Dec. 30	–		Feb. 35
97	Aug. 29	Jul. 29	Jun. 31	May. 31		Feb. 35
98	Oct. 31	Oct. 31	Oct. 31	Sep. 31		Feb. 35

No.	ATC	Partitioned	Cond	Notes
71	Jun. 43?	–	Sep. 54	'Plymouth' Nov. 32
72	Jun. 40	–	Sep. 55	'Plymouth' Nov. 32
73	Jun. 40	–	Sep. 55	'Plymouth' Nov. 32
74	Jun. 43	–	Sep. 54	'Plymouth' Nov. 32
93	Apr. 47	Jan. 43	Aug. 57	
94	Feb. 46	–	Oct. 57	
95	Aug. 40	–	Oct. 57	
96	May. 47	–	Aug. 57	
97	Oct. 41	–	Oct. 57	
98	Aug. 40	–	Oct. 58	

70 ft Trailers Nos. 75–80: Diagram T, & Nos. 81–92: Diagram U

Two Diagram T trailers on the Calne branch train at Chippenham on 21st September 1948. R. E. TUSTIN

These 18 trailers can be dealt with together, as the only difference between the two designs appears to have been that the Diagram T trailers had two less windows each side than the Diagram U vehicles. Ordering details were:

Lot	Ordered	Completed	Running nos.	Diagram	Average cost
1190	Jun.10	Jun.11	75–80	T	£1,188
1198	Mar.11	Sep.12	81–92	U	£1,192

The Diagram U trailers were built with TRG, and the others may well have been.

These trailers were a slightly-modified and modernised version of the Diagram P 70 ft trailers (see page 91). Internally they were the same, the only significant difference being that Diagrams T and U were all built with gangways at the luggage compartment end.

The vehicles were 70 ft by 9 ft, and 12 ft $3\frac{3}{4}$ in high; they had a 61 ft wheelbase with 9 ft American bogies, and had queenpost trussed underframes with no twist in the truss rods. Gas lighting with incandescent burners was fitted from new, as were Churchward pattern vacuum cylinders.

The trailers had a driver's vestibule with 2 ft wide, recessed, flat doors that opened inwards. There was an intermediate passenger vestibule with similar doors, and retractable steps below; the luggage compartment was equipped with double doors that opened outwards – these doors had tumblehome.

The luggage compartment was 7 ft $10\frac{3}{8}$ in between end wall and partition, and the other two vestibules were 3 ft 9 in deep. Between the luggage compartment and the passengers' vestibule there were five pairs of walkover seats (14 ft $7\frac{1}{4}$ in) with the end seats fixed, as usual, and a 4 ft 6 in length of longitudinal seating. Between the passengers' and the driver's vestibules there was a 9 ft length of longitudinal seating either side of another five pairs of walkover seats (15 ft $2\frac{1}{2}$ in).

The windows were to the newer pattern, with bolection mouldings that enclosed both the large lights and the twin toplights positioned above them. These twin toplights were hinged at the bottom edge, and opened and shut simultaneously. All the window units on these trailers appear to have been the same size (at least on each type of trailer), but they were unevenly spaced.

Diagram T trailers had four window units between the luggage compartment and the passengers' vestibule; Diagram U trailers had five window units. Diagram T had seven window units between the passengers' and the driver's vestibules; Diagram U coaches had eight in that area.

The curious feature of these trailers is that they were all fitted with gangway connectors at the luggage compartment end. The problem was that there were very few trailers with gangway connectors at the leading end, and these already had luggage compartments. The 'T' and 'U' trailers were also available to run with an SRM with a gangway, but there were hardly any of them either.

Between 1912 and 1914, 'wicket' gates were fitted in the gangways of some of these trailers, and some were equipped with new pattern lamp brackets from 1917 onwards. Their subsequent history is much as may be expected, but they were all equipped with electric lighting in 1929/31.

No. 77 was being used on the Yeovil Town–Pen Mill shuttle service in 1950; it was in BR carmine and cream, and numbered W77 in 1949-style lettering.

No. 78 was used on the Bearley–Alcester branch in August 1938; this service included 'mixed' trains.

No. 79 was used on the Taunton–Westbury auto train which, in 1924, was involved in an accident at Curry Rivel Junction.

No. 80 had been repainted in BR carmine and cream livery (as W80) by 1950, when it

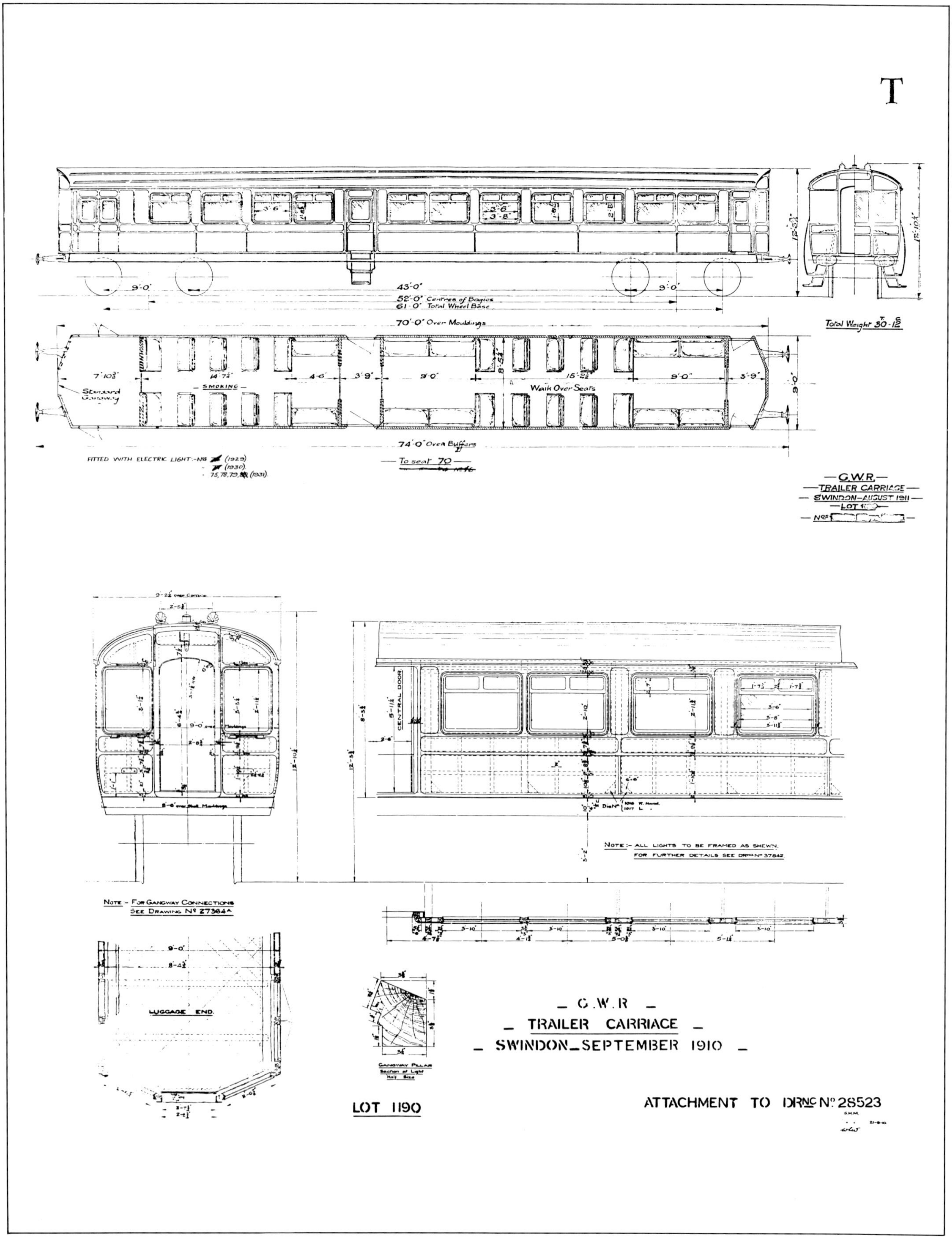
T
43'-0"
52'-0" Centres of Bogies
61'-0" Total Wheel Base
9'-0"
12'-3¾"
12'-10¼"
Total Weight 30-12
70'-0" Over Mouldings
Standard Gangway
SMOKING
Walk Over Seats
74'-0" Over Buffers
To seat 70
G.W.R.
TRAILER CARRIAGE
SWINDON—AUGUST 1911
LOT
Note:– All lights to be framed as shewn.
For further details see Drg No 37842
Note – For Gangway Connections See Drawing No 27384A
CENTRAL DOOR
LUGGAGE END.
Gangway Pillar Section of Light Half Size
G.W.R
TRAILER CARRIAGE
SWINDON_SEPTEMBER 1910
LOT 1190
ATTACHMENT TO DRG No 28523

Purpose-built 70ft Trailers

In this picture of No. 80 Diagram T at Chippenham, the wider and uneven spacing of the windows is apparent when compared with Diagram U trailers. The vehicle is in 1949 maroon and cream livery.
M. LONGRIDGE

This Diagram T trailer in 1949 carmine and cream livery may be No. 77.
COLLECTION R. C. RILEY

was photographed at Reading; the lettering was in the 1949 style.

No. 81 was photographed at Radley in BR plain maroon as W81W (in the 1951-style).

No. 82 was noted at Exeter St Davids on the same train as the Diagram R trailer No. 98, but was not coupled to that vehicle. Both were in maroon livery with 1951-style lettering (No. 82 as W82W).

No. 83 is reported to have been used in the Bristol area, and to have seen service on the Clevedon branch. During the war years it was in the Banbury area, and was also noted there in 1947 livery; later, it ran as W83 (in the 1949 style), painted in brown and cream, again at Banbury. It subsequently received carmine and cream livery, whilst still numbered W83 in the 1949-style; eventually, it was renumbered W83W, still in the same style lettering.

No. 84 ran in brown and cream as W84, in 1949-style lettering.

No. 85 seems to have been regularly used on the Yatton–Clevedon branch, as it featured in accident reports concerning two bufferstop collisions at Clevedon, in August 1920 and January 1926!

No. 87 seems to have seen regular service on the Woodstock branch in the early 1950s. It carried carmine and cream livery, and was photographed on that service in 1952, and again in February 1954.

No. 88 was photographed at Southall in 1920, in the lake livery. It also appeared in the Banbury area around the Great War, and was photographed on the Banbury–Kingham service in one-colour (lake, probably) livery.

The 6.55 Greenford–West Ealing auto at Drayton Green on 16th August 1930. The leading trailer, No. 89 of Diagram U, was newly fitted with electric light and repainted. It has been given the second gold/black waist line although the register does not record it as having cream, brown and gold lines until February 1932. The loco is '517' class 0–4–2T No. 829. The second trailer is No. 2 of Diagram A4. It is difficult to be certain exactly which livery it is carrying – possibly the autumn 1927 one. This photograph is said to show No. 2 with 7ft bogies but it is not possible to be certain and later photographs show it with 9ft 'fish-belly' bogies.

LCGB/KEN NUNN COLLECTION

Purpose-built 70ft Trailers

This picture of the interior of Diagram U trailer W83 on 2nd June 1951 also shows how the toplights open in pairs. CTY. C. TURNER

'Small Metro' 2–4–0T No. 1500 with a Diagram U trailer at Lostwithiel. DR. I. C. ALLEN

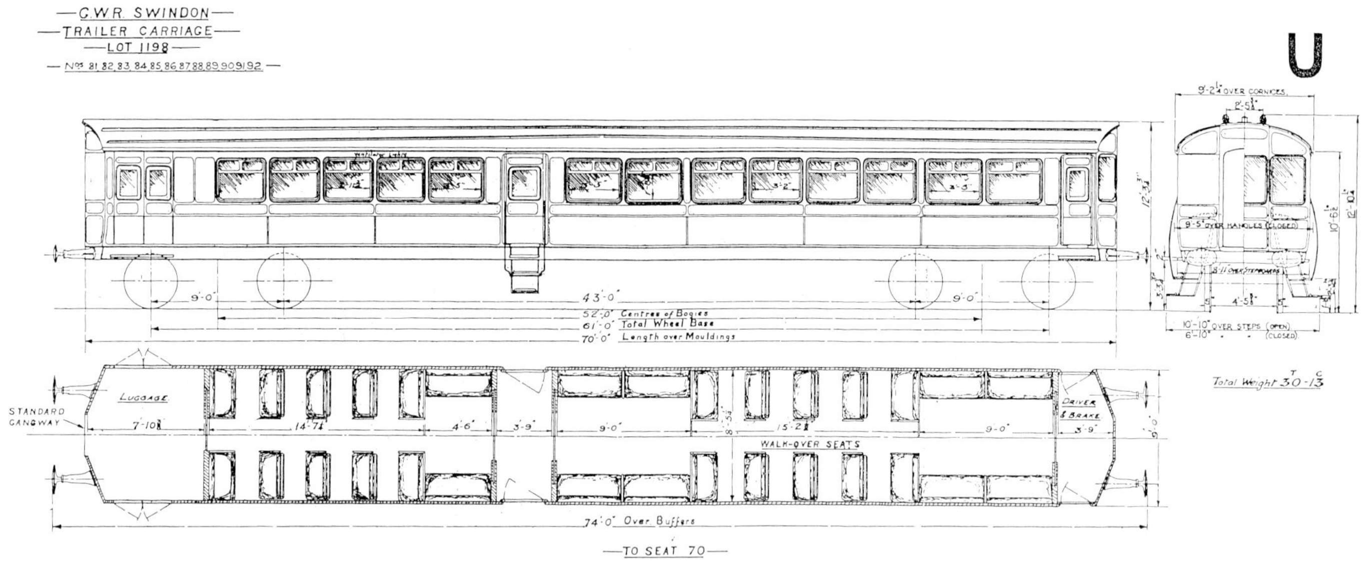
—G.W.R. SWINDON—
—TRAILER CARRIAGE—
—LOT 1198—
— Nos 81,82,83,84,85,86,87,88,89,90,91,92 —
U
9'-2¼" OVER CORNICES
43'-0"
52'-0" Centres of Bogies
61'-0" Total Wheel Base
70'-0" Length over Mouldings
LUGGAGE
STANDARD GANGWAY
DRIVER & BRAKE
WALK-OVER SEATS
74'-0" Over Buffers
—TO SEAT 70—
Total Weight 30-13

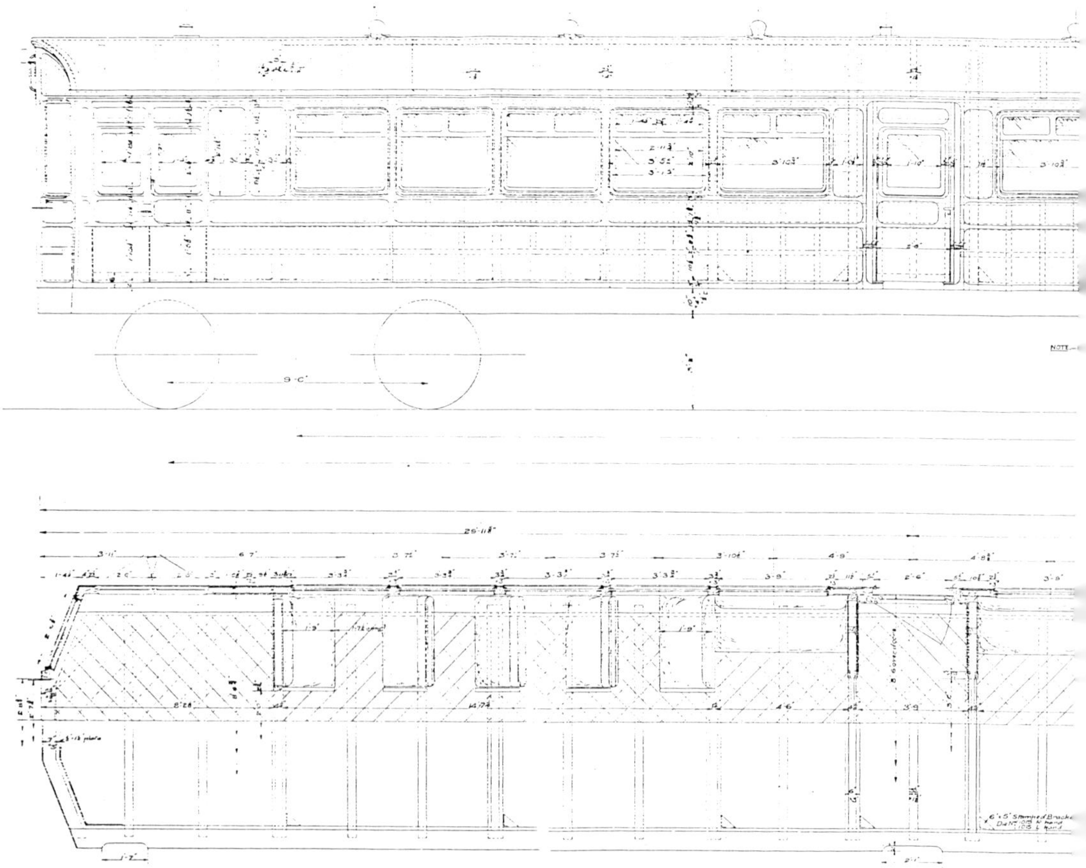

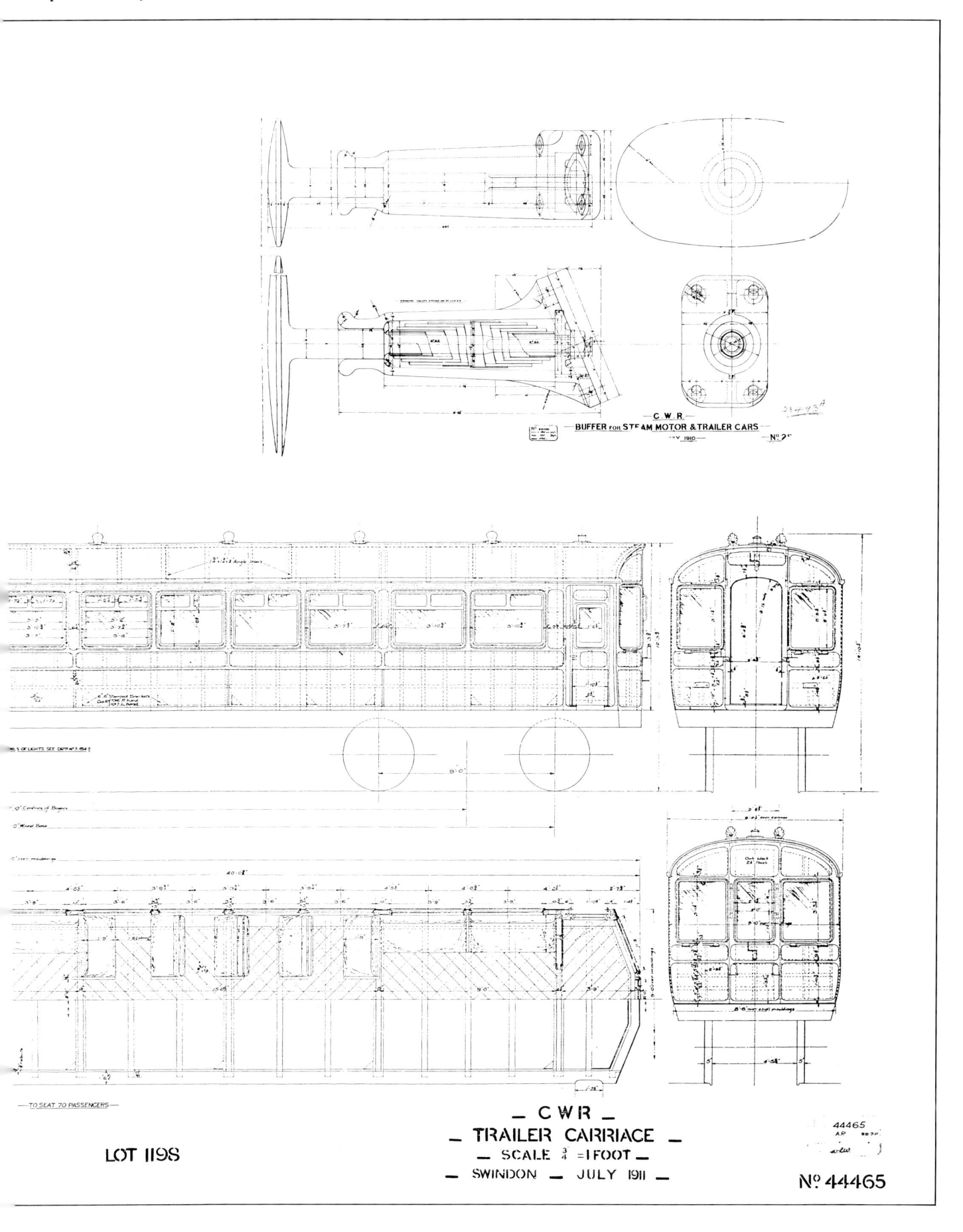

Purpose-built 70ft Trailers

G.W.R.
BUFFER for STEAM MOTOR & TRAILER CARS

LOT 1198

— C W R —
— TRAILER CARRIAGE —
— SCALE ¾ = 1 FOOT —
— SWINDON — JULY 1911 —

— TO SEAT 70 PASSENGERS —

Nº 44465

The pictures on this and the next three pages are detail views of Diagram U trailer No. 83 in 1947 livery. J. H. RUSSELL

Purpose-built 70ft Trailers 105

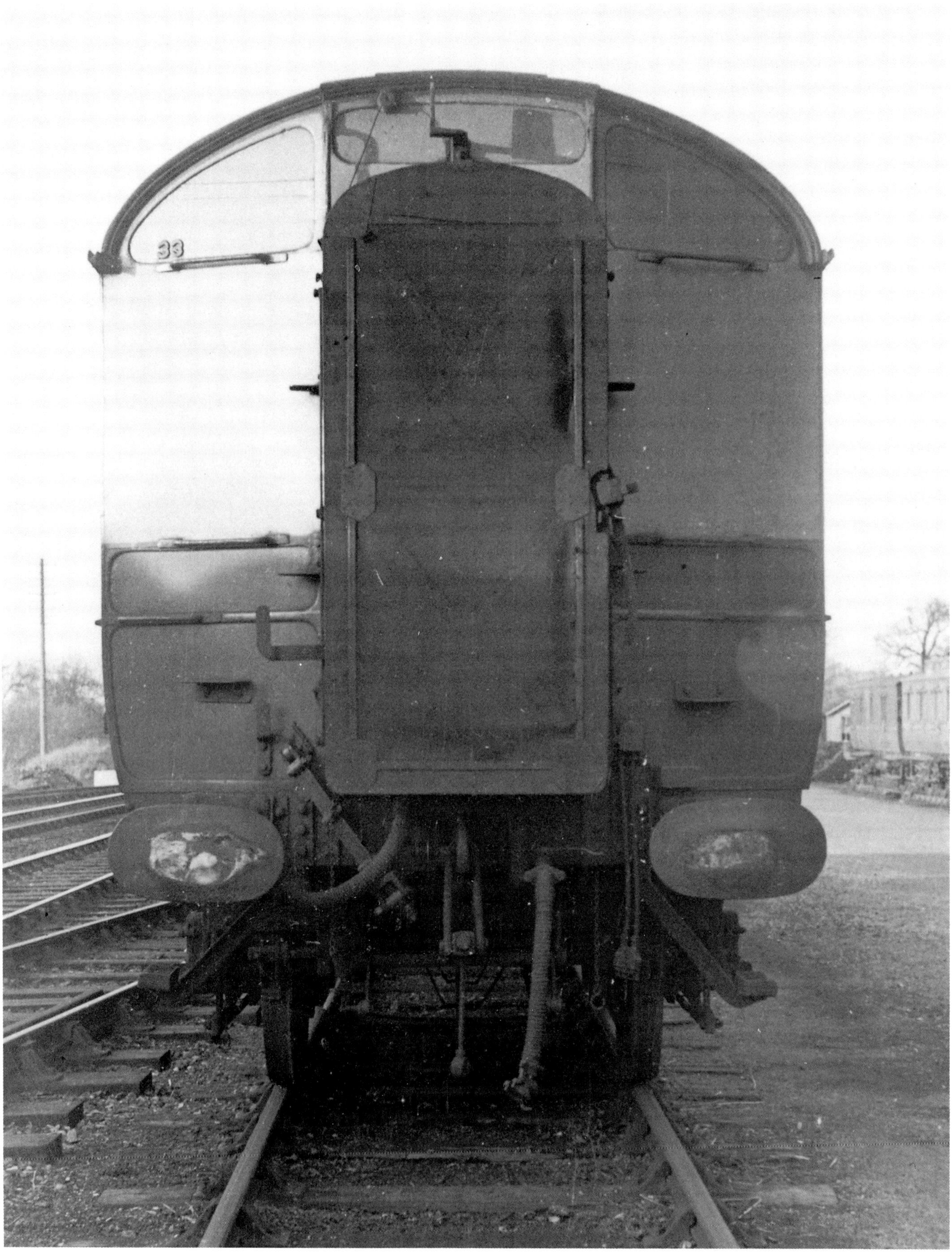
33

Purpose-built 70ft Trailers   107

W89 in BR crimson and cream livery.

J. H. RUSSELL

Purpose-built 70ft Trailers

W83W of Diagram U in crimson and cream livery. COLLECTION J. N. SLINN

No. 90 was in the Oxford area in the 1950s sporting BR carmine and cream, numbered W90 in 1949-style lettering.

No. 91 was in the Birmingham district in September 1937. It was also seen in the Banbury area during the late 1940s, and in due course was given BR maroon livery as W91W (1951-style). It had been fitted with sandboxes.

No. 92 was photographed at Leamington in BR carmine and cream, with 1949-style numbering. The maroon band below the roof may have been narrower than usual – it did not reach the tops of the window units.

A pair of Diagram T trailers were in use on the Calne branch in September 1948.

One Diagram U trailer was photographed by Mr G. H. Soole in 1937 at the front of an express leaving Bristol Temple Meads for the south-west, hauled by No. 6015 *King Richard III*. The remainder of the train consisted of only four corridor coaches, so it may be that this was the Weston-super-Mare portion of a Bristol express, and the trailer was perhaps being taken to Yatton in an emergency.

A Diagram U trailer, rather the worse for wear, in carmine and cream livery was used on the last day of the Woodstock branch service in February 1954.

A Diagram U trailer in the BR maroon livery was used on the Ealing Broadway–Greenford service in April 1955, and one in the same livery was photographed on the Old Hill – Dudley auto at Windmill End, in September 1956.

The trailers were condemned in the mid and late 1950s, except for No. 91, which seems to have survived until after 1961. No. 92 has been preserved by the Great Western Society.

Summary

No.	Built	Lot	Diag.	Sand boxes	Blue A/boxes	Chain. comm.	Smoking cpts altered	Elec. lights	Cream, brown & gold
75	May 11	1190	T			May 31	Oct.28	Aug.31	Jul.31
76	May 11	1190	T			Nov.28	Aug.28	Oct.29	Sep.31
77	May 11	1190	T	Jul.27		Dec.28	Jun.30	May 30	
78	May 11	1190	T			Feb.29	Feb.29	Dec.31	Nov.31
79	Jun.11	1190	T			Mar.29	Mar.29	Mar.31	Jan.31
80	Jun.11	1190	T			Aug.29	+	Nov.31	Oct.31
81	Aug.12	1198	U			Sep.30	Jul.28	May 30	
82	Aug.12	1198	U	Oct.31		Oct.30	Apr.29	Oct.30	Sep.30/Dec.32
83	Aug.12	1198	U			Sep.30	Jul.29	Apr.30	Oct.31
84	Aug.12	1198	U			Jun.29	Aug.28	Mar.31	
85	Aug.12	1198	U	Oct.21		Jul.29	+	May.3	May.32
86	Aug.12	1198	U			Jun.29	Jul.29	Dec.30	
87	Aug.12	1198	U	Oct.21		Jun.29	Jun.29	Jan.32	Nov.31
88	Aug.12	1198	U			Dec.30	Aug.28	Dec.30	
89	Aug.12	1198	U			Oct.29	May 28	Jun.30	Feb.32
90	Aug.12	1198	U	Oct.21		Nov.29	+	Nov.2	May 32
91	Sep.12	1198	U	Oct.21		Jun.29 9	Nr	Sep.31	Jun.31
92	Sep.12	1198	U		Dec.28	May 29	Nr	Oct.31	Aug.31

No.	Diag.	End windows black	Painted brown	ATC	Cond.	Notes
75	T	Oct.35		Sep.46	Jan.58	
76	T	Oct.35		Sep.46	Sep.57	
77	T	Apr.35		Feb.40	Nov.56	
78	T	Nov.35		Apr.41	Nov.60	Loaned temporarily to Commercial Dept Jun.58
79	T	Feb.35		Jan.41	Nov.57	
80	T	Feb.35		Oct.40	Feb.56	
81	U	Feb.35		Sep.46	Mar.58	
82	U	Feb.35	Apr.42	Jun.45	Apr.58	
83	U	Jun.35		Jul.42	Sep.57	
84	U	Feb.35		Feb.45db	Jul.56	
85	U	Feb.35		Feb.45db	Sep.57	
86	U	Mar.35		+	May.56	
87	U	Oct.35	Jul.42	Oct.40	Oct.58	
88	U	Feb.35		Jan.41	Jan.57	
89	U	Mar.35		Jan.41	Apr.57	
90	U	Mar.35		+	Oct.56	
91	U	Oct.35		Nr	?	
92	U	Feb.35		Nr	Jan.57	Preserved by GW Society

Trailer No. 8 of Diagram C with Collett 7ft bogies at Cheltenham St. James in September 1948. This photograph shows clearly the panelled end unique to the two Diagram C trailers. It is bow-ended and is painted like a hauled coach end. No. 8 is in the 1943 brown and cream livery and has ATC circuits. The whistle cord hole seems to have been moved downwards (the original is visible just below the roof) and provision seems to have been made for a destination board, the brackets for which are at the same height as the new whistle cord.
P. J. GARLAND

CHAPTER FOUR
PURPOSE-BUILT 59 ft 6 in TRAILERS

IT became normal practice on the GWR, after the introduction of 70 ft-long rolling stock, to build 57 ft carriages for situations where there were physical restrictions on using 70 ft vehicles, or where the traffic was more appropriate to the capacity of the shorter coaches. In the case of trailers, this shorter size was 57 ft (when measured over the corner pillars of the trailer body), but the over-body length, including the bow ends, was 59 ft 6 in. The pioneer matchboarded-style trailer No. 1 was also to this shorter length.

This chapter deals with the wood panelled 59 ft 6 in trailers that were 'purpose built' – the conversions from SRMs will be dealt with later.

In official literature, these 59 ft 6 in trailers were sometimes referred to as 60 ft coaches.

59 ft 6 in Trailers Nos. 7 & 8: Diagram C

These two trailers were the first 59 ft 6 in wood-panelled types to be built. They were ordered in February 1905 on Lot 1087, and delivered in August of that year, at a cost of £1,009 each.

According to the Lot list, they were built for use on the Lambourn Valley Railway, which the GWR had taken over (after some negotiations) in July 1905. The GWR had in fact hired out two SRMs to the LVR from 15th May 1904 to provide the train service. The Lambourn branch was somewhat unusual in that, although trailers were frequently used on the line throughout most of its existence as a GWR and BR(W) branch line, auto trains as such were not used. The reason for using trailers with retractable steps was that the line was constructed as a light railway (although strictly it was not one) with platforms that were very low, and lightweight construction imposed an axle weight limit of only 10 or 12 tons. The LVR was also unusual in that one of its principal *raisons d'être* was to serve a racehorse breeding and training area which resulted in irregular but appreciable flows of horsebox traffic.

It would seem that the SRMs were not a great success on this particular service. There were initially some boiler problems caused by the hard water of the area (this was overcome), but more significantly, their seating capacity was limited, and they were found to have inadequate power to haul strengthening coaches and/or horseboxes over this line with its 1 in 60 gradients. There was also a requirement for shunting at Lambourn, for which an SRM was not very suitable.

The solution adopted was initially to use these Diagram C trailers as the normal coaching stock, hauled by an 'ordinary' (ie non-auto) locomotive. This gave a much better reserve of power than an SRM, and the train could be strengthened when necessary; the locomotive could also be used for shunting when required. The use of a trailer with retractable steps simplified the serving of low platforms, and as the passengers were in an open coach, the guard could issue tickets to those who boarded at one of the unstaffed halts on the line. In due course, the GWR raised the platforms to normal height, but continued to use trailers as ordinary hauled coaches on the branch.

The advantage of using locomotives without auto fittings was that it saved the appreciable effort required in coupling and uncoupling the regulator gear, the electric bell communication circuits and the whistle circuits and the whistle chain every time the locomotive had to detach from its train to shunt any tail traffic. Because of the work involved, it was not uncommon for a trailer to remain attached to an autofitted locomotive whilst shunting operations were being carried out – not a good practice! The Lambourn branch was not unique in using trailers as ordinary hauled coaches; the Watlington branch was another. It helped, of course, that the passenger train service was not frequent, otherwise the time and effort saved in not having to couple/uncouple the auto gear for shunting was outweighed by the necessity of running round the train each journey.

Presumably because the Lambourn Valley line was worked with engines without auto control gear, trailers Nos. 7 and 8 were not provided with regulator gear either for several years. However, they looked like trailers, they were numbered in the trailer series, and were given a diagram indexed in the trailer diagram book.

A photograph exists of one of these trailers at Great Shefford station on the LVR before 1909 which shows the retractable steps in use at the low platform.

Trailers Nos. 7 and 8 were 59 ft 6 in long, 9 ft wide and 12 ft 2¾ in high from rail to roof. This was 1 inch lower than the contemporary 70 ft contemporary 70 ft trailers, but became the standard height for the shorter vehicles. The coaches were bow-ended as usual, but only the 'leading' end had the usual three large windows. The luggage compartment end was wood panelled with vertical beading, 5 panels being formed rather like that on the turnunder ends of the previous generation of non-gangwayed 8 ft wide clerestory and low-roofed coaches. The panelled bow-end was unique to this diagram. One consequence was that the luggage compartment end was painted brown or black as if it were an ordinary

Diagram C trailer at Great Shefford station on the Lambourn Valley line from Newbury. The number is unclear on the original postcard but may well be 8. The trailer has droplights and 9 ft volute or coil spring bogies. The rear van is a 21 ft example to Diagram V2.

COLLECTION P. KARAU

coach, instead of being painted like the sides of a coach, as was normal practice on GWR trailers.

A photograph of one of these coaches shows a queenpost trussed underframe like that on No. 1, which had round section truss rods (with a centre turnbuckle adjustment) and cast queenposts, similar to those provided on clerestory coaches. The diagram does not show an underframe truss or retractable steps at all. The wheelbase was 50 ft 6 in, and the bogies first fitted were of the 8 ft volute type. The coaches were gas lit.

As built, they had a brake and luggage compartment 6 ft 5⅝ in (maximum) between the end wall of the coach, and a partition with a sliding door giving access to the trailer interior. Next, there was a 10 ft compartment of two seating bays, which was originally the smoking compartment. It was followed by an intermediate passengers' vestibule, 3 ft 9 in wide. The large saloon comprised a 9 ft 10 in length of longitudinal bench seating, a 15 ft length with three transverse seating bays, and a further 9 ft length of bench seats. The 'non-driving' vestibule was 3 ft 9 in maximum between the partition and the end wall of the trailer.

The luggage compartment had double doors opening outwards, and, unusually, had the handbrake. The passengers' vestibule had a flat door, slightly recessed, which opened inwards, the same as the doors to the 'non-driving' end vestibule. Retractable steps were fitted below the passengers' vestibule doors. The 2 ft wide external door to the 'non-driving' vestibule opened inwards, but was flush with and curved to the body side.

The window arrangement is believed originally to have been two large fixed lights with twin toplights above each in the smoking compartment, and seven units in the other saloon. However, the smoking compartment soon had one pair of droplights substituted for a fixed light each side, next to the luggage compartment, and the non-smoking compartment had two double droplights substituted. This made the arrangement (each side): two fixed lights, double droplights, fixed light, double droplights, two fixed lights. The date of this alteration is not known, but it is shown on the diagram, and the Great Shefford photograph shows the droplights fitted. The droplights do not appear

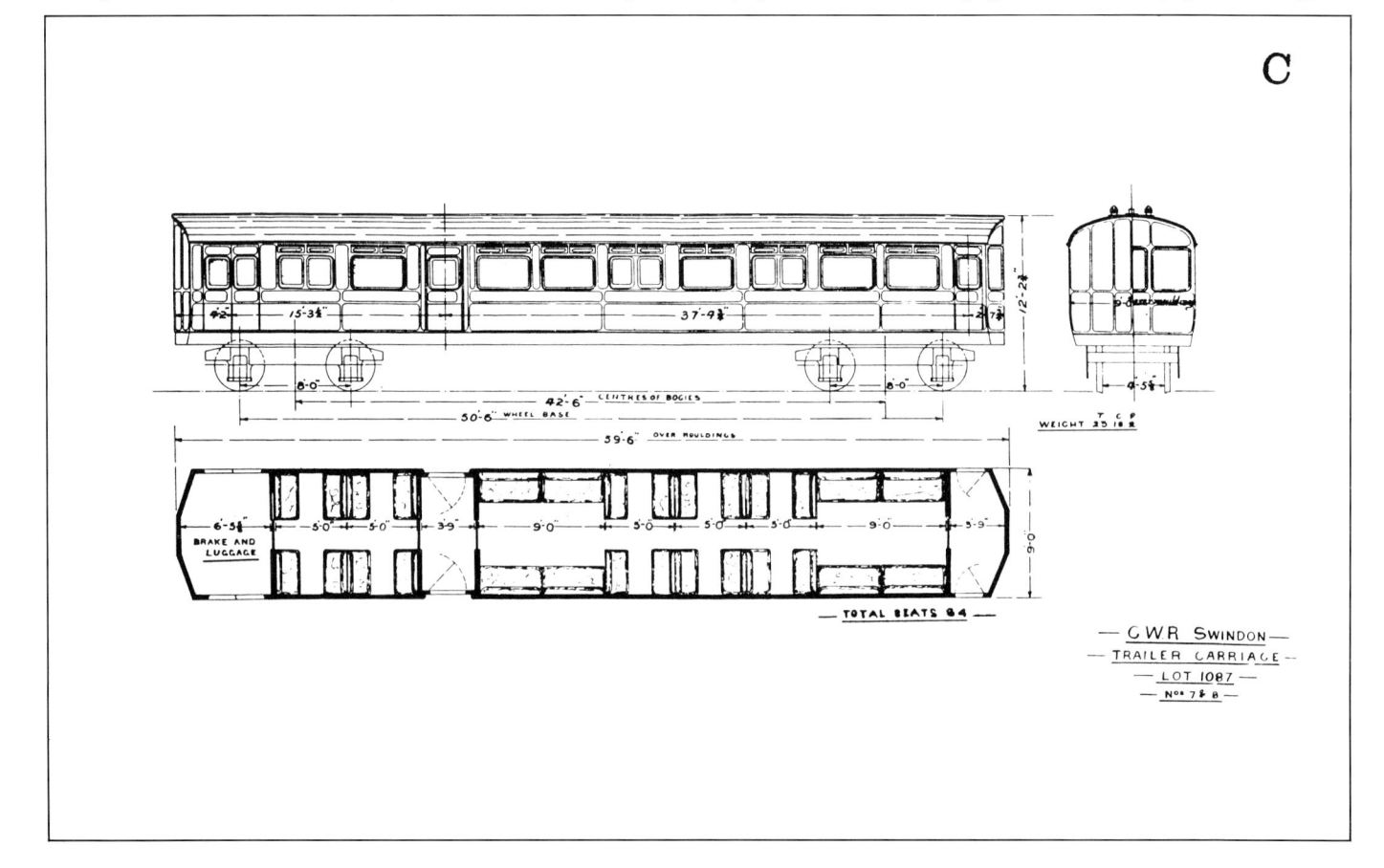

One of the ex-Cardiff Railway pairs of trailers is at the head of the 10.05 a.m. Coryton–Cardiff auto at Heath Junction on 23rd September 1953. The more interesting coach, however, is W7 which just gets a look in. This is to Diagram C and photographs are not common. S. RICKARD

Purpose-built 59ft 6in Trailers

to have bolection mouldings, which suggests that they were not fitted from new.

The 8 ft volute bogies were changed to 8 ft coil spring units in April 1907 on No. 7, and at an unrecorded date on No. 8. TRG seems not to have been fitted until July 1913, in both cases. Thereafter, they could be used as ordinary intermediate trailers, although they were not equipped with regulator handles.

No. 7 is reported to have been fitted with sandboxes in October 1927, which seems a little odd, as it had no driving apparatus. The axleboxes were painted blue in 1929/30, which may have been the dates for another change of bogie to the Collett 7 ft type.

Trailer No. 7 received replacement second-hand gas cylinders, 7 ft long × 1 ft 6 in diameter, in April 1929. The large saloon was designated as the smoking compartment at the same time as the axleboxes were painted blue. No. 8 was painted cream and brown with gold lining at this date, too; No. 7 was similarly treated in 1932.

There were no end windows in the luggage compartment, so the 'black-painting' directive did not apply. (There is an explanatory note dated 1935 in the register about them being panelled, which is a potential source of confusion, as it could be interpreted as recording an alteration.)

ATC was fitted to the trailers in 1942 and 1941 respectively.

No. 7 was condemned at Ferndale in 1954, whilst No. 8 lasted until 1955.

0–6–0T No. 6438 with the 12.45 Cardiff Clarence Road–Pontypridd auto at Ely (main line) on 11th April 1953. This is an interesting view showing the pipework for the gas lighting on the nearest trailer which is Diagram C No. 7. Unfortunately, it has lost its wooden end panelling.
S. RICKARD

Summary

No.	Lot	Built	Coil spring bogies	TRG	Collett 7ft bogies	Sand boxes	Blue A/boxes
7	1087	Aug.05	Aug.07	Jul.13	+	Oct.27	Apr.29
8	1087	Aug.05	+	Jul.13	+	–	Oct.30

No.	Smoking cpts rearranged	Chain comm. apparatus	Cream, brown & gold	ATC	Cond.
7	May 29	Feb.33	Jan.32	Jun.42	Apr.55
8	Oct.30	Oct.30	Sep.30	May.41	Mar.54

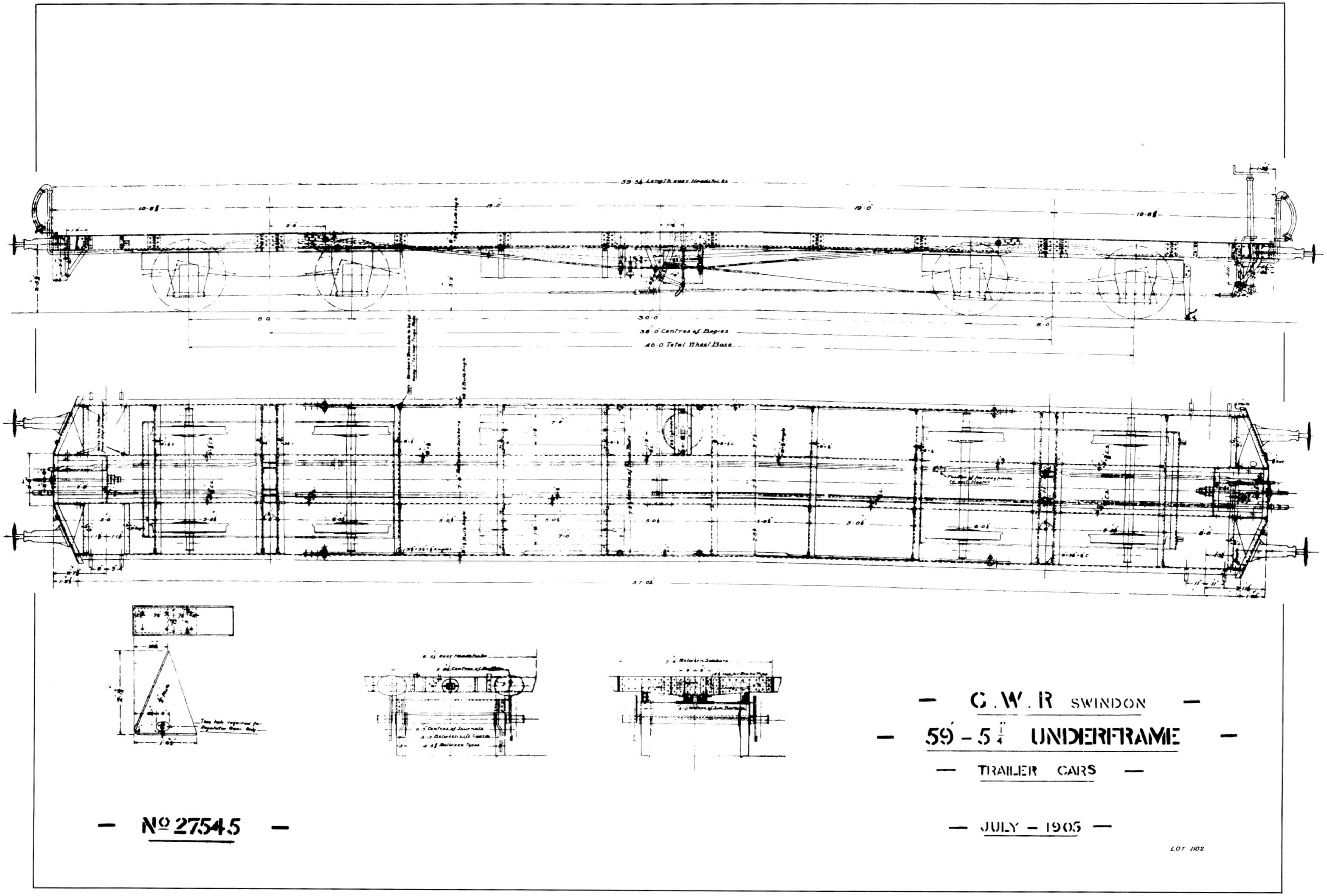
59-5¼ Length over Headstocks
10-8⅜
19-0
19-0
10-8⅜
30-0
8-0
8-0
38-0 Centres of Bogies
46-0 Total Wheel Base
57-0½
№ 27545
G.W.R SWINDON
59′-5¼″ UNDERFRAME
TRAILER CARS
JULY – 1905
LOT 1102

59 ft 6 in Trailers 19–24: Diagrams J1 & J

These six trailers were unique on the GWR in being built by an outside contractor, the Bristol Carriage & Wagon Co. Ltd. At this time Swindon was evidently very busy, and some SRMs were also built by private firms. Trailers Nos. 19–24 were ordered on GWR Lot 1102 in July 1905, and were completed in March 1906 at an average cost of £1,530, which made them the most expensive pre-Great War trailers on the railway.

They were to the standard 'short trailer' dimensions: 59 ft 6 in long × 9 ft wide × 12 ft 2¾ in high, with a wheelbase of 46 ft. The vehicles were fitted with 8 ft bogies, the diagrams showing the 8 ft volute spring bogies, but photographs indicate that the 8 ft 'Fishbelly' type (also referred to as the 'Bristol' or 'Gloucester', after the respective contractors who made them) were used instead.

As built, they had a large driver's vestibule, which was really a combined driver's and passengers' vestibule, with its functions separated by a screen incorporating angled 'wings' behind the driver. This is the same arrangement that was adopted on the contemporary 70 ft trailers Nos. 25–8 (Diagram K). There were flat, slightly-recessed doors (opening inwards) to the driver's end vestibule, with retractable steps below. When the doors were opened, they came up against the wings of the screen, and thus prevented the passengers from easily entering the driver's area. Access to the interior was via the usual sliding door in the partition. This leading vestibule was 5 ft 9 in (maximum) between the end wall of the coach and the partition.

At the guard's end there was a similar vestibule, 3 ft 9 in deep (maximum); this also had flat, inward-opening doors which were only 2 ft wide like the Diagram K trailers. In the passenger saloon, there were 10 ft 6 in lengths of longitudinal benches at each end, and a

Diagram J trailer No. 20 at the opening of the Gwaun-cae-Gurwen branch in 1908. No. 20 was also used on the first auto train from Newnham. AUTHOR'S COLLECTION

Steam Mills in the Forest of Dean in August 1907. The trailer is No. 20 of Diagram J1. The second one is of Diagram L and the third another J1. LENS OF SUTTON

The first auto train from Newnham with trailers Diag. J No. 20, Diag. L and another Diag. J.
COLLECTION A. POPE

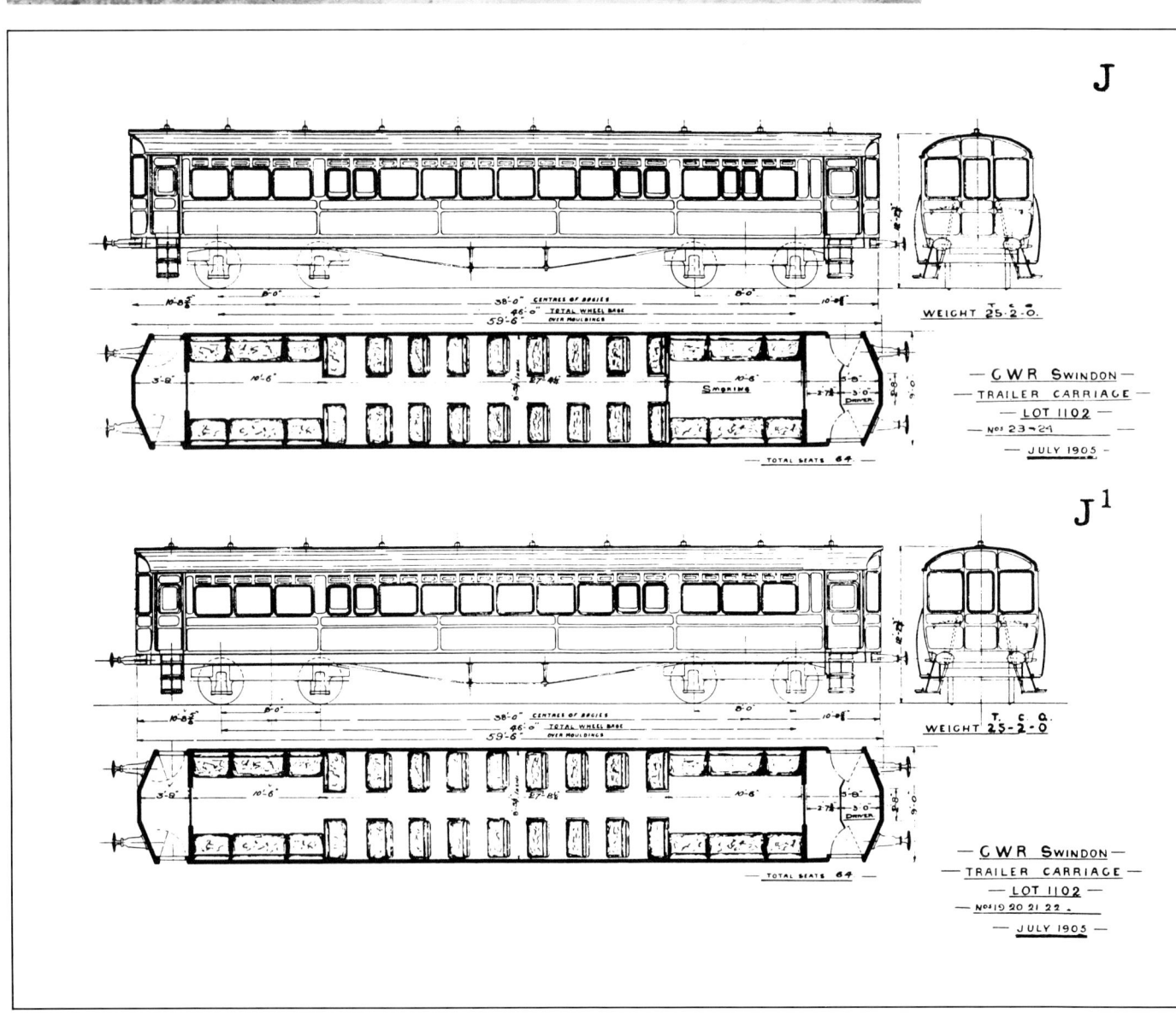

J

GWR Swindon
TRAILER CARRIAGE
LOT 1102
Nos 23-24
JULY 1905

J¹

GWR Swindon
TRAILER CARRIAGE
LOT 1102
Nos 19 20 21 22
JULY 1905

Purpose-built 59ft 6in Trailers

No. 22 Diag. J at Llantrisant. Although in BR days, the guard's compartment end windows are not plated over or painted black.
HMRS

27 ft 8½ in length of walkover seats between them. There were 9 pairs of walkover seats in this area, those at the ends having fixed backs.

The windows were the prevailing arrangement of large fixed lights or pairs of droplights, with two hinged toplights above. As built, there were three fixed window units at either end by the longitudinal seating, whilst the transverse seating had a pair of droplights at each end of a row of six fixed lights. In this condition, the trailers are shown as Diagram J1.

Evidently, it was quickly decided that the interior should be divided into two saloons, and a partition was inserted between the walkover seats and the bench seats at the driver's end; an additional pair of droplights were also inserted in place of the central fixed light in the small compartment. Although the number of seats remained the same, the length occupied by the walkover seats was reduced to 27 ft 4¼ in; the thickness of the partition was mainly due to the sliding door. The new, small compartment became 'smoking'. The trailers were shown as Diagram J in this condition. It appears that Nos. 23 and 24 were delivered in this condition, whilst Nos. 19, 20 and 22 were altered to conform; No. 21 seems to have remained unaltered. No. 22 was modified in December 1912, but a note on the J diagram states that the vehicle was not fitted with droplights in the smoking compartment.

Recorded dates for the fitting of TRG are between 1910 and 1917. No. 23 has a note against it in the register to the effect that it was fitted with driving apparatus in November 1916, although TRG had been fitted in December 1910; this implies that it may have been used as an intermediate trailer without regulator handles in the 'driving' compartment. No. 22 was fitted with sandboxes in 1913, which is an unusually early date. An apparent change to dry sanding apparatus was made at a later date.

For some reason, the number of seats in Nos. 19 and 20 is recorded as being altered from 64 to 62, and then back again in the same month, April and March 1917 respectively. The large compartment was designated 'smoking' between 1928 and 1931, and chain communication was fitted about the same time. The end windows were painted black in 1935, and No. 19 was painted red-brown in June 1942. ATC was fitted to all during the 1940s.

Before passenger services were first introduced from Newnham to Cinderford, in the Forest of Dean, a test train was run on the line using a pair of steam railmotors with a pair of Diagram J trailers between them. However, when the services were introduced, auto trains with locomotives were employed.

The combination of No. 20, a Diagram L trailer, and another (unidentified) Diagram J trailer were used on what may well have been the first Newnham – Steam Mills working in August 1907. The Diagram J trailers were both in the 'full' brown and cream livery, and carried the 1906 'prize' monogram, and appear to have been repainted for the occasion. Later photographs of this service usually show Diagram L trailers in use.

No. 22 was used on an evening Cardiff–Coryton service in the 1930s, whilst No. 23 was photographed on a Plymouth suburban working between the wars.

No. 19 was condemned in June 1949, but reinstated in November of that year; it was finally condemned in December 1956. No. 23 was condemned as 'damaged', and No. 24 was condemned at Oswestry.

Summary

No.	Lot	Built	Diag.	To diag. J	TRG	Sand boxes	Smoking cmpts rearranged
19	1102	Mar.06	J1	+	+		Apr.29
20	1102	Mar.06	J1	+	+		+
21	1102	Mar.06	J1	–	+		Jul.31
22	1102	Mar.06	J1	Dec.12	Nov.13	Mar.13	Aug.28
23	1102	Mar.06	J	–	Dec.10		Nov.28
24	1102	Mar.06	J	–	+		+

No.	Chain comm.	Cream, brown & gold	End windows black	Red-brown	ATC	Cond (1)	Notes
19	Feb.33	Aug.31	Apr.35	Jun.42	Aug.40	Jun.49	Reinstated Nov.49. Cond. Dec.56
20	Dec.28	Oct.31			May 40	Jun.58	
21	Jun.31	May 31	Feb.35		Mar.45	May 55	
22	Dec.30	–	May 35		Jun.40	Apr.56	
23	May 31	–	Nov.35		+	May 54	'Damaged'
24	Mar.29	Nov.31	Feb.35		+	Aug.55	Cond. at Oswestry

'517' class 0–4–2T No. 531 at Abbotsbury station c.1907 with a nearly new Diagram N trailer, probably No. 37 which had a long association with the Weymouth area and the Abbotsbury branch in particular.
COLLECTION J. E. KITE

59 ft 6 in Trailers Nos. 36–41: Diagram N

Trailers Nos. 36–41 were ordered on Lot 1126 in June 1906, and delivered in January and February 1907, at an average cost of £1,057 each. With two important differences, these trailers can be regarded as a slightly-updated version of the Diagram C short trailers (Nos. 7 & 8). The differences were that Diagram N vehicles were driving trailers, and they also had the usual end windows at the luggage compartment end, which were absent on Nos. 6 and 7.

Nos. 36–41 were 59 ft 6 in long, 9 ft wide and 12 ft 2¾ in high from rail to roof. Their wheelbase was 50 ft 6 in, and 8 ft American bogies were standard equipment, although the diagram shows 8 ft volute units. The trailers had the old type of queenpost trusses to the underframe, with cast queenposts at 5 ft 6 in centres, and round section truss rods with a turnbuckle for adjustment in the centre.

These coaches had a 3 ft 9 in driver's vestibule with flush doors that opened inwards. There was a 3 ft 9 in passengers' vestibule with flat, recessed doors (and with retractable steps below) towards the other end of the trailer. At the far end, there was a luggage compartment 6 ft 5⅝ in (maximum) between the end wall and the partition; this had double doors that opened outwards, and which had the same profile as the trailer sides.

Between the luggage compartment and the passengers' vestibule, there was a 10 ft saloon having two seating bays; this was originally the smoking compartment. Between the passengers' and the driver's vestibules there was the non-smoking saloon. This contained a 9 ft length of longitudinal benches, a 15 ft length with three transverse seating bays and, at the driver's end, another 9 ft length of longitudinal bench seating, giving the trailer a total of 64 seats.

The windows differed from the Diagram C trailers in that the droplights were original equipment on the Diagram N vehicles, and therefore had bolection mouldings round the frame, whereas those on the Diagram C trailers did not. Starting at the luggage end, there were a pair of droplights and a fixed light for the small saloon with toplights above each. The large saloon had two fixed lights by each of the bench seating lengths, and a pair of droplights either side of a fixed light for the transverse seating bays. Again, the usual toplights were present.

These trailers were all equipped with TRG, but the only recorded date of fitting is for No. 38, in September 1912. No. 39 was fitted with dry sand boxes (at a very early stage) in May 1913.

Chain communication was fitted in 1929/30, and the larger saloon changed to the smoking compartment in 1928–31. They were all painted in cream and brown with gold

This postcard of St. Agnes station, Cornwall, features a Diagram N trailer, possibly No. 40, which looks new (clean roof) and is in a 'full' brown and cream livery. The picture may well have been taken in 1907.
COLLECTION J. E. KITE

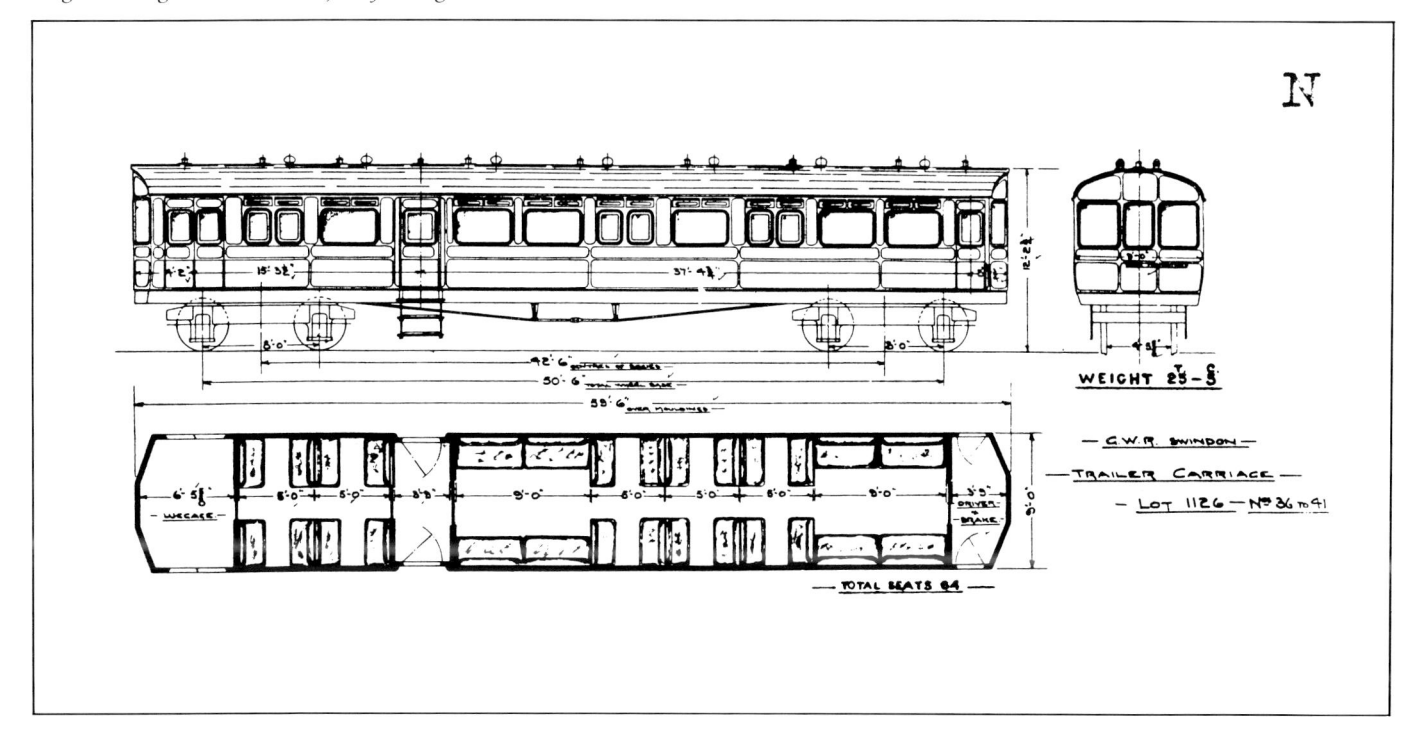

'517' class 0–4–2T No. 1157 propelling Diagram N trailer No. 41 heading an interesting train. No. 41 has sandboxes and gong and is in the 1930 livery with two gold/black waist lines. The six-wheeled passenger brake van is of Diagram V13.
R. E. TUSTIN

This Diagram N trailer, either No. 36 or No. 38, at Wallingford in June 1933, appears to be in the 1927 'plain' brown and cream livery with twin shields emblem but no gold waist line. The vehicle is fitted with 8ft American bogies. The coach beyond it is a Diagram C3 or C10 8-compartment clerestory third.
C. L. MOWAT

Diagram N No. 37 at Bridgend in July 1956 in BR plain maroon 1951-style livery. The destination board reads 'Abergwynfi'.
H. C. CASSERLEY

This picture of the locomotive end of No. 36, a Diagram N trailer, at Ebbw Vale High Level, also features the ATC connections (on the right). It is in BR maroon with 1951-style lettering.
AUTHOR'S COLLECTION

The 2 p.m. Cadoxton–Coryton auto at Neath Low Level on 6th October 1953. The leading vehicle is a Diagram N trailer, probably No. 40, in BR plain maroon with 1951-style running number. The loco is 0–6–0T No. 6416, and the vehicles behind are a newly converted A41 or A42, apparently in lined brown 1948-style, and probably an A27 steel panelled trailer without toplights.
S. RICKARD

lines in 1931/2. The end windows were painted black in February 1935, and ATC was fitted to all during the 1940s.

No. 36 was photographed in the London area in a year recorded as 1936, but as its luggage-end windows were not painted black, and it appears to have been in the 1927 livery, the date may well have been earlier. In BR days, it was photographed at Ebbw Vale (High Level) with another trailer, being hauled in a non-auto mode (the locomotive was at the wrong end for auto working). It was in BR maroon livery with W36W in small characters, 1951-style.

No. 37 was photographed on the Abbotsbury branch (at Abbotsbury) in the fully-lined brown and cream livery, when new. The trailer was also photographed in the Weymouth area on a Weymouth–Dorchester local (hauled by a tender locomotive) circa 1935; it was then in the 1934 livery. It was again photographed at Abbotsbury sometimes thereafter, with black paint on the luggage compartment end windows. It was also at Bridgend in July 1956 painted in 1951-style maroon.

No. 38 was photographed at Old Oak Common in 1950, in brown and cream livery with one waist line, as W38 (1949-style). It was at Bourne End in Spring 1951, still in the same livery, and was photographed subsequently at Newport (probably in the same livery) as W38W, still in the 1949-style.

No. 41 carried the 1943 brown and cream livery with two waist lines. It was, by then, equipped with sandboxes. Later, it ran as W41W (1949-style lettering) in brown and cream, and had received ATC.

Other examples were photographed on the Marlow branch in October 1950, and in 1951, both in brown and cream livery. (These may be pictures of No. 38.)

They all lasted until 1956/7. In September 1957, after condemnation, No. 38 became a mobile office for industrial work study consultants, and was renumbered 079022. It was originally stationed at Newport, and is now preserved.

Summary No.	Built	Lot	TRG	Sand boxes	Chain comm.	Smoking cmpts rearranged
36	Jan.07	1126	+		Apr.30	Aug.28
37	Jan.07	1126	+		Feb.29	Feb.29
38	Feb.07	1126	Sep.12		May 29	May 29
39	Feb.07	1126	+	May.13	Feb.29	Mar.30
40	Feb.07	1126	+	Sep.17	Nr	Jan.29
41	Feb.07	1126	+		Sep.29	Jun.31

No	Cream, brown & gold	End windows black	ATC	Cond.	Notes
36	Sep.31	Feb.35	Jul.40	Aug.57	
37	Oct.31	Feb.35	+	Mar.57	
38	Jul.31	Feb.35	Dec.43	Jan.57	To 079022 Sep.57.
39	Jul.32	Feb.35	Jul.40	Feb.56	
40	Mar.32	Feb.35	Nov.49	Nov.57	
41	May.32	Feb.35	Dec.44	Dec.56	

A pair of Diagram E19 coaches at Wadebridge LSWR in the 1890s. This type was converted to Diagram A1 composite trailers for the Oswestry–Gobowen service (see page 143). Here they are in early condition with oil lighting. On alteration to trailers, they retained their hauled coach running numbers, 7026 and 7028.
LENS OF SUTTON

This splendid-looking clerestory coach was built for the 'Cornishman' train in 1893. Four coaches of this type were altered in 1905 and became trailers Nos. 14–17 (see page 124).
NATIONAL RAILWAY MUSEUM

Early Conversions to Trailers

CHAPTER FIVE

EARLY CONVERSIONS TO TRAILERS

THIS chapter deals with the eight trailers produced by converting existing hauled coaches during 1905, that is, within the first 18 months of trailer operation on the GWR. There was then a gap of almost seven years before more trailers were produced from hauled stock.

There were several reasons for converting existing stock, notably that to do so would be cheaper than building completely new trailers; it would also require less workshop resources, and the trailers could be produced much more quickly. Where converted coaches were left in their original compartment form, it provided for high seating capacity and a rapid loading/unloading ability, at the expense of the capability to issue tickets on the train (unless the coach was originally gangwayed).

The GWR had several bursts of this activity. The main phases were:

1. In 1905, to increase the numbers of trailers quickly at a time when trailers were a new concept
2. In 1912–14, when a number of suburban compartment coaches were altered to compartment trailers
3. The SRM conversion programme, which lasted from 1916 to 1936
4. In the late 1930s, when a few hauled compartment coaches were converted
5. During the 1950s, when some further conversions from hauled stock took place.

Most of the trailers altered from hauled stock retained their original numbers, although many were also given diagrams included and indexed in the Trailer Diagram Book.

4-wheel, 28 ft Low-roof Driving Trailers Nos. 560 & 598

These two 4-wheel trailers were presumably intended as lightweight trailers to accompany SRMs; they seated 40 passengers each. They were never renumbered into the trailer series, nor were they given trailer diagrams.

These coaches started life as 6-wheel mainline coaches, built in 1873 on Lot 77; they were of the then standard 5-compartment all-third class design. Subject to relatively minor styling and constructional changes, this basic design of 5-compartment third started in production in the early 1870s and was still being built up to the end of 1902, by which time it had evolved into a 4-wheel vehicle, strictly for local train services.

Nos. 560 and 590 were 28 ft 0¾ in long, 8 ft 0¾ in wide, and were 11 ft 2¼ in from rail to roof (body, 7 ft 3 in tall). They had a wheelbase of 19 ft and originally were carried on six wheels (9 ft 6 in + 9 ft 6 in wheelbase) on

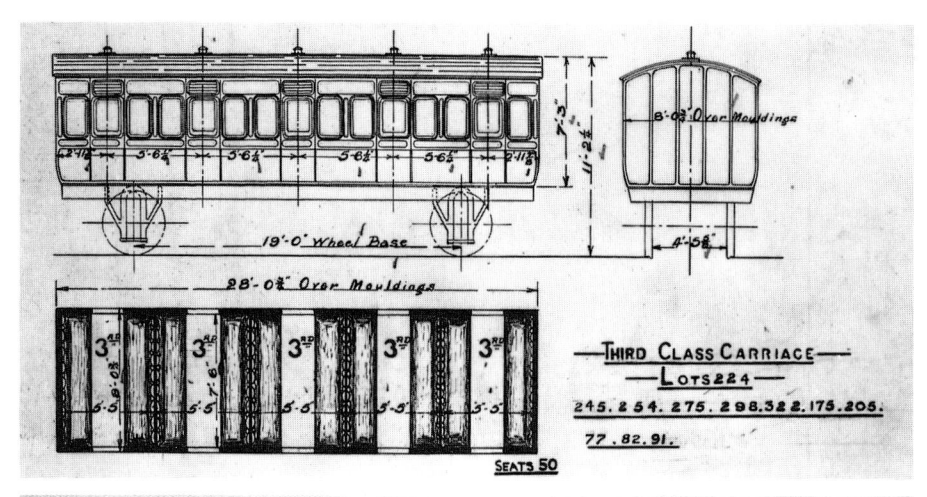

Diagram S3 as built.   COLLECTION J. N. SLINN

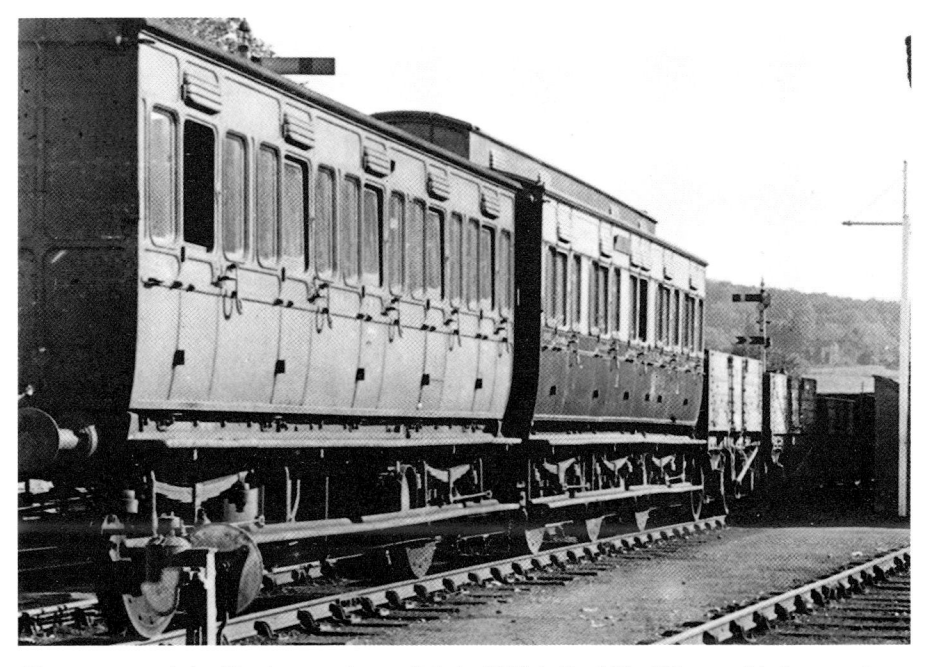

The nearer coach in this picture taken at Bala in 1924, is No. 678 of Diagram S4, the same type as those made into 4-wheel trailers.   H. S. NEWCOMBE

wood underframes. They were designed with low-roof bodies, the roofs themselves being of an arc profile. The bodies were wood panelled, with $\frac{3}{8}$ in beading, and had turn-under ends. The sides had $9\frac{1}{4}$ in eaves panels over the quarterlights, and the doors had matching eaves panels with ventilators. Coaches of this particular design were eventually shown on Diagrams S3 (6-wheel) and S4 (4-wheel).

As built, they had oil lighting, but did not have automatic vacuum (or indeed any) brakes, or steam heating; they seated 50 passengers. Continuous lower footboards were fitted in 1882/80 and No. 598 received the automatic vacuum brake in March 1882. They received gas lighting (flat flame) in 1894/5, but there is no record of them being fitted with steam heating. At some time, No. 560 had its 6 ft bearing springs changed to 4 ft 6 in units.

By 1905, they had been reduced to 4-wheel vehicles by the simple process of removing the centre wheelset and associated running gear. In that year, one of the end compartments was stripped, and converted for use by a driver. This presumably involved cutting windows in the coach end, and equipping the compartment with regulator gear, vacuum brake setter, electric bell communication apparatus and a screw handbrake; the register is silent about this equipment, except for the handbrake.

No. 598's record in the register has a note dated February 1913 indicating that the driver's compartment was also to be available for a guard.

Unfortunately, nothing more is known about them, not even where they worked, and no pictures of them have come to light. Their success as trailers is questionable. They only lasted until February 1913 and December 1914 respectively, by which time they were fully 40 years old.

Summary

No.	Blt	Lot	AVB	Cont. footboards	Gas light FF	To four wheels	To trailer	Cond.	Tare
560	Jan.73	77	+	Mar.82	Nov.95	+	Jul.05	Feb.13	
598	May 73	77	Mar.82	Feb.84	Sep.94	+	Jul.05	Dec.14	9 ct 15 cwts

52 ft Clerestory Trailers Nos. 14–17: Trailer Diagrams G, G1 & H

These four main-line, 3rd class clerestory coaches had been built in 1893 on Lot 692 for the 'Cornishman' express, which ran between Paddington and Penzance, and was a precursor of the 'Cornish Riviera Express'. Their original numbers as hauled coaches were 2833, 2839, 2841 and 2842.

They were 52 ft $0\frac{3}{4}$ in long, 8 ft $6\frac{3}{4}$ in wide, and were 12 ft $6\frac{1}{4}$ in from rail to the top of the upper roof, whilst their body height, also to the upper roof, was 8 ft 7 in. Their roof profiles were '3-arc+3-arc', and they were amongst the first clerestory coaches to have a 3-arc profile to the upper (clerestory) roof.

Their layout originally comprised five 'no-smoking' compartments, 5 ft 7 in between partitions, with a lavatory (2 ft $10\frac{5}{8}$ in between partitions each side), all of which were served by a side corridor; the smoking accommodation was in the form of three bays in an open saloon with a central aisle, 16 ft $8\frac{1}{2}$ in between the final partition and the coach end wall. Each compartment and seating bay, except for the central seating bay in the smoking saloon, had its own door with droplight, flanked by quarterlights. In the central bay of the smoking saloon, the coach was panelled and lined as if the door were present, and there were the droplight and quarterlights, but the 'door' did not open! The corridor side (which did not have any longlights) had the same arrangement of doors, droplights and quarterlights as the compartment side. The windows were relatively tall, and the eaves panels were 7 in deep with matching door ventilators. The coaches had been built as gangwayed stock with side gangway connectors, which were of the standard GWR type with double 'scissors', and were not so wide as a Post Office side gangway, although they were very similar in appearance.

SRM No. 85 hauling one of the clerestory trailers. Unfortunately, from this angle it is not possible to be certain which trailer it is. It might be 14 or 15 of Diagram G as there seems to be only two passenger doors on the side that is visible, evidenced by the commode handles. The other trailers ought to have had a full set of doors this side. The SRM and trailer are in the lake livery.
L & GRP, CTY. DAVID & CHARLES

These vehicles had a wheelbase of 44 ft, and were mounted on Dean's 8 ft 6 in wheelbase bogies. The underframe was of iron, and had queen post trusses. The queenposts themselves were castings, and were 4 ft apart, instead of the more usual 2 ft. The truss rods were of round section, and had a central turnbuckle to permit some adjustment to the underframe. The coaches were built with automatic vacuum brakes, using Armstrong's moving cylinder design, and had gas lighting (flat flame) from new, but not steam heating.

As hauled coaches, they were shown on coaching stock Diagram C8.

All four were rebuilt at Swindon, and emerged as trailers in July 1905. Nos. 2833 and 2841 had had their interiors removed, and were re-equipped on a pattern similar to that of the purpose-built trailers. They became trailers Nos. 14 & 15, and were shown as trailer Diagram G. Coaches Nos. 2839 and 2842, on the other hand, largely retained their existing accommodation; they were renumbered into the trailer series as

Early Conversions to Trailers

Nos. 16 & 17, and were shown as trailer Diagram H.

One possible reason for the rebuilding of these four coaches was that they may well have still had their side gangways intact, and were due for a fairly drastic rebuild to incorporate centre gangways if they were to remain in main-line service. This would have meant modifying the coach ends, the lavatory at the compartment end of the coach, and the seating at the other end.

All four coaches had their gangways removed, and the end walls made good. Three large windows were fitted into the 'compartment' end of the coach and the lavatory compartment changed into a vestibule for the driver. In Nos. 14 and 15, this driver's compartment had two doors to the outside opening outwards, and a central hinged door in the partition opening into the passenger area. In Nos. 16 and 17, there appears to have been an internal door opening into the side corridor, and only one external door opening outwards, on the compartment side of the coach.

The trailers were fitted with the usual driving equipment and electrical communication with the guard and fireman. In all cases, the original arrangement of droplights and quarterlights remained. The vehicles were not equipped with the retractable steps. The driver's end of the coach was painted in the same manner as the coach sides, as was usual with trailers, but the other end was panelled conventionally, and is believed to have been painted brown or black, as on hauled stock.

In Nos. 14 and 15, the driver's compartment was 3 ft 0$\frac{7}{8}$ in between the coach end wall and the partition. It had ordinary opening doors in the sides of the coach (with droplights), and there was a central door in the partition, allowing the driver easy access to the passenger accommodation.

The passenger accommodation had a central aisle, and the interior was divided into three areas. Starting from the driver's end, 2$\frac{1}{2}$ pairs of seating bays were followed by an external door to each side. Beyond the doors were lengths of longitudinal bench seating, with a partition and sliding door across the coach at their further extremity. These two parts formed the large saloon, 31 ft 6$\frac{1}{8}$ in long, and this became the non-smoking area. Next came three seating bays, with an external door to each side in the bay next to the non-smoking compartment. The seat against the end of the coach extended across the whole width of the vehicle. This formed the small saloon, used for smoking accommodation, and was 16 ft 8$\frac{1}{2}$ in long.

The previous arrangement of droplights with adjacent pairs of quarterlights was retained, although the number of passenger doors was reduced to two each side. In this form they seated 65, forty of which were

This is a Barry–Pontypridd auto train unusually headed by two clerestory trailers. The leading one is either 14 or 15 because there are only two external doors to the passenger accommodation. The second trailer is one of 16, 17, 18 or 35 because a full complement of doors is present. These trailers are in the autumn 1927 brown and cream livery with the twin shield device. Note in particular the end of the clerestory is cream, also the white lines across the end windows. The third trailer (behind the loco) is an ex-Rhymney Railway one and the last one looks like a GWR matchboarded example.
COLLECTION R. C. RILEY

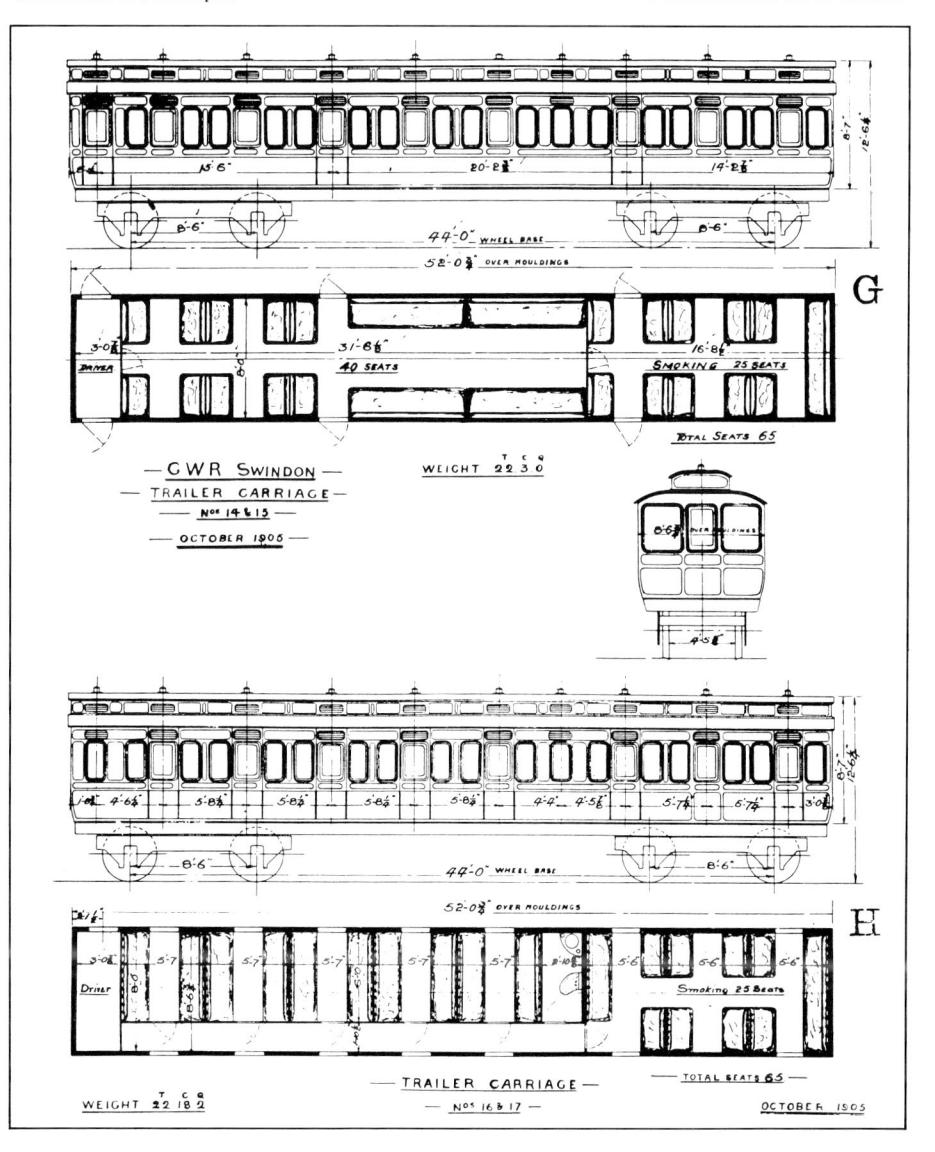

in the non-smoking compartment, and the trailers were shown on Diagram G.

In July 1910, No. 15 had the smoking compartment enlarged to 25 ft 6 in by the addition of $1\frac{1}{2}$ seating bays; the partition was moved to near the centre of the coach, and the non-smoking area and its bench seating correspondingly reduced. As altered, it was shown as Diagram G1, and it is thought the larger compartment became 'non-smoking' as usual at this period. The number of seats was increased to 67 of which 37 were in the enlarged compartment, and 30 in the reduced saloon.

Nos. 16 and 17 had a minimal conversion. The end lavatory was converted into a driver's compartment, and remained at 3 ft $0\frac{7}{8}$ in between the coach end wall and the partition. The remainder of the coach remained more or less unaltered, and even the internal lavatory apparently remained! The seat at the end of the coach in the smoking compartment was, however, extended across the whole width of the coach. This gave a passenger seating capacity of 65, 25 of which were in the smoking saloon. The side doors to the passenger accommodation remained unchanged, and all still opened.

Incandescent gas lighting was fitted to the four trailers between 1908 and 1913, and TRG to all four coaches around 1912/13. In the case of No. 16 (and some other examples) we have a clue to just what comprised 'Through Regulator Gear'; there is a note to the effect that the alteration comprised a connection at the driver's end.

The next noteworthy record indicates that the internal lavatory (fittings) were removed from Nos. 16 and 17, and four 'emergency' tip-up seats were fitted in that compartment (and clear glass, presumably!). This compartment was designated for luggage in February (No. 16) and September (No. 17). It is possible that the lavatory had been taken out of use before then. A new Diagram H was issued showing the 69 seats, but no new index number. It showed the luggage compartment width as 3 ft $0\frac{3}{4}$ in; originally the lavatory tank was concealed in a partition.

No. 17 is the only example recorded as being fitted with sandboxes, the date being August 1927. All of the coaches are recorded as being equipped with chain alarm communication apparatus in 1933; it is almost certain that all had received this whilst they were still hauled coaches, and it was removed on conversion to trailers.

Nos. 14 and 15 are recorded as having the larger compartment made into smoking accommodation. There is no record for No. 16, and No. 17 has the remark 'Not dealt with at Swindon' (December 1931) against it.

No. 14 had dual bell ATC communication circuits fitted in February 1945. It was condemned in April 1951, but reinstated. By the time it was finally condemned in December 1953 (in BR carmine and cream livery, as W14W in 1949-style lettering), it had all the wood panelling on the front covered over with steel sheet, but the date of this modification is not recorded.

No 14 was allocated to Southall and No. 16 to Croes Newydd in January 1906.

A photograph taken by Mr R. C. Riley shows a four-coach auto train on the Pontypridd–Barry service, which has one of Nos. 14–15 as the leading coach, and another clerestory trailer (16–18, or 35) as the second vehicle. The leading coach has a cream end to the clerestory, but it is not known how common this feature was on the clerestory trailers.

No. 15 was condemned in April 1938, No. 16 in June 1939 and No. 17 in April 1944.

The last days of trailer 14, showing how most of the side doors had been permanently 'fastened up'. Even in BR days it had a cream end to the clerestory roof.
COLLECTION J. N. SLINN

Trailer No. 14 of Diagram G condemned in 1951 and again in 1953 after being reinstated. The date of this photograph is not recorded, but is probably after 1953 as the coach has lost its gong and ATC. No. 14 is in the maroon and cream livery and seems to have the end of the clerestory painted in cream. There are side doors at the driver's compartment and where the ladders have been placed against the footboard.
COLLECTION J. N. SLINN

Summary

Coach no.	Lot	Built	Diag.	To trailer	Trailer no.	Trailer diag	Incand. gas	To diag. G1
2833	692	Jun.93	C8	Jul.05	14	G	Aug.08	?
2841	692	Oct.93	C8	Jul.05	15	G	Nov.08	Jul.10
2839	692	Oct.93	C8	Jul.05	16	H	Jun.13	—
2842	692	Aug.93	C8	Jul.05	17	H	Nov.12	—

Trailer No.	TRG	Sand	Lav cpt to luggage	Smoking cpts changed	Chain comm.	ATC	Cond. (1)	Cond. (2)
14	Mar.13			Feb.32	Feb.33	Feb.45db	Apr.51	Dec.53
15	Nov.12			Oct.29	Feb.33	—	Apr.38	—
16	Jun.13		Feb.27	Nr	Feb.33	—	Jun.39	—
17	+	Aug.27	Sep.27	NOT	Feb.33	—	Apr.44	—

db = dual bell

Early Conversions to Trailers

54 ft Clerestory Trailers Nos. 18 & 35: Trailer Diagrams I, A8, M & M1

These two trailers were converted from Diagram C17 main-line gangwayed clerestory thirds Nos. 3148 (Trailer 18) and 3152 (No. 35). They were relatively new coaches at the time of the conversions (September 1905) having been built on Lot 905 in December 1898 and January 1899 respectively. Diagram C17 coaches were the standard main-line gangwayed third of the period 1898 to 1903, by which date 81 examples had been built.

They were to the then standard style of clerestory coach, with 7 in eaves panels, matching door ventilators, and tall windows. They were 54 ft 0¾ in long, 8 ft 6¾ in wide and 12 ft 6¼ in high from rail to the top of the clerestory roof. They had Dean 10 ft wheelbase bogies, and the usual round section queen post truss underframe with a central turnbuckle for adjustment purposes. They were gas lit with flat flame burners, and steam heated.

As constructed, they had central gangway connections at each end. At one end, there was a lavatory compartment 3 ft 8¼ in wide between the end wall of the coach and the adjacent compartment partition. Then came five compartments served by a side gangway. These were 5 ft 7¾ in between partitions, and each had a door to the outside with the usual droplight in it, and quarterlights either side. The corridor had a door opposite each compartment, but with longlights between the doors, which is how Nos. 18 and 35 can be differentiated from Nos. 14–17. However, the diagrams relating to Nos. 18 and 35 seem to have been based on hauled coaching stock Diagram C8 rather than the correct C17, and they do not show the longlights. Next, there was a cross vestibule, extending about halfway across the coach; the remaining half of its width was taken up by a second lavatory, about the same size as the other. The half-vestibule gave access to the smoking saloon, which had three seating bays, each having doors (and quarterlights) on both sides of the coach. The seating here was two either side of the central aisle.

The conversion involved the removal of the gangway connectors at both ends of the coach, and making the end walls good. The end lavatory compartment was stripped out to provide a driving compartment the width of the coach, with three large windows fitted into the end. In the case of No. 18, the driver's compartment had an exterior door both sides, but No. 35 had a droplight only on the corridor side and a door between the driver's compartment and the corridor. It appears that the central pair of doors in the smoking compartment were fastened shut at this time.

In February 1907, No. 18 had the compartment next to the driver's made into first class, and at the same time the 'lavatory door

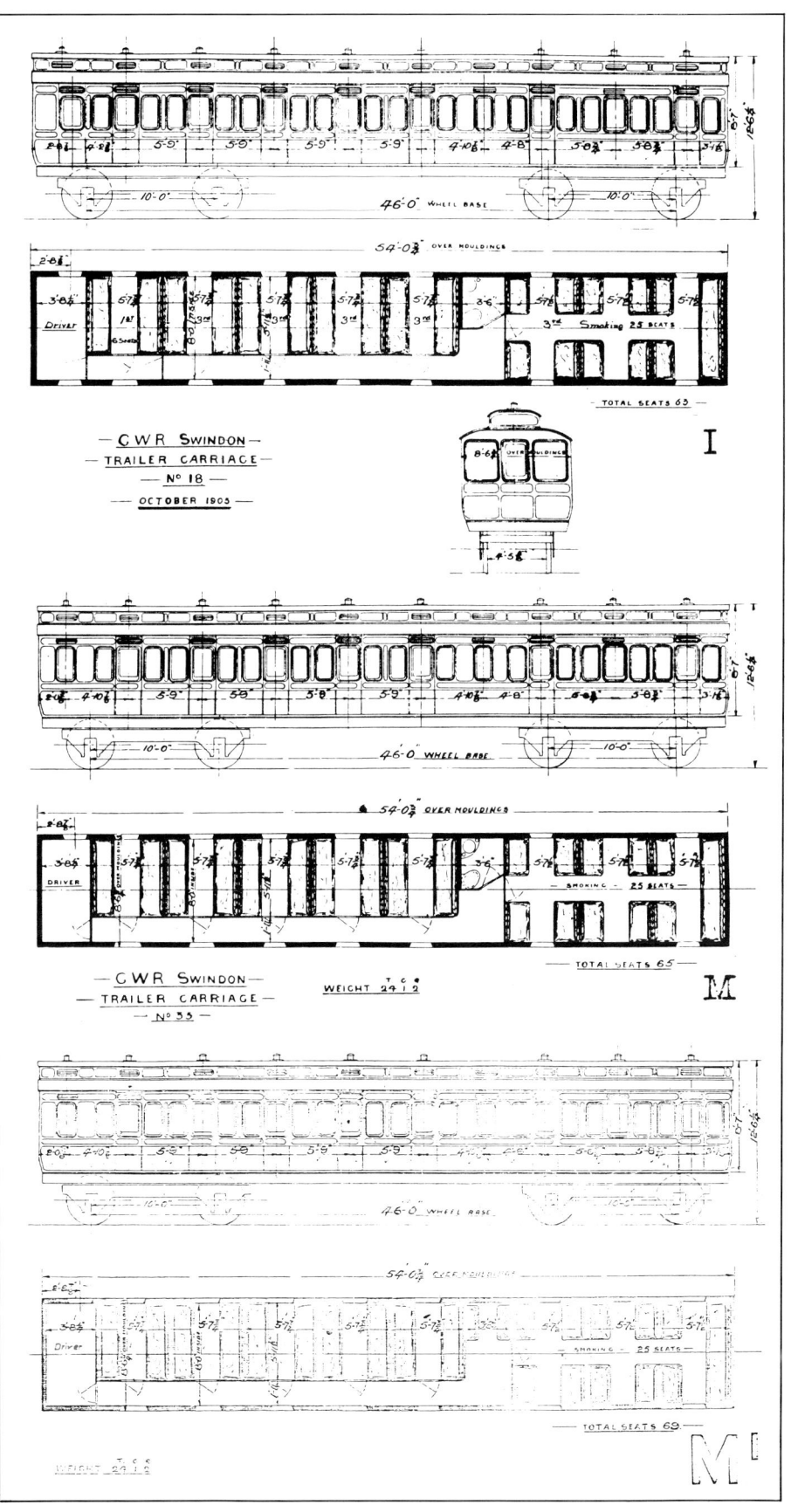

'Large Metro' 2-4-0T No. 3586 and clerestory trailer 35 of Diagram M at Cowbridge in 1947, a couple of years before 35 was condemned. It seems to have spent its latter years at least based there.
I. L. WRIGHT

was fastened shut'. In this condition it is illustrated as trailer Diagram I, and it ran on the Calne branch. Its allocation to this branch is recorded, and it was allocated to Chippenham in March 1906. Diagram F trailer No. 13 was also allocated to the Calne service.

No. 35 was allocated to Croes Newydd (Wrexham) in February 1907. It remained an 'all-third', and also had its lavatory taken out of use at an unrecorded date. It was shown on Diagram M1, and at some stage was allocated to Ruabon. No. 35 had its flat flame gas lighting changed to incandescent in October 1908, whilst No. 18's lighting was not changed until June 1911. These coaches received through regulator gear in December and October 1913 respectively.

In October 1917, No. 18 reverted to an all-third, and at the same time the centre doors in the smoking compartment were restored; it was then shown as Diagram A8. No. 35 had these doors restored too, and an exterior door was fitted to the corridor side of the driver's compartment, but the date is not recorded. It received the diagram index 'M' [the history of what diagram had the index letter 'M' is complicated, and the surviving diagrams are as indicated above]. The next alteration was the reopening of the central lavatory compartment, being equipped with tip-up seats in place of the old fittings. This was done in December 1925 in the case of No. 35, and the coach's seating capacity was thus increased from 65 to 69. Presumably the obscured glass in the window was replaced by clear. No. 18 was similarly dealt with in September 1927.

Both coaches are reported to have had the large compartment allocated for smoking, but it is doubtful whether this represented any change. They were fitted with chain communication in February 1933 and September 1930 respectively.

No. 18 was condemned in December 1938, but No. 35 was equipped with ATC in July 1940, and lasted until October 1949, when it was condemned at Llantrisant. Latterly at least, it had been in use on the Llantrisant–Cowbridge service.

Summary

Coach no.	Lot	Built	Diag.	To trailer	Trailer no.	Trailer diag.	To compo	Lav. cmpt door fastened
3148	905	Dec.98	C17	Sep.05	18	I	Feb.07	Feb.07
3152	905	Jan.99	C17	Sep.05	35	M1	–	+

No.	TRG	To 3rd class (A8)	Extra doors in saloon	Large cmpt smoking	Chain comm	ATC	Cond	Notes
18	Dec.13	Oct.17	Oct.17	Oct.28	Feb.33	–	Dec.38	'Calne' (N/
35	Oct.13	–	+(M)	Oct.28	Sep.30	Jul.40	Oct.49	

Low Roof Conversions to Trailers 1912–1914

CHAPTER SIX

LOW ROOF CONVERSIONS TO TRAILERS
1912–1914/1931

Non-auto-fitted 'Metro' class 2–4–2T No. 3593 with a Clifton Downs set at Twyford with the Henley branch train in 1927. The Clifton Downs coaches are possibly 3335 (nearest) and 3276.
M. W. EARLEY

IN this chapter, we look at a number of trailer conversions from low-roof (as opposed to clerestory roofed) compartment coaches that took place just before the beginning of the Great War plus one in 1931. These had a few unusual features, although the conversions of the 4-wheel thirds was a precedent in some respects.

These were all non-corridor coaches, so the advantages of the guard being able to issue tickets had to be foregone in the interest of higher seating capacity. None of these vehicles were renumbered into the trailer series, but instead kept their original running numbers. The driving trailers were given diagrams in the trailer book, but the intermediate trailers were not so favoured. The intermediate trailers remained as such for the rest of their existence. Almost half of these vehicles ran for some time as composite trailers, with first class accommodation.

A total of 18 coaches were involved in the pre-war conversion programme. The main batch comprised eight driving trailers converted from brake thirds of Diagram D27, and eight intermediate trailers converted from six composites and two all-thirds. These sixteen trailers were altered for the Bristol–Clifton Downs service, and are commonly known as 'Clifton' or 'Clifton Downs' trailers. The other two trailers were converted from brake tricomposites of Diagram E19.

The surviving records for these coaches in the registers do not tell the whole story.

51 FT DRIVING TRAILERS Nos. 3331/32/35–40
Trailer Diagrams A2 & A3 – 'Clifton Downs' Stock

These eight trailers were altered from brake thirds built in May and June 1898 on Lot 872, which originally had 5 third class compartments plus separate ones for the guard and for luggage. The guard's compartment had projections (or 'wings'), and the luggage compartments had a dog locker, which was a box across the coach with small external doors. These were in the then standard style for low roof coaches: a 3-arc profile roof, wooden panelled body with turn-under ends, tall windows, 7 in eaves panels and matching door ventilators. They were 51 ft 0¾ in long, 8 ft 0¾ in wide, and the body height was 7 ft 6 in. They had Dean 8 ft 6 in bogies, and the total wheelbase was 43 ft.

Gas lighting (with flat flame burners) was fitted from new, and with the possible excep-

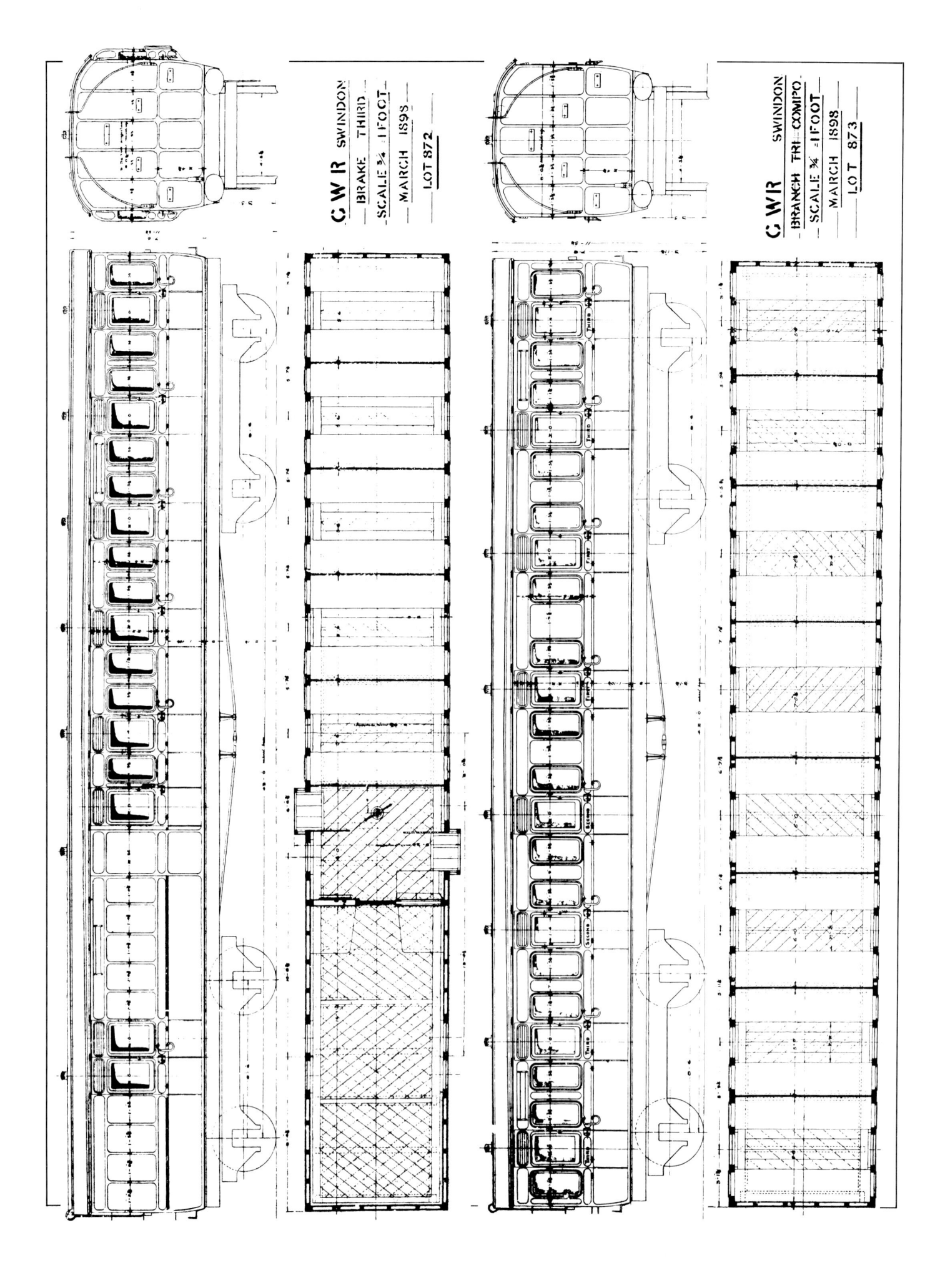

GWR SWINDON
BRAKE THIRD
SCALE ¾ = 1 FOOT
MARCH 1898
LOT 872

GWR SWINDON
BRANCH TRI-COMPO.
SCALE ¾ = 1 FOOT
MARCH 1898
LOT 873

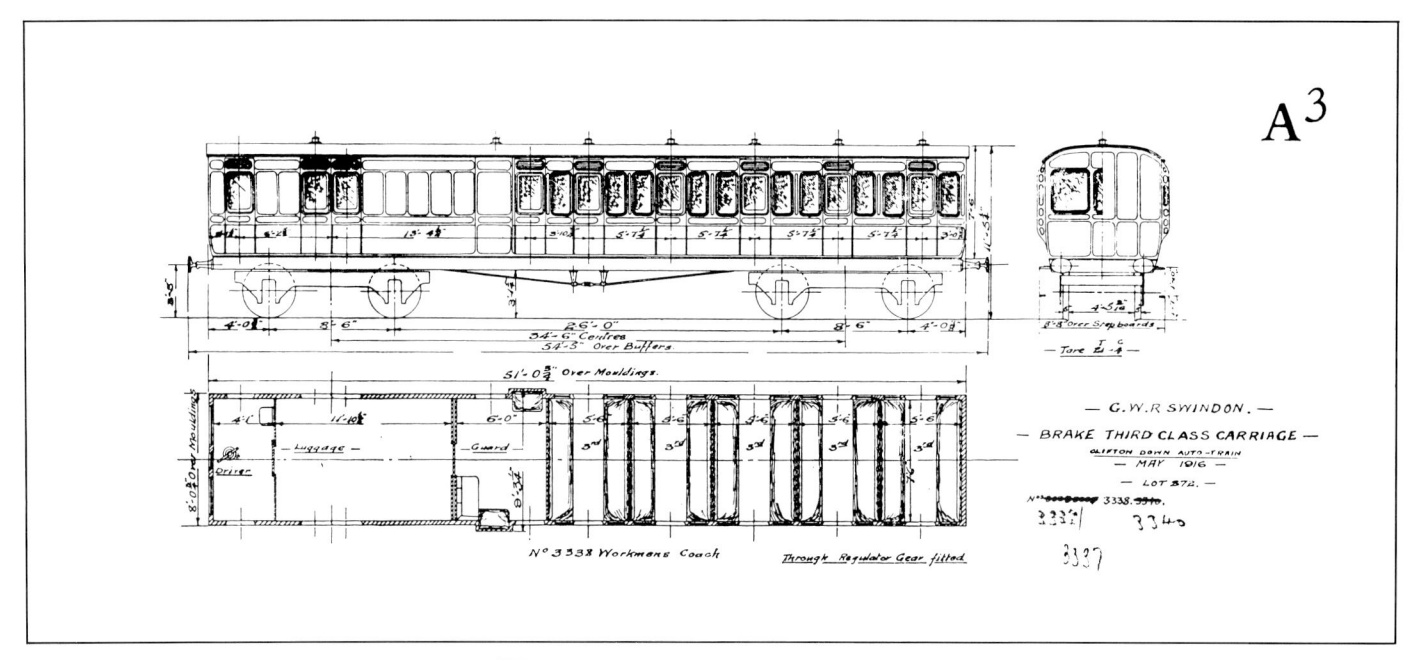

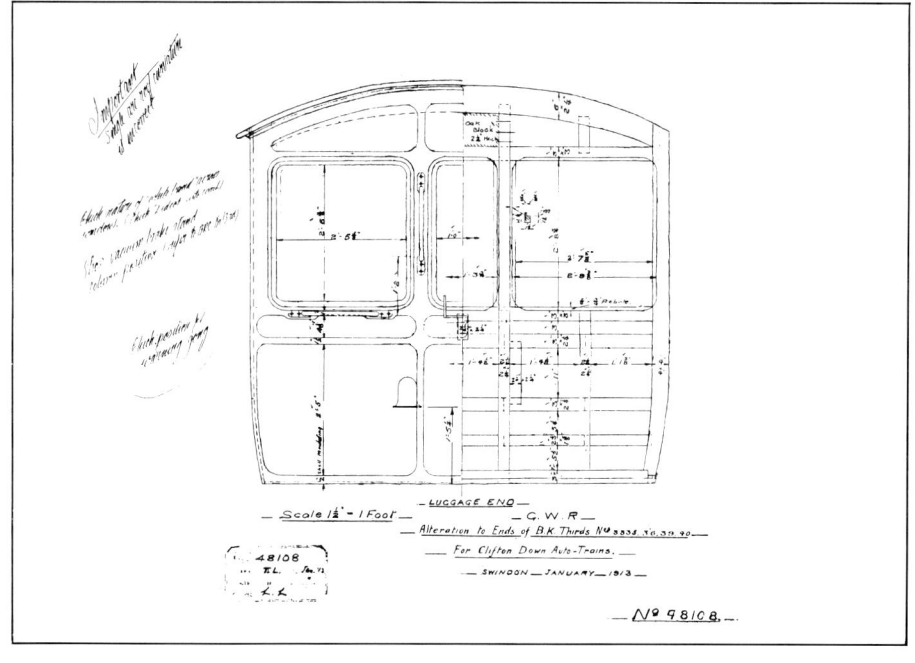

tion of 3340, they were re-equipped with incandescent lighting between June 1910 and December 1911. In the period between July 1912 and November 1913, the dog lockers were removed. Around 1915 and 1916, shelves were fitted in the guard's compartment above the site of the dog lockers, as was standard practice for brake coaches of the period.

There has been some confusion as to the dates of conversion of these trailers, perhaps caused by the different dates of modifications to the driver's compartments and the fitting of through regulator gear. The dates of allocation to the Bristol–Clifton Downs service, which in some cases *preceded* their conversion to a trailer, add to the puzzle, and the registers are not always as clear or complete as might be wished. In this account, the date on which the addition of the driver's compartment was effected is taken as defining the conversion date of the driving trailers.

The first two conversions took place in June 1913, and involved Nos. 3335 and 3340; these were followed by the remaining six vehicles during the following three months. They were altered to trailers by partitioning off the end of the luggage compartment to form a driver's compartment, measuring 4 ft 1 in between the coach end wall and the partition. There were three fixed windows placed in the end of the coach for the driver; the centre window had a glass width of 1 ft, whilst those on either side were 2 ft $5\frac{5}{8}$ in wide. They were all 2 ft $6\frac{3}{8}$ in tall, and were positioned rather higher than the side windows. The panelling on the driving end was altered so that it effectively divided the coach end into three, corresponding to the windows.

Unlike the purpose-built trailers, the ends retained their turn-under, and were not bowed. There were even waist panels on the driver's end, like the sides, but because the windows were positioned higher than those on the sides, the bottom moulding of the waist panels at the end corresponded to the top mouldings of the side waist panels. In due course, much of this panelling was replaced by steel sheet in many cases. The non-driving end remained unchanged, with five vertical panels divided by a horizontal waist level moulding.

Through regulator gear was fitted as part of the conversion process, and the handbrake was moved from the guard's compartment into the new driver's vestibule. The guard lookouts remained unchanged. Unusually for a trailer, these coaches had a bracket for roof destination boards, which were retained after conversion; however, photographs show that they had been removed from those vehicles that survived beyond WW2. There was also a pair of brackets for a destination board on the front, immediately above the centre window.

There were a number of variations and alterations in the arrangement of the driver's compartment in the first three years after the conversions.

Some were initially fitted with a door in the partition between the driver's compartment and the luggage van, though by the end of 1913 the doors had been removed, and the partition made solid. On those trailers which had no external doors in the driver's vestibule at the time the solid partition was erected, two such doors had to be provided.

The official photograph of the Clifton Downs stock, with '517' class 0–4–2T No. 833. The leading coaches are brake third 3332 and composite 7176 forming set No. 3. Only 7176 has 'G.W.R' once in the waist panel. This implies that the others are in brown 1908 livery whilst 7176 is in lake. The leading trailer has no gong or sand apparatus, but it does seem to have the bell wiring at the driver's end, so presumably had TRG. On the front, behind the vacuum pipe, it seems to have a protrusion similar to that on slip coaches. On slips this concealed a foot-operated horn. No. 7176 still has the chain alarm.
AUTHOR'S COLLECTION

In 1916, the door in the partition between the driver's and the luggage compartments was restored (or in some instances, provided for the first time); this modification was carried out on all the trailers.

With a full complement of driver's doors and droplights, and with a solid partition between the driver's and luggage compartments, the coaches were shown as Diagram A2 (dated June 1913), and after the modification providing the door in the partition as Diagram A3 (dated May 1916).

On conversion to trailers, all these coaches were allocated to the Bristol–Clifton Downs service, with Nos. 3331/5/6/8 being recorded in the register as 'Workmen's coaches' on this service. The A3 diagram shows No. 3332 as being a workmen's coach. They were allocated to this service until 1922, when they were dispersed, with most going initially to the Birmingham Division. Their known allocations are set out in the table on page 141, with those of the intermediate trailers involved.

Subsequently, Nos. 3337 and 3338 are recorded as being equipped with sand boxes in August 1927 and May 1926 respectively. Photographs show No. 3331 as having them, and the remainder were probably fitted too. There is no record of the trailers being fitted with chain communication, but the official photograph of two sets (as rebuilt) seems to show all coaches already fitted with it. All the vehicles were probably equipped with a gong in the 1920s, and photographs taken in the 1930s show this feature, although the official 'as rebuilt' picture does not. However, as usual, there are no records of gongs being fitted.

Trailer No. 3331 is recorded as having its guard's lookouts removed, and a seat fitted for the guard, in March 1927; no new diagram was included in the trailer diagram book for it. No. 3331 was the only trailer to lose its wings. Four examples were recorded as being painted 'cream and brown with gold lines' in 1930/1. Four were fitted with special door locks for use on the Severn & Wye Joint Railway in 1936; New Works Order 9/3/43 covered this, and these were the first four to be withdrawn, the other four surviving the war. None are recorded as being painted brown during WW2, but it is thought that the four survivors were. Only two are recorded as being fitted with ATC: No. 3335 in February 1946, and No. 3338 in October 1944.

No. 3337 was the first to go, in December 1938; the others followed at intervals, the last survivor being No. 3338, which was condemned in September 1948 but not cut up. It was reinstated in November 1949, and finally condemned in March 1954.

Summary to 1920

No.	Built	Incand. gas light	Dog locker remvd.	To trailer	Door in partition
3331	May 98	Dec.10	Aug.13	Aug.13	No
3332	Jun.98	Dec.11	Jul.13	Aug.13	No
3335	Jun.98	Sep.10	Feb.13	Jun.13	Yes
3336	Jun.98	Sep.10	Apr.13	Jul.13	Yes
3337	Jun.98	Dec.10	Jul.13	Sep.13	No*
3338	Jun.98	Dec.10	Jun.13	Sep.13	No*
3339	Jun.98	Jul.10	Mar.13	Jul.13	Yes
3340	Jun.98	?	Feb.13	Jun.13	Yes

No.	Driver's doors	Partition made solid	Driver's cpt doors provided	Shelf in guards cpt	Door put in partition	Workmen's (Br–CD) service
3331	2	Aug.13	–	Dec.15	Nov.16	No
3332	2	Jul.13	–	Dec.15	+	Yes (Diag A3)
3335	0	Nov.13	Nov.13		Jul.16	Yes
3336	0	Dec.13	Dec.13		May 16	Yes
3337	2	Jul.13*	–	May 16	May 16	No
3338	2	Sep.13*	–	May 16	May 16	Yes
3339	0	Dec.13	Dec.13		Sep.16	No
3340	2	Nov.13	–		+	No

* Note: These trailers are shown in the register as being fitted with doors in the driver's compartment partition, but the partition was made solid before they were released to traffic as trailers.

Summary (cont)

No.	Wings removed	Sand boxes fitted	Cream, brown & gold	Door locks for S & W	ATC	Cond.	Reinstated	Cond.
3331	Mar.27	+	Jul.30	–	–	Nov.46		
3332	–	Nr	Aug.30	Sep.36	–	Aug.39		
3335	–	Nr		–	Feb.46	Jul.48		
3336	–	Nr		–	–	Dec.50		
3337	–	Aug.27		Sep.36	–	Dec.38		
3338	–	May 26	Jun.31	–	Oct.44	Sep.48	Nov.49	Mar.54
3339	–	Nr	Sep.31	Sep.36	–	Jun.39		
3340	–	Nr	Sep.36	–	–	Dec.40		

Low Roof Conversions to Trailers 1912–1914

Perranporth where auto trains crossed on the Newquay branch. On the left of this 1936 view is a Clifton Downs driving trailer, possibly 3332 which was allocated to Truro between December 1933 and about September 1936. Attached to the Clifton Downs trailer is an A30 example. The trailer on the right is unidentified.
G. N. SOUTHERDEN

The auto train in the centre of this picture of Heathfield on 9th September 1933 consists of a Clifton Downs set with 3331 leading, trailer 3275 in the middle, and loco 1487 at the far end. No. 3331 was the only one to lose its guard's look-outs. This photograph provides a useful view of the roofs of these trailers with their ventilators, gas lamps, gas pipes and roof board holders. To the right is an SRM hauling a saloon.
G. N. SOUTHERDEN

A Clifton Downs set on a Reading–Basingstoke working near Reading West station. The mostly hidden loco is '517' class 0–4–2T No. 526 which is also hauling a horse-box. Fairly close examination of the photograph shows the set to be in the 1930 livery with two gold waist lines.
H. PATTERSON RUTHERFORD

Low Roof Conversions to Trailers 1912–1914

'517' class 0–4–2T No. 526 and a Clifton Downs set at Reading shed. The leading vehicle is intermediate trailer 3387. It is believed that the whole train was taken on shed to avoid uncoupling and recoupling the auto-gear again.
LENS OF SUTTON

A 'Clifton Downs' driving trailer with an A30 steel panelled trailer.
T. E. LAINE

One of the last workings of a Clifton Downs set on the Marlow branch in 1947. The leading trailer is in the 1943 brown livery with a single waist line, but unfortunately the running number is not visible. It is fitted with ATC. The vehicle nearest the camera ia probably 3335 with 3276 behind.
J. H. RUSSELL

Low Roof Conversions to Trailers 1912–1914

0-6-0PT No. 6401 with the Porth auto at Pontypridd in May 1953. The trailer is ex-Clifton Downs driving trailer No. 3338, which seems to be in BR plain maroon. It lasted for nearly another year before finally succumbing.
COLLECTION
R. C. RILEY

Above & right: No. W3338 at Cardiff Queen Street. This may be another example of the lined maroon (unofficial version).
M. LONGRIDGE

THE 'CLIFTON DOWNS' INTERMEDIATE TRAILERS

There were no less than four varieties of intermediate trailers converted for the Clifton Downs service. Two were adapted from a rather old 8-wheel all-third compartment design, and the remaining six from three varieties of 8 wheel non-corridor composite. None were ever renumbered into the trailer series, or given indexed diagrams in the trailer diagram book.

45 ft Intermediate Trailers Nos. 2293/4: Diagram C1 'Clifton Downs' Stock

Trailers Nos. 2293/4 & 2294 were the solitary examples of one of the earliest designs of eight compartment, 8-wheel all-third on the GWR. They were built on Lot 187 in 1879 as Nos. 370 and 371, so they had already seen over thirty years service when they were made into trailers. They were 45 ft 0¾ in long, 8 ft 0¾ in wide, and had bodies that were 7 ft 2½ in high. By the time they were altered to trailers, they had Dean 6 ft 4 in bogies, with a total wheelbase of 34 ft 6 in.

They had a single-arc profile roof and 'low' windows. The eaves panels should have been 9¼ in deep, but the weight diagram seems to show rather deeper ones. The only photograph of these coaches to come to light so far is a rather distant view at Neyland, which does not answer these questions. The coaches had the usual turn-under ends of the period, with five vertical panels, originally without a waist moulding, but one may have been added in due course. The compartments varied marginally, and were either 5 ft 5⅝ in or 5 ft 5¾ in between partitions.

They were renumbered 2293 and 2294 in July 1894. Originally, these coaches were oil lit and unheated. No. 2293 received flat flame gas lighting in July 1894, and steam heating in January 1906, whilst the corresponding dates for No. 2294 were June 1891 and January 1905 respectively.

No. 2293 was the first to be altered to a trailer, in May 1913 (just preceding the first of the brake thirds), and was followed by No. 2294 in July 1913. Both coaches were given incandescent gas lighting. The conversion to an intermediate trailer involved fitting through regulator gear, a cable with connectors for the electrical bell communication (between the driver in the leading trailer, and the fireman on the engine), and the cord for the locomotive whistle.

Their recorded allocations are set out on page 142. They were condemned in July 1931 and February 1933 respectively, the first GWR-built (or rebuilt) 8-wheel trailers to go.

Summary

No.	Built	Lot	Avb	Oil A/boxes	FF gas light	Renumbered To	Date	Steam heat	Incand. gas light	To trailer	Cond.
370	Mar.79	187	Feb.81	Jul.94	Jul.94	2293	Jul.94	Jan.06	Apr.12	May.13	Jul.31
371	Mar.79	187	Mar.82	Nr	Jun.91	2294	Jul.94	Jan.05	Jul.13	Jul.13	Feb.33

51 ft Intermediate Trailer No. 6734 (later 3273): Coaching Stock Diagram E56/C42 'Clifton Downs' Stock

This coach was one of three built on Lot 837 in June 1897; it was originally numbered 734, but became 6734 as a result of the 1907 renumbering scheme. It was 51 ft 0¾ in long, 8 ft 6¾ in wide, and the body height was 7 ft 6 in. It was the only one of the 'Clifton Downs' trailers to be of this width, and instead of having the usual six vertical panels at the ends, it had the design known as 'pseudo-gangway', with what looked like a panel in the centre with wide surrounds, as if a gangway could be fitted there if required (none ever were!). The coach had the usual style 3-arc profile roof. The sides were in the standard style of the period with 7 in deep eaves panels, matching door ventilators and tall windows.

No. 374 was built with flat-flame gas lighting and steam heating. It had Dean 10 ft bogies, with a total wheelbase of 43 ft. The accommodation was arranged, 2nd, 2nd, 2nd, 1st, 1st, 1st, 3rd, 3rd, but the second class compartments became thirds on the abolition of the second class in 1909. The third class compartments were 5 ft 6 in between partitions, second class 6 ft, and first class either 6 ft 11 in or 6 ft 11⅛ in.

The vehicle received incandescent gas lighting in September 1910.

It was altered to a trailer in September 1913, the changes being the fitting of control gear as for No. 2293/4. It continued as a composite trailer until November 1923, when it was reclassified as all-third, renumbered 3273, then being shown on the coaching diagram C42. However, the first class trimmings were left in situ – presumably until overhaul.

It remained as a trailer until June 1931, when the control gear was removed and it reverted to an ordinary hauled coach. It was prepared for use on the continent in 'Overseas Train No. 1' in July 1945, but reverted to ordinary traffic in December 1945. It was condemned in April 1950.

Summary

No.	Built	Lot	Compo. diag.	1907 no.	Incandescent gas lighting	To trailer	To third class	3rd no.	3rd diag.	Control gear removed
734	Jun.97	837	E56	6734	Sep.10	Sep.13	Nov.23	3273	C42	Jun.31

No.	Painted brown	To workmen's coach	Prepared for continent	To ordinary traffic	Cond.
3273	Sep.37	July 38	July 45	Dec.45	Apl.50

51 ft Intermediate Trailer No. 7173 (later 3390): Coaching Stock Diagrams E59/C41 – 'Clifton Downs' Stock

This was a 'one-off' coach built in June 1898 on Lot 882. It was 51 ft 0¾ in long, very similar to No. 6734, though it differed in being 8 ft 0¾ in wide, with standard 5-panelled ends. Dean 8 ft 6 in wheelbase bogies were fitted, and the accommodation was arranged 3rd, 2nd, 2nd, 2nd, 1st, 1st, 1st, 3rd. The third class compartments measured 5 ft 5 in between partitions, second class 5 ft 11¾ in, and first class compartments 7 ft.

The coach received incandescent gas lighting in July 1910, and was altered to an intermediate trailer at a date that is not recorded in the register. It ran as a trailer until April 1922 when it was reclassified as an all-third, renumbered 3390, and given coaching stock diagram index C41. Unfortunately, most of its record in the register has been obliterated, so all that is known of its subsequent history is that it was condemned in June 1949 as an ATC-fitted trailer.

Summary

No.	Built	Lot	Compo. diag.	1907 no.	Incandescent gas lighting	To trailer	To third class	3rd no.	3rd diag.	ATC	Cond.
1173	Jun.98	882	E59	7173	July 10	+	Apl.22	3390	C41	+	Jun.49

50 ft Intermediate Trailers Nos. 7169–72 (later 3274–6 & 3387): Coaching Stock Diagrams E58/C40 – 'Clifton Downs' Stock

These four coaches were yet another example of the GWR's apparent ability to produce an almost infinite number of variations in the design of composite coaches built in the same style (and thus achieving a very high degree of 'low level' standardisation). In this case, they were just 12 inches shorter (at 50 ft 0¾ in) than their contemporary No. 7173 (considered immediately above), but they were the same width – 8 ft 0¾ in; they were 11 ft 5¼ in high from rail to roof. Their accommodation was arranged: 3rd, 3rd, 2nd, 2nd, 1st, 1st, 3rd, 3rd. The compartment sizes were slightly larger than in No. 7173, with third class compartments 5 ft 8 in between partitions, second class 6 ft exactly, and first class measuring 7 ft 0⅝ in.

The coaches were built on Lot 873 in June 1898, and numbered 1169–72; they became Nos. 7169–72 as a result of the 1907 renumbering. Their second class compartments were reduced to third on the abolition of second class. They had Dean 8 ft 6 in bogies, with a total wheelbase of 42 ft, and were gas lit from new with flat flame burners. They had steam heating, and all received incandescent gas lighting between October 1909 and October 1911.

All four were altered to intermediate non-driving trailers in August and September 1913 by the fitting of control gear. They remained composites in their new role, until transferred away from the Bristol area in 1922 when they were reclassified all-third. They then became Nos. 3274, 3275, 3387 and 3276 respectively. Notes against all of these vehicles in the register show that they retained their first class trimmings after reclassification to all-third. No. 3387 is also known to have been painted cream and brown with gold lines in June 1932; it is recorded as receiving ATC apparatus in October 1944. This would have meant that it

'517' class 0–4–2T No. 526 again, with a Clifton Downs set on a local train from Reading to Twyford and/or Maidenhead. The coaches are to Diagrams C40 and A3 or A2 ('Third' appears on the doors).
HMRS

No. 3387 Clifton Downs intermediate trailer, Diagram C40, at Reading in August 1933.
H. C. CASSERLEY

acquired the appropriate electrical cables; it may then have been running with Driving Trailer No. 3338, which received ATC fittings at the same time. No. 3276 may also have been fitted with ATC in February 1946, as it was reported as running with driving trailer No. 3335, which itself received ATC at that date.

There is one unexplained feature that was fitted to these intermediate trailers: an angle iron strip was placed across the coach roof at the locomotive end. It was quite prominent, and must have protruded 2 to 3 inches above the roof line. It was not applied to the trailers when converted, because it does not appear in the official photograph, but it had been applied to all vehicles by the late 1920s. It is possible that it was fitted to the other types of 'Clifton Downs' intermediate trailers. No. 3273 did not have this fitting when photographed in 1947, but by then it was no longer in use as a trailer.

All were condemned between 1946 and 1950. The last survivors were painted brown; it is possible that others were too.

Summary

No.	Built	Lot	Compo. diag.	1907 no.	Incandescent gas lighting	To trailer
1169	Jun.98	873	E58	7169	Oct.09	Aug.13
1170	Jun.98	873	E58	7170	May 11	Aug.13
1171	Jun.98	873	E58	7171	Sep.10	Sep.13
1172	Jun.98	873	E58	7172	Oct.11	Sep.13

No.	To third class	3rd No.	3rd Diag.	Cream, brown & gold	Painted brown	ATC circuit fitted	Cond.
1169	Aug.22	3274	C40	–	+	–	Dec.50
1170	Aug.22	3275	C40	–	–	–	Nov.46
1171	Apr.22	3387	C40	Jun.32	–	Oct.44	Sep.48
1172	Apr.22	3276	C40	–	–	–	Jul.48

'517' class 0-4-2T No. 1427 at Heathfield on 9th September 1933 with a Clifton Downs set. No. 3275 is nearest the camera whilst the driving trailer is No. 3331. The coaches appear to be in the 1929 brown and cream livery and both are fitted with roof destination board holders, but I have not seen a photo of them in use on a Clifton Downs set. Eventually they were removed.   G. N. SOUTHERDEN

Low Roof Conversions to Trailers 1912–1914

Ex-Clifton Downs trailer (probably 3332) and Diagram A30 steel-panelled trailer (190?) entering Shepherds station in June 1936.
G. N. SOUTHERDEN

'Clifton Downs' Trailers – Allocations

More is known about the allocations of the Clifton Downs trailers than most of the others. They are also fairly readily identifiable in photographs. In addition, David Rouse has kindly provided details of observations on the subject by the late Mr R. P. Walford. Despite such information, the whole story is still not entirely clear, and probably never will be. What follows is a 'best possible' reconstruction from the official records, and what is known from other sources. It should be noted that the register of composite coaches does not include any allocation information on the intermediate trailers.

Nos. 3331 and 3335 were allocated to the Clifton Downs service in 1912, before being made into trailers.

The coaches were all converted into trailers in 1913, and are believed to have been allocated to the Bristol–Clifton Downs service. It would appear that, initially, four-coach trains were run, as in the official photograph; hence, Trains Nos. 3 and 4 are recorded as having two driving trailers allocated to each.

By April 1918, the Bristol–Clifton Downs–Avonmouth services only required two of the 'Clifton auto sets' on weekdays, with an additional set on Saturdays. These workings included a daily trip to Portishead and back. On Saturdays, most trains were strengthened with two additional thirds, and the services on the line required a 10/12 coach train of 6-wheeled stock plus (in the rush hours) a 9/11 coach train of 8-wheel coaches. On Sundays, a 'B set' was used, which in 1918 was a four coach, close-coupled set of 4-wheelers.

In 1922, all the sets left the Bristol Division and most went (at least initially) to the Birmingham Division, but they were fairly rapidly dispersed thereafter.

Withdrawals were not made as sets, or pairs, but on an individual basis. From 1931 until 1940, there was an excess of driving trailers; from 1941 until 1949, there were more intermediate than driving trailers, and between 1950 and 1954 there was only driving trailer No. 3338 in service.

At January:	1931	1932	1933	1934	1940	1941	1946	1947	1948	1949	1950
No of sets possible	8	6	6	5	5	4	4	3	3	1	1

Driving Trailers
No. 3331
Bristol–Clifton Downs No. 3 workmen's (August 1912).
Converted into a trailer in August 1913.
Bristol–Clifton Downs
Birmingham auto train No. 1. Accident Report 1924: with 3275.
Neyland auto train No. 2 (April 1925)
Swindon (No date)
Exeter Division (September 1930)

No. 3331 is believed to have been based at Newton Abbot and normally ran with intermediate trailer No. 3275. This combination was photographed in September 1933 on the Moretonhampstead service, and at Heathfield. They regularly ran on the Moretonhampstead branch between April 1940 and December 1945 (at least). No. 3331 and a trailer (possibly 3275) were photographed at Paignton in September 1946.
Both Nos. 3331 and 3275 were withdrawn in November 1946.

No. 3332
Converted into a trailer in August 1913
Bristol–Clifton Downs No. 3 (Diagram A3 gives this as a workmen's coach)
Birmingham auto train (August 1922)
Swansea auto No. 3 (December 1922 to May 1932)
Truro (December 1933)

An unidentified 'Clifton Downs' type driving trailer was photographed on the Newquay–Chacewater line in June 1936. It was accompanied by an ordinary driving trailer, rather than an ex-Clifton intermediate type.
The door locks were altered for use on the Severn & Wye Joint Railway (NWO 9/3143 –

September 1936). This implied use on the Lydney Town–Berkeley Road service.
No. 3332 was withdrawn in August 1939.

No. 3335
Bristol–Clifton Downs workmen's (May 1912)
Converted into a trailer in June 1913.
Bristol–Clifton Downs workmen's
Birmingham auto train No. 3 (not dated), probably with No. 3387 in August 1922.
Reading, early 1940s, probably from 1930s until withdrawal. Running with 3276.
No. 3335 was withdrawn in July 1948, as was No. 3276.

No. 3336
Converted into a trailer in July 1913
Bristol–Clifton Downs workmen's
Birmingham auto train – not written (November 1922)
Cardiff Division auto train No. 60 (Sept 1931) with No. 2294
    Also (not dated): Swansea No. 2
               Garw Valley
               ? & Pontycwmr
No. 2294 was condemned in February 1933; No. 3336 may have been partnered with intermediate trailer No. 3274 some time after this date, as both were condemned at the same time.
One set which may have been Nos. 3336 + 3274 was photographed in July 1938 in sidings at Llantrisant.
No. 3336 was condemned in December 1950, possibly with No. 3274

No. 3337
Cnverted into a trailer in August 1913
Bristol–Clifton Downs auto train No. 4
Birmingham auto No. 2 (September 1922)
'To work between Lydney Town and Berkeley Road' (August 1936). The door locks were altered for use on the Severn & Wye Joint Railway (NWO 9/3143–September 1936).
No. 3337 was condemned in December 1938.

No. 3338
Converted into a trailer in August 1913
Bristol–Clifton Downs Auto Train No. 4 workmen's
Swindon No. 6 (December 1922)
Photographed at Reading in 1929
Marlow Branch (per Mr Walford)
ATC October 1944
No. 3338 was condemned in August 1948, but reinstated in November 1949.
Oxford May 1951 in maroon livery (per Mr R. C. Riley)
Cardiff (1952 photograph taken at Queen Street in single colour livery, possibly maroon, as W3338)
No. 3338 was finally condemned in March 1954.

No. 3339
Converted into a trailer in July 1913
Bristol–Clifton Downs auto train
Neyland No. 1 (September 1925) with No. 2294, until September 1933.
'To work between Lydney Town and Berkeley Road' (September 1936). The door locks were altered for use on the Severn & Wye Joint Railway (NWO 9/3143–September 1936).
No. 3339 was condemned in June 1939.

No. 3340
Bristol–Clifton Downs (May 1913)
Converted into a trailer in June 1913
Bristol–Clifton Downs
Swansea auto train No. 1 (December 1922 obliterated July 1932) with No. 2293 (Mr Walford)
Neyland No. 2 (Mr Walford) with No. 2293, until July 1931
Swansea auto train (March 1932)
'To work between Lydney Town and Berkeley Road' (September 1936). The door locks were altered for use on the Severn & Wye Joint Railway (NWO 9/3143–September 1936).
No. 3340 was condemned in December 1940.

Intermediate Trailers

No. 2293
Converted into a trailer in May 1913
Bristol–Clifton Downs auto train
Swansea (December 1922) with No. 3340
Neyland No. 2 with No. 3340 (Mr Walford)
No. 2293 was condemned in July 1931.

No. 2294
Converted into a trailer in July 1913
Bristol–Clifton Downs auto train
Neyland No. 1 (January 1925) with No. 3339
Cardiff Division No. 60 (September 1931) with No. 3336
No. 2294 was condemned in February 1933.

No. 6734
Converted into an intermediate composite trailer in September 1913
Bristol–Clifton Downs
Made all third No. 3273 September 1922. (1st class trimmings remained),
    then as No. 3273, Birmingham auto train No. 2 (November 1923)
    Regulator gear removed June 1931.

No. 7169
Converted into an intermediate composite trailer in August 1913
Bristol–Clifton Downs
Made all third No. 3274 August 1922 (1st class trimmings remained)
    then as No. 3274, Birmingham auto train (August 1922)
    Swansea No. 3 (December 1926), possibly with No. 3332
    If No. 3274 ran as a pair with No. 3332, subsequent allocations would have been:
        Truro (December 1935)
        Lydney Town–Berkeley Road (August 1936)
As no records exist of the door locks being altered on No. 3274 for use on the Severn & Wye Joint line, it is more probable that it ran with a different trailer. A possible partner is No. 3336, which was condemned on the same date, December 1950. No dated allocations beyond 1931 have survived for No. 3336, or after 1926 for No. 3274, but a photograph showing a Clifton Downs set at Llantrisant was taken in July 1939, which may be of this pair.

No. 7170
Converted into an intermediate composite trailer in August 1913
Bristol–Clifton Downs
Made all third No. 3275 August 1922 (1st class trimmings remained),
    then as No. 3275, Birmingham Division auto train No. 1 (not dated, but probably August 1922, with No. 3331)
    Neyland auto No. 2?
    Exeter Division (September 1930) with No. 3331.
Nos. 3331 and 3275 were photographed in Devon in September 1933, although there is a note that 3275 was transferred to Neyland auto No. 2 in August 1933. ('Neyland' is written above 'Exeter Division' in the register)
3275 was noted regularly on the Moretonhampstead branch with No. 3331 between April 1940 and December 1945.
Nos. 3275 and 3331 were both condemned in November 1946, so may have remained as a pair until the end.

No. 7171
Converted into intermediate composite trailer in September 1913
Bristol–Clifton Downs
Made all third No. 3387 April 1922 (1st class trimmings remained),
    then as No. 3387, Birmingham auto train (presumably with No. 3335)
Birmingham auto train No. 3 (not dated)
Swindon (not dated)
Reading August 1933 (photo)
Marlow Branch (Mr Walford – not dated, with No. 3338)
Both Nos. 3338 and 3387 were condemned in September 1948, although 3338 was later reprieved.

No. 7172
Converted into an intermediate composite trailer in August 1913
Bristol–Clifton Downs
Made all-third No. 3276 April 1922 (1st class trimmings remained)
    then as No. 3276, Birmingham auto train (November 1922): not written on the coach.
Swindon (not dated)
Ran with No. 3335 (Mr Walford).
Reading – 1930
Reading – early 1940s with 3335
Both Nos. 3335 and 3276 were condemned in July 1948.

No. 7173
Converted into an intermediate composite trailer, but date not recorded. 1913?
Bristol–Clifton Downs
To all-third No. 3390, April 1922.
    then as No. 3390. All allocations in register obliterated.
    At Landore in early 1940s without a Clifton Downs driving trailer.
    Condemned June 1949. It may have been 'spare' from 1940.

One 'Clifton Downs' set, including either No. 2293 or No. 2294, is visible in an official photograph of the 'Neyland Complex', said to have been taken in 1921; but because a reasonable proportion of the coaches in the photograph are in a brown and cream livery, it was more likely to have been in 1923–5.

At least one set is known to have been in the London Division by 1927; it was photographed by Maurice Earley, and seen in a non-auto mode with the unique 2–4–2T No. 3593, at Twyford. The London Division *Working of Coaches* programme had workings for two two-coach trailer sets. These worked services along the main line to Slough and Didcot, and on the branches to Basingstoke, Henley-on-Thames, and Marlow, but one working was used for the experimental ATC auto train from May 1935. One 'Clifton Downs' set (at least) was in use on the Marlow branch in September 1947.

A photograph of one of these trailers in use on the Severn & Wye Joint Railway appears to show 'Clifton Downs' type driving trailers working without the corresponding intermediate trailers. Another photograph shows an A34 compartment type driving trailer paired with a Clifton Downs driving trailer.

One set was still at Newton Abbot in 1946, and was photographed at Paignton on 10th September that year in the 10.05 to Newton Abbot. This was a rather odd train hauled by 2–6–2T No. 5551, and consisted of the 'Clifton Downs' set, probably 3275 & 3331, an ordinary trailer, and what appears to be a main line coach. Needless to say, the rake was not running as an auto train!

46 ft 6 in Composite Driving Trailers Nos. 7026/8: Trailer Diagram A1

These were two coaches of which little is known, because the register entries have been partly obliterated.

They started life as two broad gauge brake composites, Nos. 559 and 561, built in May and April 1889 respectively on lot 460. Being constructed for the broad gauge at this rather late date, they were believed to have been 'convertible' with a narrow gauge underframe and body, but with broad gauge bogies ('narrow gauge' in this context was the GWR term for 'standard gauge'!). The wings were of the type fitted to coaches that might run on the broad gauge, that is, they were not tucked in to the body side just below the waist panelling, but extended downwards, almost to the bottom of the coach body.

These coaches were 46 ft 6¾ in long and the standard 8 ft 0¾ in wide, and had a body height of 7 ft 6 in; they were carried on Dean 6 ft 4 in bogies (on both the BG and NG), and had an overall wheelbase of 36 ft. They were a typical low-roofed coach of the latest standard, with 7 in eaves panels, matching door ventilators and tall windows, three-arc roofs, and oil lighting. Their accommodation was arranged guard/luggage, 3rd, 3rd, 3rd, 3rd, 2nd, 1st.

The guard's/luggage compartment was 11 ft 4¾ in long between the end wall of the coach and the partition. It was a little unusual in having the wings almost (but not quite) at the end of the coach. There was a single door next to the wing for the guard, and a double door for luggage towards the other end of the compartment. The thirds were 5 ft 5 in between partitions, the second class compartment 5 ft 10 in, and the first class 6 ft 6 in.

Lot 460 covered six coaches (BG Nos. 557–62); there had been a previous six built on Lot 414 to the same body design in February 1888, but these had all been built for the NG only. One example of the latter, then No. 706, had the double luggage doors removed and the guard's door replaced by a pair of doors.

Nos. 559 and 561 were converted to the NG, and renumbered 1026 and 1028 respectively, in May 1892. They were equipped with gas lighting and steam heating, No. 1026 having this done in March 1896, but the record for No. 1028 is incomplete. They both

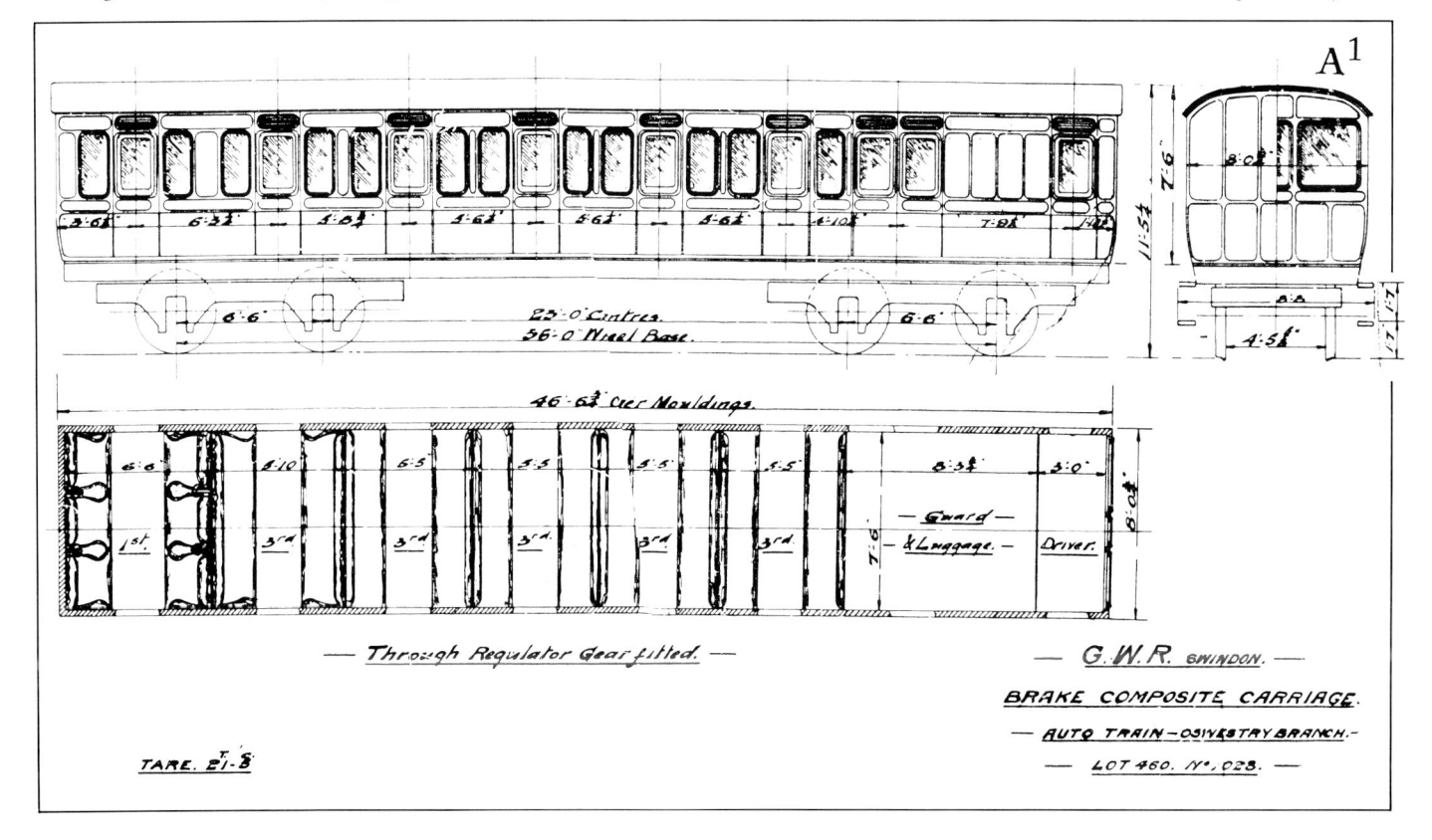

Oswestry with an auto train just visible. 7026 or 7028 is nearer the camera with 7216 behind. This is the only picture I know of showing either of these types of trailer.
H. F. WHEELER

received incandescent gas lighting in 1906, and were renumbered 7026 and 7028 as a result of the 1907 renumbering scheme. The second class compartment became third class following the abolition of second class.

The vehicles were converted to driving trailers in 1914, the alterations including the removal of the wings and the adjacent guard's door. The luggage compartment was divided by a partition 3 ft (only) from the coach end. The new driver's compartment was fitted with external doors in the sides, and three windows in the coach end; like those on the 'Clifton Downs' stock, the central window was much narrower than those on either side.

It is possible that these coaches had end-panelling like the 'Clifton Downs' stock, but so far no photograph has been found to confirm this. They were shown on trailer Diagram A1. TRG is believed to have been fitted at this time.

Both trailers were condemned in 1936, and as far as can be ascertained, they remained as composites all their lives, which was most unusual for trailers on the GWR. At some time, No. 7028 was allocated to Oswestry but the entry is not dated. It is believed that both coaches were based there and were replaced by the A32 composite trailers in 1936. A 1935 picture confirms that their driving end was like that of the 'Clifton Downs' conversions, but is too distant to reveal any details of the end panelling.

Summary

BG no.	Built	Convtd	NG No.	Gas FF	Steam heat	Gas incand.	To trailer	Cond.
559	May 89	May 92	1026	Mar. 96	Mar. 96	Dec. 06	1914	Aug. 36
561	Apr. 89	May 92	1028	+	+	Sep. 06	Jun. 14	Mar. 36

56 ft Composite Intermediate Trailer No. 7216: Coaching Stock Diagram E120

This coach was a low-roofed vehicle similar in style to the 'Clifton Downs' trailers and those of Diagram A1, so it is best dealt with here.

Coach No. 7126 was built (as No. 1126) in October 1896 on Lot 813, in the form of a brake tricomposite. It was of the standard style of the period with a three-arc profile roof, 7 in deep eaves panels, and tall windows. It was 56 ft 0$\frac{3}{4}$ in long, 8 ft 6$\frac{3}{4}$ in wide, a height of 11 ft 5$\frac{1}{4}$ in from rail to roof. The vehicle ran on Dean 10 ft bogies, and had a total wheelbase of 46 ft.

The guard and luggage compartments were combined, measuring 7 ft 6 in between partition and coach end, with double doors and end 'wings'. The passenger accommodation comprised four third class compartments (5 ft 5 in between partitions), two second class (5 ft 9 in between partitions) and two first class compartments, 6 ft 9 in between partitions. It had flat flame gas lighting and steam heating fitted from new; the weight was 23 tons 13 cwts.

The coach's early history was fairly typical for a brake tricomposite. In September 1905, it was given gas lighting with incandescent burners, and was renumbered 7216 following the 1907 renumbering scheme; about 1909, the second class accommodation was reclassified third. In December 1922, the wings were removed and a new seat provided for the guard; in this condition, it conformed to Diagram E120.

In 1931 it was taken into Swindon, and in December of that year emerged, fitted with (through) regulator gear, and bell communication between the train driver and the guard for use on Oswestry auto trains; it then operated on the Oswestry–Gobowen service. Note that there is no record of No. 7216 being fitted with a driver's compartment or end windows.

It is thought that this trailer appears in a rather distant view of Oswestry station, coupled to a Diagram A1 trailer (nearer the camera), so that the luggage compartment would have been next to the engine; this would indicate that it ran as an intermediate trailer, not too uncommon for conventional trailers with luggage compartments, but unique for what had been a brake compartment coach.

In February 1935, Oswestry works altered it further, so that the passenger compartment next to the guard's vestibule was absorbed by it; the trailer now had five third class compartments, which seated 50 passengers. This was done on New Works Order 9/1963 at an estimated cost of £10/10s/0d. In the register, the work is described as follows:

Compartment H taken into existing luggage body.
Cupboard and letter rack removed; tool box, ambulance box displaced from the partition of compartment H to be refixed in their place.
Outer doors of compartment H fixed up.
Electric bell communication from the guard's compartment.

I think they actually meant 'reprovide' bell installation!

No. 7216 was condemned in December 1937.

Summary

No.	Built	Lot	Incand. gas light	Wings removed	TRG etc.	Modified NWO9/1963	Cond.
7126	Oct. 96	813	Sep. 05	Dec. 22	Dec. 31	Feb. 35	Dec. 37

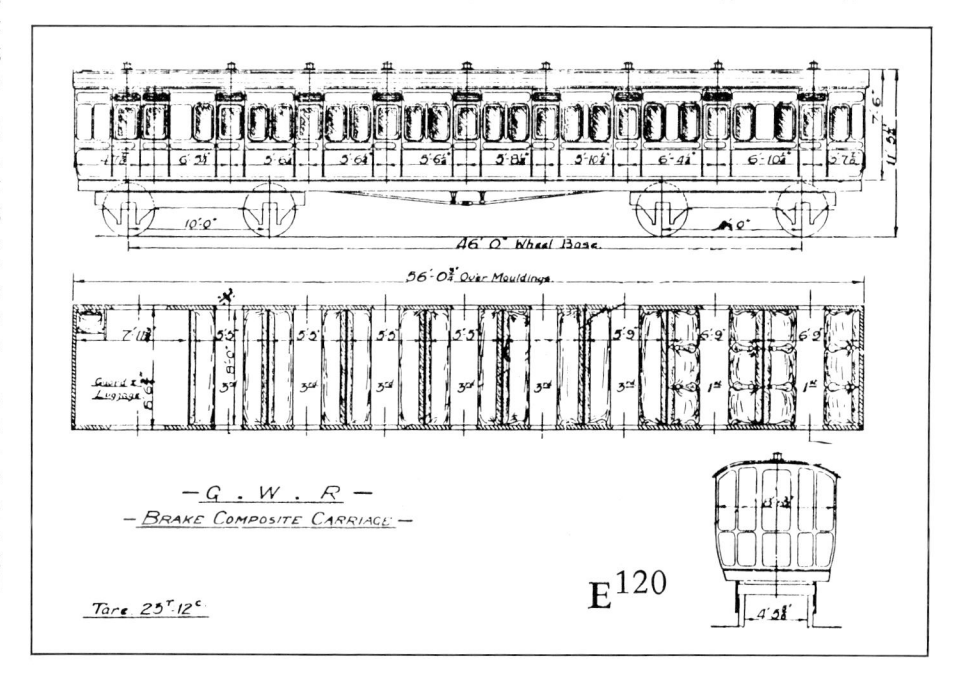

A31 trailer No. 202 on its last journey. This picture shows the 8ft 'fish-belly' bogies and the double doors to the passengers' vestibule.
COLLECTION J. N. SLINN

No. 73 of Diagram Q at Exeter in May 1932. It was altered to trailer 202 (above).
F. M. BUTTERFIELD

CHAPTER SEVEN
CONVERSION OF THE STEAM RAIL MOTORS

THE GWR started to convert their steam railmotors into trailers in 1915, the year after the last of the conversions of ordinary compartment coaches to trailers (dealt with in the preceding chapter). The process was carried out only approximately in order of the age of the SRMs, but the matchboarded units were dealt with before the wood panelled examples. Not all the SRMs were altered to trailers; a few were sold or scrapped instead. There were a number of years in which no conversions took place; in particular, there was a hiatus during 1924–1927, when the GWR was dealing with the rolling stock absorbed at the grouping. The last rebuild of an SRM was not completed until 1936.

No. 57 of Diagram O at Weymouth shed about 1905. COLLECTION R. C. RILEY

Number of steam railmotors converted to trailers

Year	No.	Year	No.	Year	No.
1915	6	1922	6	1929	0
1916	3	1923	6	1930	6
1917	3	1924	0	1931	0
1918	1	1925	0	1932	0
1919	5	1926	0	1933	4
1920	12	1927	0	1934	9
1921	0	1928	13	1935	7
				1936	3

Because the GWR had chosen a design in which the 'engine' portion of the SRM was built into the body of the unit, conversion was not as simple a process as it might otherwise have been. The very non-standard SRMs, Nos.15 and 16, which did not have the power units built into the coachwork, were not converted.

The boiler had to be detached from the power bogie, and lifted out of the body by crane; then the bogie could be removed (all this had to be done every time a major service was carried out on the power unit anyway). The coal bunker at the front of the unit and the water tank (underneath) had to be removed. The underframe and the body were separated, because the underframe had to be modified at the locomotive end to take a conventional bogie, and the body had to be rebuilt at that end to make use of the space vacated by the power unit. It was the practice to alter this end to accommodate the guard (and any luggage), leaving the original driver's compartment at the other end of the unit as part of the 'new' trailer. The alterations to the passenger accommodation had to include alterations to the doors, and a rearrangement of part of the seating and windows, so that only about half of the accommodation was left in its original state. The roof had to be made good, by closing up the aperture that had allowed the boiler to be removed; additional lighting and ventilators were then fitted. Through regulator gear was fitted on conversion.

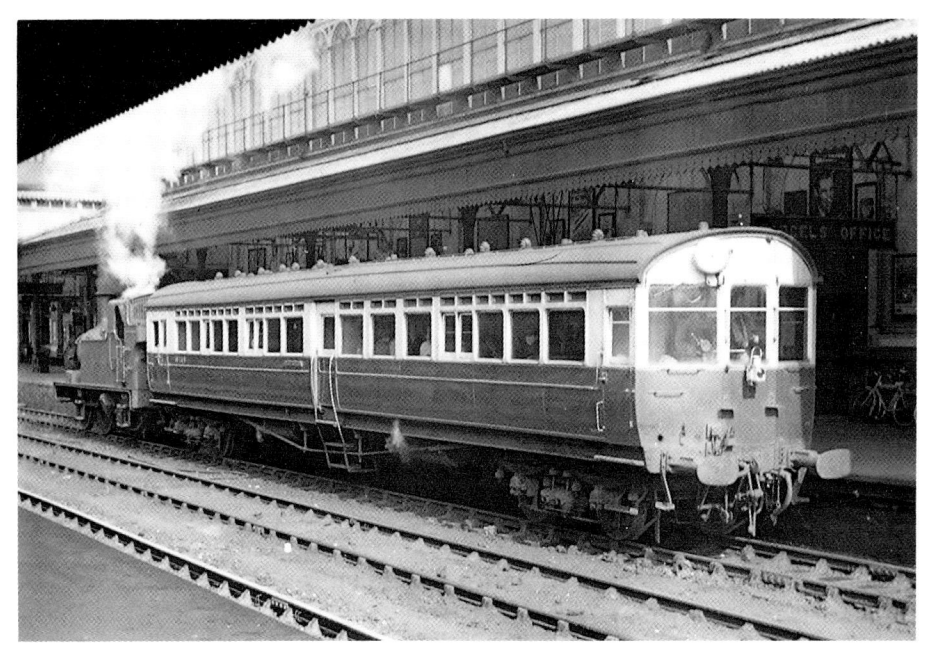

No. 149 of Diagram A26 at Exeter St. David's in BR maroon and cream livery. It has 7ft bogies, ATC, sandboxes, is gas-lit, and has the communication chain tell-tale at the luggage end. Originally it had been SRM No. 57. HMRS

This rebuilding process gave rise to three interesting points:

1. The earliest SRMs had Dean 8 ft 6 in bogies at the non-powered end, whilst later units had a variety of 8 or 9 ft bogies (the volute or coil spring, the 'Fishbelly' types, or the 'American'). But each conversion only produced one conventional bogie suitable for use under a trailer. An additional bogie had to be obtained from somewhere; this could be a problem, particularly as the existing one on the SRM was normally an obsolete design by the time the unit was converted to a trailer, but not so old that spares were common from scrapped coaches. This gave rise to some swapping of bogies on conversion, and some trailers appeared with new bogies.

2. On the SRMs, the power bogie was set back a different distance from the headstock than the bogie at the other end of the coach. The power bogie was of 8 ft wheelbase, and the bogie centre was usually 10 ft 0$\frac{5}{8}$ in from the headstock, whilst the other bogie centre was either 8 ft 5$\frac{3}{8}$ in or 11 ft 2$\frac{5}{8}$ in from its headstock, depending on whether or not retractable steps were fitted below the end door of the unit. On some of the last units to be converted, this non-symmetrical arrangement of the bogie centres was not entirely corrected whilst the underframe was being altered.

3. The underframe and the body were separated during the rebuilding work, and there is photographic evidence to show that a few trailers did not get their original underframes back.

It would appear that all had received incandescent gas lighting by the time they reappeared as trailers. All the SRMs which were altered to trailers were renumbered into the trailer series, and were given diagrams included in the Trailer Diagram Book.

MATCHBOARDED TRAILERS CONVERTED FROM SRMs

The conversions of SRMs to trailers did not strictly follow their building date order, but the oldest SRMs, which were characterised by 'matchboarded' sides and ends below the waist line, were dealt with before the wood panelled SRMs. In the early years of the century, there seem to have been occasional instances where coaches on various railways in the country had been matchboarded, for example on the North Eastern Railway and the Highland Railway. Matchboarding did have the advantage of using smaller pieces of timber, and did not require the large sheets of wood which were necessary in the ordinary wood panel style. On the GWR matchboarded trailers, the panelling above the waist line had square corners, which was unusual for the company. In addition, all window apertures had their lower corners set at right-angles, but the upper corners were rounded, again a most unusual feature for the GWR, (although standard on some other railways in South Wales). The toplights were of clear glass, whereas on hauled stock they were usually of hammered glass. The toplights were hinged at the bottom, and opened individually.

'517' class 0-4-2T No. 561 at Abbotsbury about 1925 with Diagram K4 passenger luggage van, a Diagram Z matchboard-sided trailer and a Diagram U 70ft trailer. The Z trailer is in the 1922 brown and cream livery, the K4 and U are in lake. COLLECTION J. E. KITE

59 ft 6 in Trailers Nos. 99–104: Trailer Diagram Z

The first SRMs to be converted to trailers were Nos. 3–8 of Lot 1054, built in April and May 1904. Nos. 3–5 were originally shown as SRM Diagram B, but were later included on Diagram C; Nos. 6–8 had always been Diagram C.

These SRMs were in the matchboarded style, 59 ft 6¾ in long, 8 ft 6 in wide, and 12 ft 6 in high from rail to the roof. They were thus ¾ in longer than most other matchboarded SRM conversions. They had bow ends, Dean 8 ft 6 in suspension bogie at the non-power end, and the usual round section queenpost truss, with an adjustable turnbuckle in its centre. The queenposts were the cast type.

All these SRMs were altered to trailers during the first six months of 1915. Four of them were given Dean 8 ft 6 in bogies at both ends, the other four receiving new 9 ft light duty 'fishbelly' bogies. This resulted in the bogie centres differing between the two batches; those with 9 ft bogies were at 41 ft 3 in and the others at 42 ft. The overall wheelbase was therefore 50 ft 3 in (9 ft bogies) and 50 ft 6 in (8 ft 6 in bogies).

As altered, the accommodation consisted of a 7 ft 8 in guards/luggage compartment with double doors; then a small saloon with bench seating, divided into four, apparently by arm rests; this saloon was 18 ft long. Then came a 3 ft 9 in vestibule with inward-opening doors, followed by a large saloon (23 ft 4⅝ in long) which was divided in two.

The first portion contained two seating bays each side, whilst the second length (13 ft 5⅛ in) was equipped with longitudinal bench seating, divided into three by arm rests. Finally came a driver's compartment (4 ft 9 in maximum width) with inward-opening external doors, and a sliding door into the large saloon.

The sides were arranged to give a panel between the end of the coach and the double doors of the luggage compartment. These doors had a droplight in each with a wooden panel (square-cornered) above it. This panel matched the toplights, but does not ever seem to have been used as one. The luggage doors were flat, flush with the trailer sides and opened inwards. Originally there was a pair of window-height panels between the luggage doors and the small saloon windows, but these were often combined into a single panel in due course.

The small saloon had a large fixed window next to the guard's compartment with a pair of toplights above; this was about 4 ft 7 in wide. Together with the luggage compartment, this represented the original power unit end of the old SRM. There was next what had originally been an external door in the SRM; this was allegedly 'screwed up', but in practice the only clue to its original identity (in a photograph, at least) was the droplight with a solid panel above. The panels either side of this droplight were of different sizes, with the larger nearer the luggage compartment. This, too, was unaltered from the SRM design. The next was another large window, this time 3 ft 8 in wide, with a pair of toplights above it. Then came a pair of droplights, each with a toplight; these droplights had replaced a large window in the SRM whilst it was still in service as such, in a similar way to some of the early trailers, which had also undergone this alteration.

One of the original large windows was removed, and a new inward-opening vestibule door, also with uneven panels either side, was fitted in its place; The wider panel was again the one nearer the luggage end. This door had retractable steps fitted below it. The seating bays in the large saloon had a large fixed window (with two toplights) next to the vestibule, and a pair of droplights with toplights. The bench seating had large windows flanking a pair of droplights, all with toplights as before. Again, the droplights were not original. The driver's doors opened inwards, and contained droplights as usual.

On these trailers, the droplights that were not mounted in the doors seem to have orig-

Conversion of the Steam Rail Motors

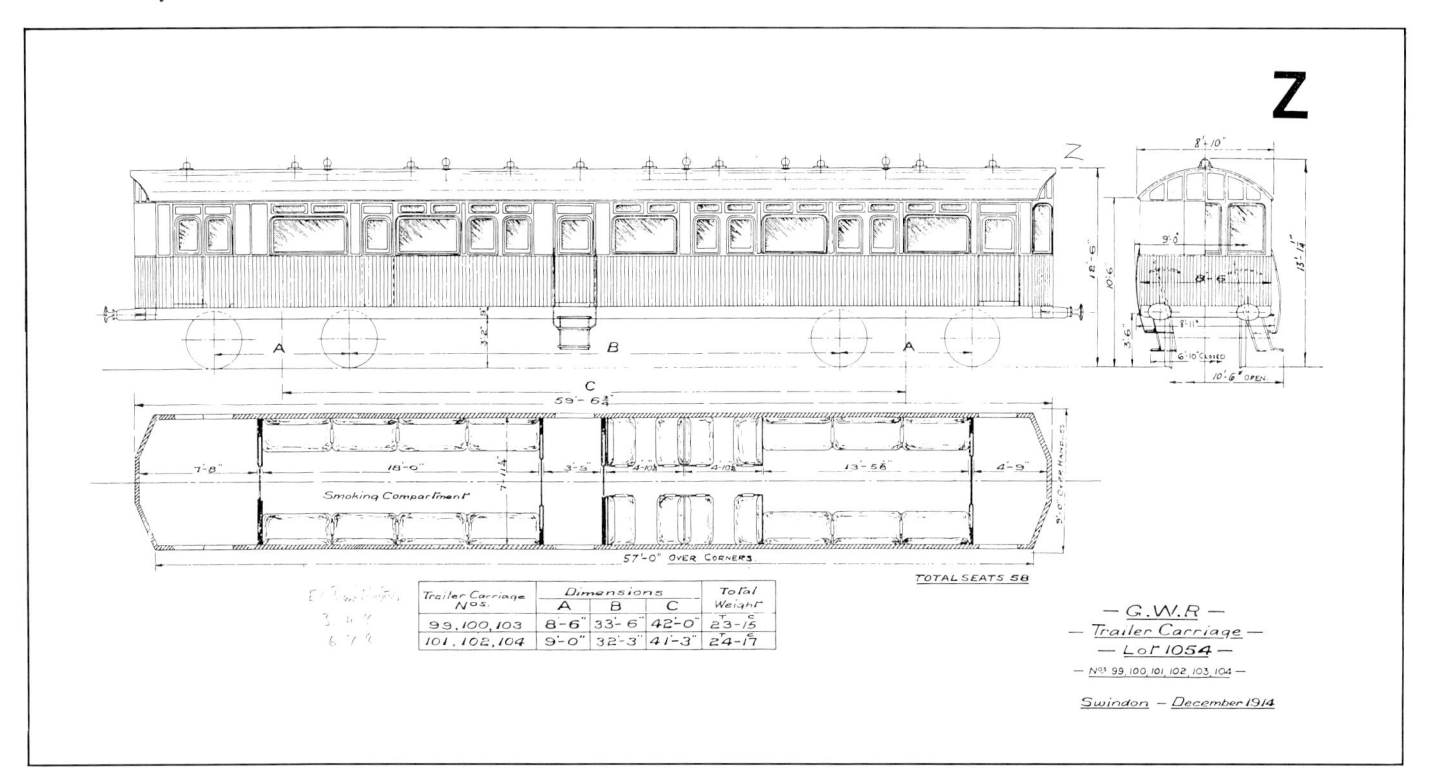

G.W.R
Trailer Carriage
Lot 1054
Nos. 99, 100, 101, 102, 103, 104
Swindon – December 1914

Trailer Carriage Nos.	A	B	C	Total Weight
99, 100, 103	8'-6"	33'-6"	42'-0"	23-15
101, 102, 104	9'-0"	32'-3"	41'-3"	24-17

'517' class 0–4–2T No. 562 with a pair of Diagram Z trailers near Cheltenham Racecourse station on the Winchcombe–Cheltenham service on 24th July 1924. Both trailers are in the lake livery. As running numbers and insignia are scarcely visible, it is open to question if they received a repaint between conversion and when this picture was taken.
J. E. KITE

inally had single bars across them, and photographs show that the driver's compartment droplight had a white line painted across the glass (perhaps to remind him when the window was closed?).

The ends had the usual three windows in them. The area above was originally divided into panels by vertical beading, but this feature was generally panelled over in the course of time.

The subsequent history of these trailers is much as usual. No. 102 was the only one recorded as being fitted with sanding gear (in 1927), although No. 100 is known to have been fitted with it. The others probably were, too. Chain communication was fitted in 1929/30, and the large compartment was made 'smoking' in 1928–30.

No. 100 had its steps altered somehow in September 1928, and it was fitted with additional brake gear operated by two brake cylinders for the Newport – Blaenavon – Brynmawr service in November 1931. Some are recorded as being painted in cream and brown livery with gold lines in the early 1930s, and the end windows were painted black in 1935. All except 99 are officially recorded as being fitted with ATC.

SRM No.	Built	To Trailer	Trailer No.	Bogies	Overall Wheelbase
3	Apr. 04	Jun. 15	99	Dean 8 ft 6 in	50 ft 6 in
4	Apr. 04	Jan. 15	100	Dean 8 ft 6 in	50 ft 6 in
5	Apr. 04	May. 15	101	9 ft Light 'fishbelly'	50 ft 3 in
6	Apr. 04	Jan. 15	102	9 ft Light 'fishbelly'	50 ft 3 in
7	May. 04	Jan. 15	103	Dean 8 ft 6 in	50 ft 6 in
8	May. 04	Feb. 15	104	9 ft Light 'fishbelly'	50 ft 3 in

As usual, the dates for fitting warning gongs, and of plating over the guard's end windows, are not recorded. There are no dates given for blue axle boxes, or for the trailers being painted in 1940s brown, although they probably were.

No. 99 had its official portrait taken on its conversion in 1915 (although the lowest-

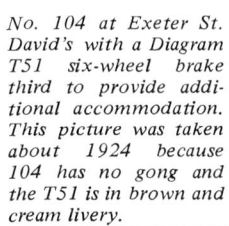

No. 104 at Exeter St. David's with a Diagram T51 six-wheel brake third to provide additional accommodation. This picture was taken about 1924 because 104 has no gong and the T51 is in brown and cream livery.
G. N. SOUTHERDEN

'Metro' class 2–4–0T No. 1446 with trailer 103 of Diagram Z in the 1927 'simple' livery. There appears to be a 'supporter' on the garter crest and there do not seem to be any lines between the brown and cream. Note how the bolection mouldings contrast with the cream at the end. COLLECTION J. E. KITE

Conversion of the Steam Rail Motors

Diagram Z trailer No. 99, at Cardiff on 1st July 1948, appears to be in 1943 brown livery, but the 'G.W.R' is not visible. The running numbers are not as large as they were previously.
P. J. GARLAND

Diagram Z No. 99 at Whitchurch (Glam) in August 1951, still with its luggage end windows which have not been painted black. It is equipped with ATC and is in 1948 brown and cream livery.
H. C. CASSERLEY

Trailer 103 of Diagram Z being propelled into Pontypridd by 0-6-0PT No. 5421 in July 1952. The train was the 5.8 p.m. from Old Ynysybwl and the trailer in BR's 1949 carmine and cream livery.
R. C. RILEY

0-6-0PT No. 5421 on the last day of service on the Ynysybwl branch, with Diagram Z trailer No. 103 in the bay platform at Pontypridd on 26th July 1952. For some reason, matchboarded trailers had always been favoured for this service. R. C. RILEY

Conversion of the Steam Rail Motors

numbered of the SRM conversions, it was the last of the first batch to be dealt with); this shows it in the 1912 lake livery. It is noteworthy that only the panelling above the waist is picked out with gold lines, and there is only a single gold line at the waist itself, at the top of the matchboarding. Unfortunately, the ends are not visible. The area on the roof below the rainstrip appears to be marginally darker, as if it might have been painted in a colour other than white (i.e. lake) but this may be a trick of the light as it appears much lighter in colour that the coach sides.

No. 99 was in the Oxford district in 1927, and was used on the Woodstock branch on 5th April that year. It may have been in the 1922 livery. It was in the Cardiff area in 1951, fitted with ATC and with its luggage end windows still intact.

No.100 ran in BR carmine and cream, numbered W100W in 1949-style. Photographs show it to have sand pipes.

No.102 was photographed in the 1922 (full) two-colour livery, and it was also seen at Pontyscill in BR days as W102 in what appears to be brown and cream livery, with the running number at both ends of the trailer in large characters, GWR-style; it had sandboxes and ATC.

No.103 was included in an official photograph of Weymouth station taken in the 1920s. It was then in the 'full' 1922 livery with '103' on the end to the right of the vacuum pipe (the luggage end is visible in the picture). It was used on the Machen–Pontypool service in BR carmine and cream livery, as W103W (1949-style). It had sand boxes fitted, although this was not recorded in the register.

No.104 was photographed at Exeter St. Davids in the 1920s in lake livery, in the company of a '517' class 0–4–2T locomotive and a 6-wheel low roof centre brake third (Diagram T51) which was in brown and cream.

Other services where Diagram Z trailers were photographed include:

The Abbotsbury branch, in the 1920s in the full two colour livery with a Diagram U trailer, a Diagram K4 passenger luggage van and a '517' class locomotive. The other coaches in the train were in the lake livery.

The Cowbridge – Llantrisant branch in 1949, the trailer being in an all-brown livery.

With a Diagram A9 matchboarded trailer on a Pontypridd – St. Fagans – Cardiff train in 1946. Both trailers appear to be in the 1943 plain brown livery.

They were all condemned between December 1950 and April 1955.

Summary

Trailer No.	Sand app.	Chain comm.	Smoking cpt. changed	Cream brown & gold	End windows black	ATC	Cond.
99	nr	May. 29	Feb.29	Sep. 31	Feb. 35	yes	Sep. 52
100	yes	Sep. 29	Oct.29	Dec. 31	Feb. 35	Oct. 45	Apr. 55
101	nr	Jly. 30	Aug. 30	?	Feb. 35	Mar. 43	Dec. 50
102	Apr. 27	Nov. 29	Aug. 29	Feb. 32	Nov. 35	yes	Nov. 51
103	yes	Apr. 30	Apr. 30	?	Feb. 35	Oct. 45	Sep. 53
104	nr	Oct. 30	Aug. 28	Sep. 30	Feb. 35	Sep. 45	Jun. 52

Diagram Z No. 100 in BR maroon and cream livery as W100W but with the number in the 1949 style. It is, however, positioned as if in a waist panel, close to the bottom of the window.
H. C. CASSERLEY

No. 103 in BR 1950 carmine and cream at Machen on the Machen–Pontypool service.
M. E. J. DEANE

57 ft Trailers Nos.105 & 106: Diagram A6
ex- SRM Diagrams A & A1

These were the conversions of the first two SRMs to be built on the GWR, Nos.1 and 2, built in October 1903 on Lot 1037. These two SRMs were matchboarded, but were unique amongst those built by the GWR because they had flat ends as well as flat sides.

There were other features common only to these two SRMs that affected their conversion to trailers. The ends, as originally built, had three windows which were only about 2 ft 1 in high. If a driver was standing at the controls, this meant that he had to duck his head to see out. Consequently, No.2 was provided with a fixed toplight above each end window so as to improve the visibility, although the outer toplights were narrower than the central one. However, SRM Diagram A shows No.1 as having the outer toplights plus a tall centre window, and the trailer Diagram A6 also shows this feature (for both units); photographs confirm this arrangement which was also fitted to SRM No.2 eventually. The wood-panelled, bow-ended SRMs, by way of contrast, had full-height end windows at the non-power end; whilst the windows at the power end were short, their bottom edges were well above the waist line of the unit. On conversion to trailers, these windows in the bow-ended SRMs were usually made full height.

SRMs Nos.1 and 2, unlike other SRMs, had large sliding doors in the power compartment with two droplights. Between these

An early view of trailer No. 105 Diagram A6, probably around Dawlish. This photo shows it inherited the modified front end from SRM No. 1. In this picture it is in the lake livery and has rather odd-looking white lines to the driving windows. The bell cable has also been painted white and there is no sign of the regulator pivot plate.
LCGB/KEN NUNN COLLECTION

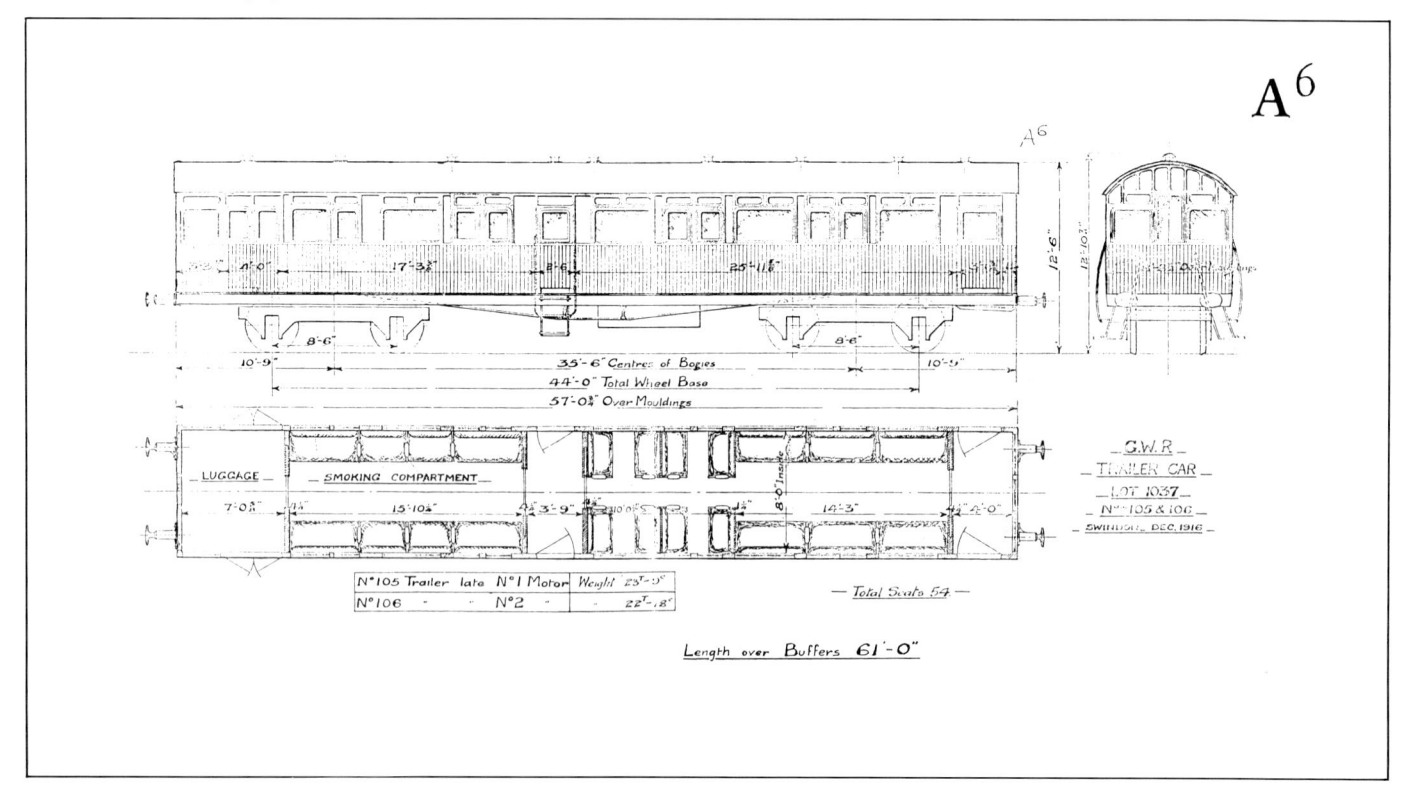

Conversion of the Steam Rail Motors

This photograph of Diagram A6 No. 106 at Llantrisant in June 1948, confirms that it had the unusual end windows of its previous existence as SRM No. 2. It also had flat ends which meant that the buffers were non-standard. The driver's door was unusually wide and the droplight divided into two parts, a feature not shown on the diagrams. Under the considerable grime it appears to be in brown and cream livery. Again the regulator pivot plate cannot be seen. I. L. WRIGHT

Diagram A6 No. 106 at Llantrisant c.1951, in 1948-style brown and cream with the running number twice at the waist. P. J. GARLAND

'Metro' class 2–4–0T No. 3586 at Cowbridge in 1949 with trailer No. 106. The window between the open luggage doors and the end of the trailer was a distinguishing feature of these cars. C. CHAPMAN

doors and the corners of the SRM there was a fixed window with a toplight above. A further 'feature' of these two units was that passengers could only board and alight from the end doors at the non-powered end (when end doors were fitted; originally they were left open!).

The passenger compartment originally had eight large fixed windows with two toplights above each. According to SRM Diagram A, three of these large windows in each side were each replaced by a droplight flanked by two quarterlights, leaving the twin toplights above each intact. However, on conversion to trailers, they had twin droplights in these positions instead.

SRM No. 1 was converted to trailer No. 105 in June 1917; No. 2 had preceded it in January of that year, when it became trailer No. 106.

As rebuilt, they were 57 ft $0\frac{3}{4}$ in long, 8 ft $6\frac{3}{4}$ in wide and 12 ft 6 in from rail to roof. It appears that both were fitted with Dean 8 ft 6 in bogies and the total wheelbase was 44 ft. Since these two SRMs had flat ends, there was no requirement for them to be fitted with the long buffers of bow-ended SRMs and trailers. The diagram shows the bogie centre – headstock distance to have been 10 ft 9 in at each end; this was appreciably more than on other matchboarded converted trailers, in spite of the fact that Nos. 105 and 106 had flat ends, and the others were bow-ended.

The accommodation was arranged to give a guard's/luggage compartment 7 ft $5\frac{1}{8}$ in long with double doors opening outwards, and a sliding door to, the small saloon. This saloon was 15 ft $10\frac{1}{2}$ in long, and had longitudinal bench seating, unevenly divided into four. The central vestibule was 3 ft 9 in wide, and had inward-opening doors with retractable steps below. The large saloon had a 10 ft $0\frac{1}{2}$ in

0–6–0PT No. 6409 with trailer 106 of Diagram A6 at Llantrisant in July 1950. This view shows the luggage end and confirms the additional end window 'outboard' of the luggage compartment doors. No. 106 is in the 1948 brown and cream livery with the running number twice each side.
W. H. G. BOOT

Conversion of the Steam Rail Motors

length with two seating bays each side, and a 14 ft 3 in length of bench seating, divided into three. The driver's compartment was 4 ft wide, and had inward-opening doors.

The guard's/luggage compartment (most unusually) had a fixed window with a toplight above it, as well as the double doors with droplights. This fixed window was originally a feature of the parent SRMs. The small saloon had, from the luggage end, a fixed window with a droplight, then a panel, another fixed window, followed by two droplights. All had toplights above. The vestibule door had panels either side, and the large saloon had a large fixed window, two droplights, another fixed window, two more droplights and a final fixed window. Again, all had toplights and the doors were flat and flush with the body sides.

Subsequently, No.105 is recorded as having chain communication fitted, and the large saloon made 'smoking' in January 1929; in respect of No.106, these modifications were made in April 1930 and July 1928 respectively.

Both vehicles had their guard's end windows painted black in October 1935. No.105 was painted brown in 1942, and 106 received ATC in 1945.

No.105 was condemned in 1948, and 106 lasted until 1952. The latter trailer is known to have been used in South Wales in the late 1940s, and in July 1950 was working from Llantrisant on the Cowbridge service as W106, in brown and cream livery.

Summary

SRM No.	Built	SRM Diagram	To Trailer	Trailer No.	Chain comm.	Smoking cmpts altered	End windows black	Painted brown	ATC
1	Oct. 03	A	Jun. 17	105	Jan. 29	Jan. 29	Oct. 35	May. 42	–
2	Oct. 03	A1	Jan. 17	106	Aug. 30	Jul. 28	Oct. 35		Aug. 45

59 ft 6 in Trailers Nos.107–112: Diagram A7 (ex-SRM Diagrams D & D1)

As well as SRMs Nos.3–8, Lot 1054 covered the building of SRMs 9–14. These were very similar to Nos.3–8, having the same dimensions, and being in the matchboarded style with bow ends. They differed slightly in internal accommodation and window arrangement, and were shown on SRM diagrams D and D1.

Their conversion was very similar to the earlier vehicles, but was spread over the years between 1916 and 1919. As converted, they were 59 ft 6 in long (¾ in less than Diagram Z trailers), 8 ft 6 in wide and 12 ft 6 in high from rail to roof (the same as the Diagram Z trailers). The total wheelbase varied according to the bogie fitted, being 50ft 6in with Dean 8ft 6in bogies, and 50ft 3in where 9ft light 'fishbelly' types were fitted. The bogie centres were both the same distance from the adjacent headstock.

The internal accommodation comprised a guard's and luggage compartment, 7 ft 7½ in long, with double doors opening outwards, followed by a small saloon (17 ft 11¾ in long) with bench seating each side, divided into six by arm rests. There was a 3 ft 9 in central vestibule with inward-opening doors. The large saloon was again divided into two areas, the first 9 ft 11½ in long with two seating bays, and a 13 ft 5½ in long area of bench seating.

The driver's compartment was 4 ft 9 in (maximum) between the trailer end wall and the partition. The reason for the small differences quoted between these trailers and Nos.99–204 is not known, and they may just be the result of measuring errors.

The external doors were all flat, and flush with the body sides. The window arrangements also differed slightly from the earlier SRM conversions to Diagram Z. The doors of the guard/luggage compartment opened outwards, as on the Diagram Z trailers. On the Diagram A7 trailers, there was originally only a single panel between these doors and the adjacent window. This window was a

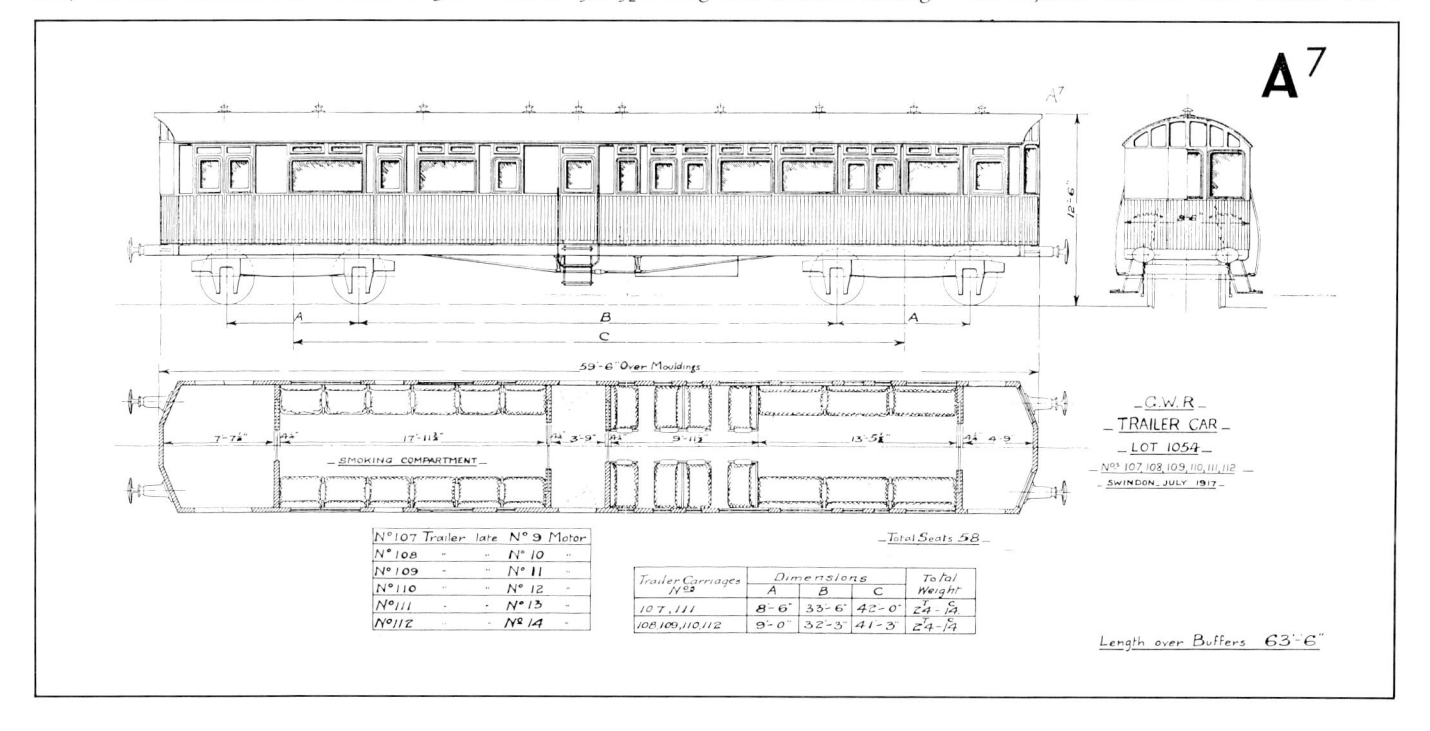

A Princes Risborough auto train at Aylesbury station. The trailer, No. 112 Diagram A7, is in the October 1927 'plain' brown and cream livery.
LENS OF SUTTON

large fixed light with two toplights above it, followed by a droplight that had originally belonged to the vestibule door of the SRM, but which was now incorporated into the small saloon. There was then another large fixed window (though smaller than the first) with toplights, a narrow panel and then another droplight, this time with a toplight. Next came a wide panel, and the vestibule door with retractable steps below it. The large saloon had a narrow fixed window (about the same size as a droplight) with a small toplight above it, a pair of droplights, two fixed large windows, another pair of droplights and a final fixed, large window, all with toplights above. The driver's door opened inwards.

Their history as trailers was very much standard; sand apparatus was fitted in the 1920s, chain communication in 1927–1930, and the large saloon was designated 'smoking' in 1928–30. No.112 was painted cream and brown with gold lines in 1932, and in all cases the end windows of the guard's compartment were painted black in 1935. No.112 is recorded as having been painted in red-brown in June 1942, and ATC was fitted to 110 in November 1946 and to 112 in April 1941.

No.107 was condemned in February 1952 in brown and cream livery as W107, 1949-style, without any GWR markings and without any visible gold lines. It was fitted with sandboxes, and was still extant thus at Swindon in July 1955.

Diagram A7 trailer No. 109 at Cardiff in July 1948, probably in a wartime all-brown livery, but with 'G.W.R' omitted.
P. J. GARLAND

SRM	Built	To Trailer	Trailer No.	Bogies	Wheelbase
9	May 04	Dec. 16	107	Dean 8 ft 6 in	50 ft 6 in
10	May 04	Dec. 16	108	9 ft f/b	50 ft 3 in
11	Jun. 04	Mar. 17	109	9 ft f/b	50 ft 3 in
12	Jun. 04	Dec. 16	110	9 ft f/b	50 ft 3 in
13	Jun. 04	Mar. 19	111	Dean 8 ft 6 in	50 ft 6 in
14	Jul. 04	Nov. 18	112	9 ft f/b	50 ft 3 in

Conversion of the Steam Rail Motors

No. 3586 with a Diagram A7 trailer, possibly No. 108, near Llantwit Fardre on a Llantrisant–Pontypridd train in May 1948.
I. L. WRIGHT

'Metro' class 2–4–0T No. 3588 at Llantrisant in June 1948 with A7 trailer No. 108 in 1943 brown and cream.
COLLECTION R. C. RILEY

A Diagram A7 trailer at Llantrisant. HMRS

ATC-fitted No. 110 at Oxford loco shed with damage or rot in the side boarding. Some panelling at the front, above the windows, is still intact.

J. H. RUSSELL

Conversion of the Steam Rail Motors 161

Diagram A7 trailer No. 108 at Cowbridge, Glam. The loss of its toplights changed its appearance considerably. It had 9ft 'fish-belly' bogies and appears to be in 1948 brown and cream with 1949-style running numbers.
W. A. CAMWELL

No.108 was photographed (undated, unfortunately) in what was presumably the 'fully lined' 1922 livery. However, the only detail to inform the viewer that it was not in the 1927 livery were the mouldings at window height, which were picked out in brown. There appears to be no gold lining at all – not even a lower waist line. Together with a Diagram U trailer, it was photographed sandwiching a '517' class 0–4–2T. No.108 also ran as W108 in BR days on the Cowbridge branch in South Wales. By this time, it has lost its toplights and was numbered in 1949 style; however, it is thought that it was still in brown and cream.

No.109 was photographed in South Wales sporting BR plain maroon livery with 1951 position numbers as W109W, but they appear to have been in the large size characters. It had ATC, sanding apparatus, and still had the luggage end windows intact; they were no longer partially painted over.

No.110 was operating in the Oxford area in the late 1940s in GWR 1947 livery, with two gold waist lines. It is known to have been used on the Woodstock branch in this condition in July 1947.

A pair of A7 trailers in lake livery were photographed on a Winchcombe–Cheltenham train with a '517' class 0–4–2T locomotive in July 1924.

All were condemned in the 1950s, the last to go being No.111 in October 1957.

Diagram A7 trailer No. W107 at Swindon in July 1955 with Dean 8ft 6in bogies and brown and cream livery. It had been condemned in February 1952!
P. J. KELLEY

Summary

Trailer No.	Sand boxes	Chain comm.	Smoking cmpts. changed	Cream brown & gold	End windows black	Painted red-brown	ATC fitted	Cond.
107	+	Jul. 30	Aug. 30		Jun. 35		–	Feb. 52
108	+	Jul. 30	Jul. 30		Mar. 35		–	Sep. 54
109	+	Jul. 30	Jul. 30		May 35		+	Jul. 53
110	+	Aug. 30	Aug. 30		Feb. 35		Nov. 46	Sep. 53
111	Apl. 27	Mar. 30	Mar. 30		Apr. 35		–	Oct. 57
112	+	Mar. 29	Apl. 29	Feb. 32	Feb. 35	Jun. 42	Apr. 41	May 52

This photo, taken in May 1930 at Blenheim, shows the non-standard livery of A9 No. 119 clearly. The mouldings are not lined out, but the trailer has the garter crest with supporters plus double waist lining. The loco is Fair Rosamund.
H. C. CASSERLEY

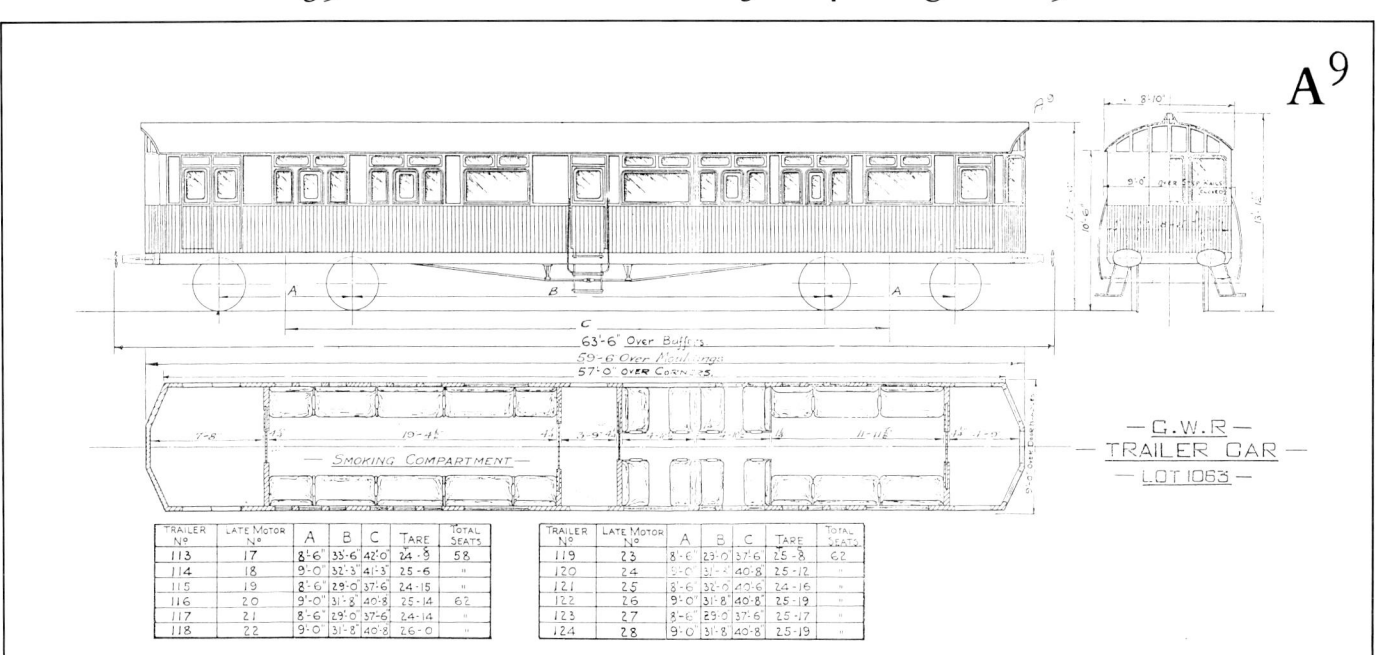

59 ft 6 in Trailers Nos. 113–124: Diagram A9

Diagram A9 trailer No. 117 with '517' class 0–4–2T No. 527 and an L or P trailer at Staines West. No. 117 is in the 1924 brown and cream livery. Note that the black lining to the end mouldings above the windows does not extend to the whole width of the mouldings.

COLLECTION R. C. RILEY

There was yet another variation on the theme of matchboarded trailers, this time converted from SRMs Nos.17–28 built in 1904, and shown as Diagrams F, G and G1. Diagram F SRMs differed from those of G and G1 in having 48 ft 9 in wheelbase instead of 45 ft 9 in, and no retractable steps; G differed from G1 by having three of the large fixed windows each replaced by quarterlight/droplight/quarterlight sets. Diagram F had the same window arrangement as G. Diagram G1 appears to have been the original window arrangement of all these trailers: no droplights or quarterlights.

These SRMs differed from the matchboarded examples considered so far in that they already possessed a luggage compartment, and were therefore 'branch' rather than 'suburban' units. The luggage area was situated next to the engine compartment, and gave passengers an alternative doorway to the one in the driver's compartment at the non-power end. The original luggage compartment was not left in situ on conversion, since it would have been near the middle of the trailer; instead, a new compartment was provided in the normal place at the end of the trailer where the driving and engine compartment had been, so rather more rebuilding work was required on these twelve SRMs than on the units already converted.

The A9 trailers were bow-ended, and measured 59 ft 6 in long, 8 ft 6 in wide, and the usual 12 ft 6 in from rail. The wheelbase depended on the source SRM, and on the bogies fitted. The odd-numbered ones received Dean 8 ft 6 in bogies, whilst the even-numbered vehicles had 9 ft 'fishbelly' ones. The wheelbase of individual trailers is set out in the summary table.

The interior arrangement of the trailers followed the now standard practice of luggage compartment, small saloon, passenger vestibule, large saloon and driver's vestibule. As usual, the dimensions differed from similar trailers on Diagrams Z, A6 and A7.

The luggage compartment was 7 ft 8 in between the end of the trailer and the partition, which had a central sliding door to the small saloon. The area was served by double exterior doors which opened outwards. The small saloon was 19 ft 4½ in long, and had bench seating divided into five, with the three central sections being wider than the outer pair. The central vestibule was 3 ft 9 in wide with retractable steps below its inwardly-opening doors. The large saloon was 22 ft 0⅜ in long. It had two seating bays, each of 4 ft 10½ in, and bench seating (divided unevenly into three) which was 11 ft 11⅞ in long. (The individual lengths quoted do not take into account partitions between the seats, which is why the sum of the parts is less than the whole). The driver's compartment was 4 ft 9 in (maximum) between the partition and the end wall. The driver's door opened inwards.

Curiously, Nos.113–115 are recorded on the diagram as having 58 seats, as compared with 62 seats for the rest. Either one person extra was supposed to squeeze onto each length of longitudinal seating, or else four extra tip up seats were provided in the luggage compartment, though no such seats are shown on the diagram. The tare weights are also recorded individually on the diagram, and vary between 24 tons 9 cwts (No.113) and 26 tons (No.118).

The overall design of the trailer sides followed familiar lines, with the luggage compartment having double doors and a panel. Then followed the small saloon, which had two sets of droplights with flanking quarterlights (each set having two toplights) plus a single large fixed window, also wih two toplights. Each was separated by a medium width panel. There was then another wide panel, the central vestibule door, and a narrower panel. The large saloon had a large fixed window, two sets of droplights plus quarterlights, and another large window; all these had toplights, as before. The panels between the windows were all of different sizes. The driver's door had panels on each side.

There are no real surprises in their subsequent history, except possibly the rather late painting date recorded for blue axleboxes of two examples. No.119 is known (from a photograph) to have been painted in the brown livery. Only five out of the twelve were recorded as being fitted with ATC apparatus, and No.124 did not receive it until October 1950 (it only survived for three more years).

No.114 was used on the Ynysbwl service in August 1951. It was probably in carmine and cream with lettering W114 in the 1949 style. No.114 was condemned at Llantrisant.

No.115 was used on the Kingham – Chipping Norton branch in lake livery soon after conversion, and was on the Woodstock branch in the 1930s, running in 1927 livery with a single gold line.

No.116 was used on the Clyndwern – Letterston line in the 1920s.

No.117 was used on the Staines branch in the 1920s (in the 1922 'full' brown and cream livery), on the Woodstock branch about 1930, and on the Staines and Watlington branches carrying the early 1927 livery, with no gold lines.

No.118 was condemned in November 1957, but not broken up; then in June 1961(!), it was renumbered into internal use service stock as DW079044, and formally made into a classroom at Monmouth (it may have been there all the time). It was condemned finally in March 1963, and sold to Birds of Morriston for breaking up in February 1964.

No. 117 of Diagram A9 in the 1927 simple brown and cream livery. On this coach the TRG link to the locomotive is held vertically against the coach end. Quite often this was at an angle. The communication circuit wiring cable can be seen emerging just above the buffer beam, above the right-hand buffer. The triangular 'No Smoking' and the longer 'Smoking' signs are also easily visible in this view. This trailer was frequently used on the Watlington branch in the '20s and early '30s.
G. HEMMINGWAY

Old Ynysybwl Halt before the line was cut back to this point. The trailer is No. 119 of Diagram A9 and may well be in a 1943 all-brown livery.
I. L. WRIGHT

No.119 was used on the Woodstock branch periodically from 1930 until (at least) 1935. In May 1930, it was in what may have been a partial repaint of the 1922 livery: brown and cream, with none of the mouldings picked out in brown or black, but with two gold waist lines. However, it was still carrying the garter crest with supporters. After the Second World War, it was photographed at Craven Arms in the 1943 all-brown livery, apparently without any waist lines, but it was in such a filthy condition externally that it is difficult to be certain of this point. It was fitted with sanding apparatus.

No.124 was at Caerphilly works during May 1952 in brown and cream livery, as W124 in the 1949-style of lettering.

Other services on which Diagram, A9 trailers were used include:

Clydach–Pontypridd (September 1951)
Cowbridge branch (1949, and May 1950)
Cardiff–Coryton (brown 1943 livery)
Pontypridd–St Fagans–Cardiff in 1946, with a Diagram Z matchboarded trailer; both were in the 1943 all-brown livery.
The Princes Risborough–Watlington branch in 1929

They were condemned between April 1949 (Nos.119/20) and November 1957 (No.118).

Conversion of the Steam Rail Motors

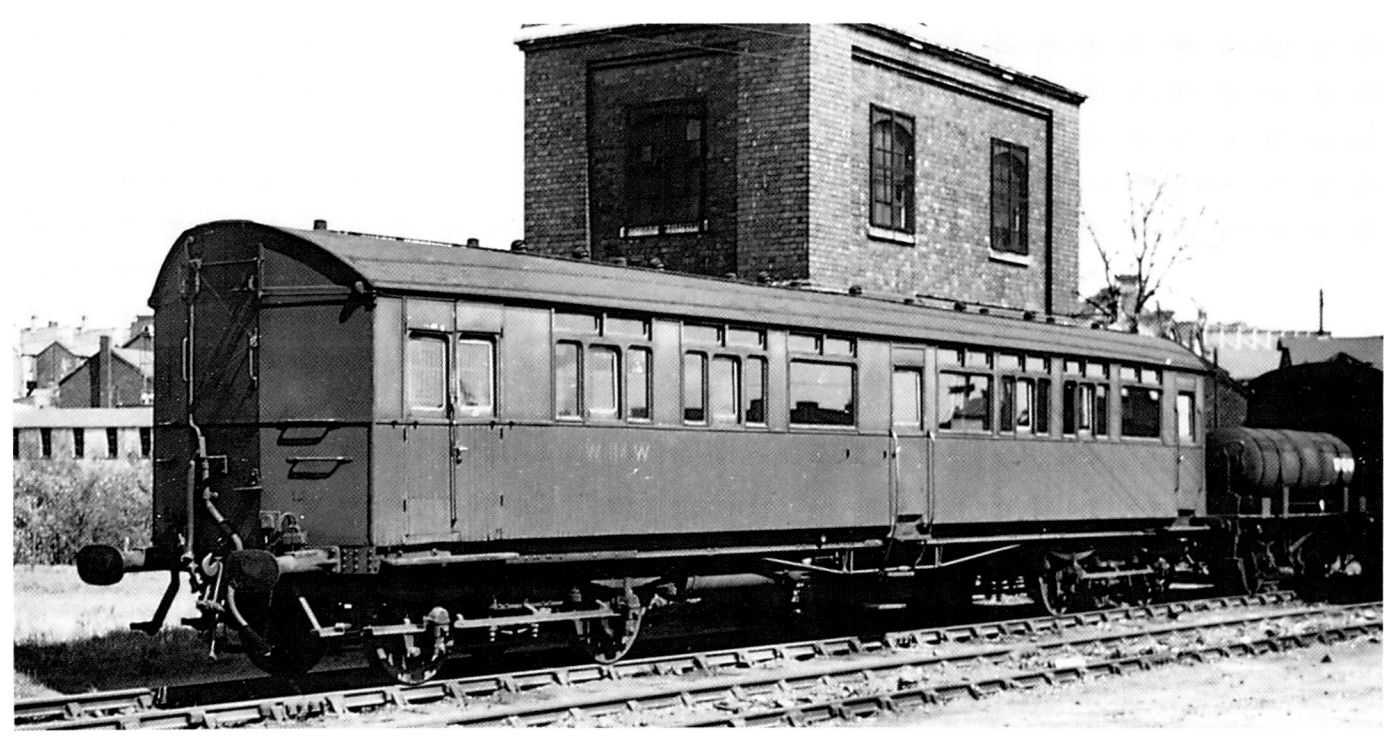

Diagram A9 No. 114, probably in 1948 brown and cream, with 'W' suffix. COLLECTION J. N. SLINN

RECOGNITION GUIDE FOR MATCHBOARD TRAILERS

Diagram A: No. 1
No central passengers' vestibule (all the others have one)
Steps have treads at an angle when retracted (unique)
End retractable steps (all the others have central ones)

Diagram A6: Nos. 105–106
Flat ends (all other matchboarded trailers were bow ended) with unique end window arrangement.
Window between end and the luggage doors (unique)

Diagram A9 Nos. 113–124
Four sets of quarterlight/droplight/quarterlight: two between the luggage and passengers' vestibule doors, and two more between the passengers' and the driver's doors (unique in matchboarded trailers)

Diagram A7 Nos. 107–112
Three quarterlight-sized windows next to the passengers' vestibule door (one fixed, two droplights – unique in matchboarded trailers)

Diagram Z: Nos. 99–104
The remainder. The Diagram Z trailers were a bow-ended version of the Diagram A6 vehicles, without the additional window between the luggage doors and the end of the trailer. Some of the window sizes were a little different, too. The end windows were normal.

Summary

SRM No.	Built	SRM Diag.	To trailer	Trailer No.	Bogie type	Overall wheelbase	No. of seats	Tare t-cwts
17	Apr. 04	F	Apr. 19	113	Dean 8 ft 6 in	50 ft 6 in	58	24–9
18	Apr. 04	F	May 19	114	9 ft F/B	50 ft 3 in	58	25–6
19	Jul. 04	G	Aug. 19	115	Dean 8 ft 6 in	46 ft 0 in	58	24–15
20	Aug. 04	G	Sep. 19	116	9 ft F/B	49 ft 8 in	62	25–14
21	Jun. 04	G	May 20	117	Dean 8 ft 6 in	46 ft 0 in	62	24–14
22	Jul. 04	G	Feb. 20	118	9 ft F/B	49 ft 8 in	62	26–0
23	Aug. 04	G	Mar. 20	119	Dean 8 ft 6 in	46 ft 0 in	62	25–8
24	Jul. 04	G	May 20	120	9 ft F/B	49 ft 8 in	62	25–12
25	May 04	F	Apr. 20	121	Dean 8 ft 6 in	49 ft 0 in	62	24–16
26	Jun. 04	G	Feb. 20	122	9 ft F/B	49 ft 8 in	62	25–19
27	Aug. 04	G1	Mar. 20	123	Dean 8 ft 6 in	46 ft 0 in	62	25–17
28	Sep. 04	G	Feb. 20	124	9 ft F/B	49 ft 8 in	62	25–19

Summary

Trailer	Sand boxes	Blue a/boxes	Chain comm.	Smoking cpts changed	Cream brown & gold	End windows black	ATC	Cond.
113	—	—	Nov. 29	Nov. 29	Sep. 32	Feb. 35	—	Jun 49
114	—	—	May 29	Nov. 29	—	Apr. 35	Feb. 45	Sep. 55
115	—	—	Mar. 29	Mar. 29	Jan. 32	Feb. 35	Aug. 46	Apr. 51
116	—	May 35	Dec. 29	Jul. 28	May 31	Feb. 35	Aug. 40	Nov. 45
117	—	—	Apr. 30	Apr. 30	—	Jun. 35	—	Feb. 52
118	—	—	Jan. 29	Jul. 29	Feb. 31	Jun. 35	—	Nov. 57 (see text)
119	+	—	Feb. 29	Aug. 29	—	Feb. 35	—	Apr. 49
120	—	—	Apr. 29	May 29	Feb. 32	Feb. 35	—	Apr. 49
121	—	—	Sept. 29	Jul. 28	Apr. 32	Feb. 35	Mar. 49	Jun. 52
122	Oct. 26	—	May 29	May 29	—	Mar. 35	Nov. 46	Mar. 55
123	Apl. 28	—	Mar. 29	May 28	Jul. 30	Apr. 35	—	Oct. 50
124	—	Jun. 35	Feb. 30	Feb. 30	Sept. 32	May 35	Jan. 50	Oct. 53

Nos. 126 and 127, Diags. A13 and A14, on the Yealmpton branch in July 1924, appear to be in lake livery and still have plate frame bogies.

H. C. CASSERLEY

CHAPTER EIGHT
THE CONVERSION OF WOOD PANELLED SRMs TO TRAILERS

THERE were major differences between the matchboarded style SRMs and the later wood panelled units. These included the width (the matchboarded vehicles were 8 ft 6 in (against 9 ft of the wood panelled), and the shape of the sides – the wood panelled coaches having turn-under sides whereas the matchboarded SRMs had slab sides. The toplights on the wood panelled trailers appear to have been of hammered glass, which was by then standard on hauled stock.

Larger capacity coal bunkers were fitted to the wood panelled SRMs than were provided in the matchboarded units. Because of the height of the coal bunker, the external waist panel at the power unit end was made deeper than standard, and the end windows at this end of the vehicle only were correspondingly shorter. As with the matchboarded SRMs, the non-power unit end of the SRM became the driver's end on conversion, leaving the power unit end to be rebuilt into the luggage compartment, guard's vestibule, or passenger accommodation as required. In most cases, trailers rebuilt from wood panelled SRMs were given standard waist panels, and windows at both ends. Where the original window and waist panels from the power unit end of the SRM are known to have been retained, this is noted in the text.

70 FT GANGWAYED TRAILERS
Nos.126 & 127, Diagrams A13 and A14

These two trailers started life as SRMs 59 and 60, originally shown on SRM Diagram P and later on Diagram T, the changes apparently being in the heating surface of the power units, and the provision of a gangway connector on Diagram T. They were built in November and October 1905 (respectively) on Lot 1089, and had 'open gangways', i.e. doorways, (later, gangways – 1911) at the non-power unit end. They were allocated to Plymouth, and trailers 9 and 10 (Diagram D) were built at the same time to accompany them. They appear to have run as a four-car unit, with the SRMs at the outer ends of the sets. The method of control is not recorded, but may have been by bell communication between the driving compartments of the SRMs.

Nos.59 and 60 were the first 70 ft SRMs to be rebuilt into trailers, becoming Nos.126 and

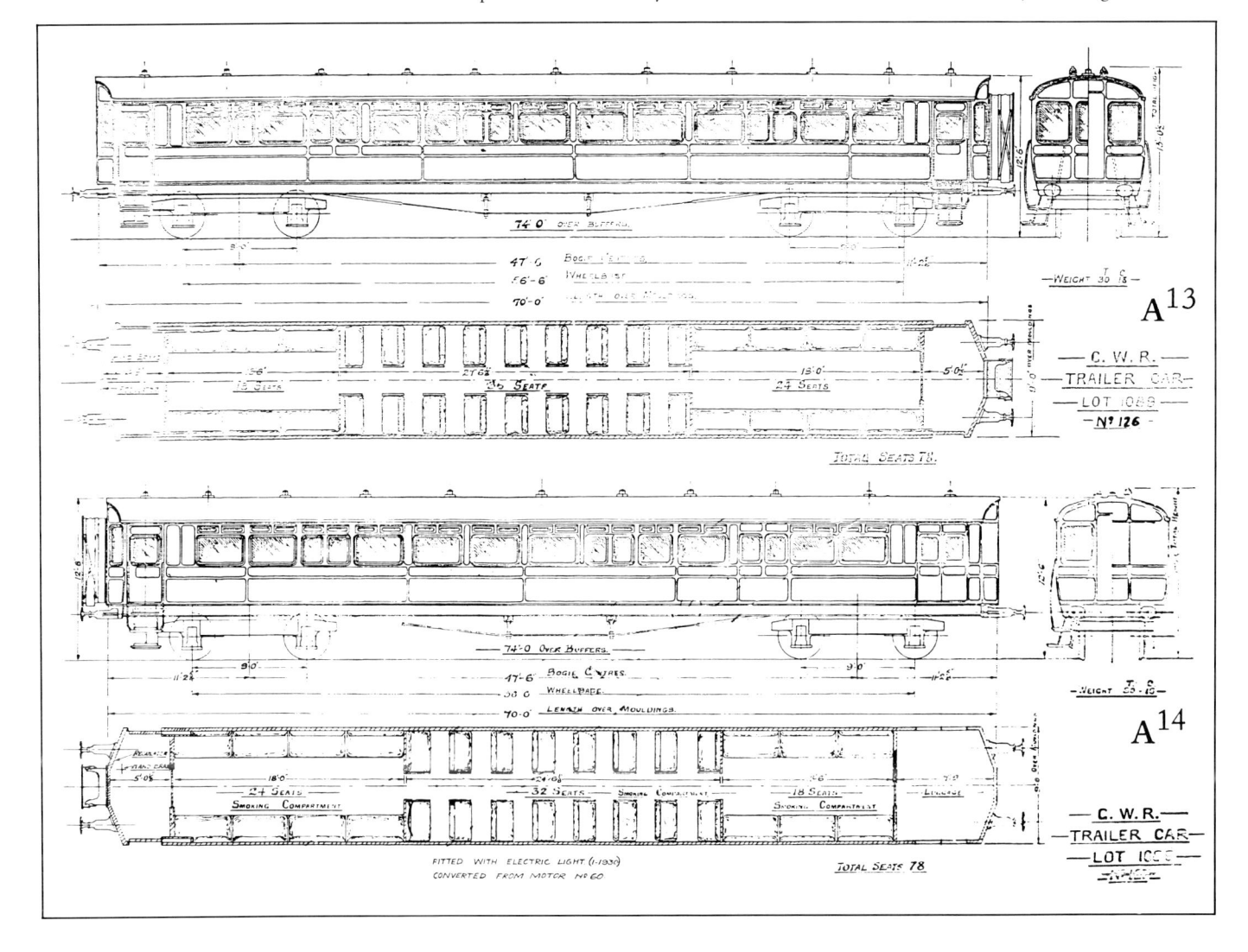

Top: *DW079017, previously Diagram A14 No. 127, shown here with 7ft bogies.* Above: *Detail views of Diagram A14 No. 127 after condemnation as 079017.*
COLLECTION J. N. SLINN and C. M. STREVENS

Conversion of Wood Panelled SRMs to Trailers

127 respectively; the conversions of both vehicles were completed in June 1920. They were altered so that they could thereafter run as a pair, with No.127 as an intermediate non-driving trailer. At the same period, trailers Nos. 9 and 10 were likewise altered so that they too could run together – see the chapter on 70 ft wood panelled trailers (Diagrams A11 and A12).

As rebuilt, both were 70 ft long, 9 ft wide and 12 ft 6 in high from rail to the roof. They had a 56 ft 6 in wheelbase, and the diagrams show 9 ft coil spring bogies. The diagrams also show them with the locomotive end to the right; most other diagrams were drawn the other way round.

The internal arrangement of No.126 (Diag A13) gave a 4 ft 9 in driver's compartment with slightly recessed, flat, sliding external doors (an unusual feature). It also had an internal sliding door to the passenger accommodation. This was in the form of one open saloon, but was divided into three areas. There was a 13 ft 6 in length of longitudinal benches (seating a total of 18 passengers), then nine walkover seats each side of the central corridor (these occupied a 27 ft 6½ in length, and seated 36), and finally an 18 ft length of bench seats, divided into four (seating 24), giving a total seating capacity for the trailer of 78. The end vestibule which was 5 ft 0½ in between the partition and the end of the coach, had the same external sliding doors as the driver's compartment and gave access to the gangway connector between the coaches.

No.127 (Diag A14) was laid out in a similar manner to No.126, but reversed, and with a luggage compartment. Internally, (starting at the gangwayed end) it had an end vestibule (5 ft 0½ in wide) with a handbrake, and external sliding doors; a further door gave access to the gangway connector, like the end vestibule on No.126. Then came the open saloon for passengers, which was again divided into three areas. An 18 ft length of longitudinal benches, with seats for 24 passengers, was followed by eight walkover seats on each side of the central corridor occupying a length of 24 ft 10½ in and seating 32; finally, a 13 ft 6 in length of bench seats, divided into three, seated 18. The total seating capacity of the trailer, according to the diagram, was 74. At the end, the luggage compartment was 7 ft 9 in long, and had flush external double doors which opened outwards, as well as an internal sliding door to the passenger accommodation.

Externally, No.126 was equipped with retractable steps beneath the driver's door, as well as those to the end vestibule. There was a pair of panels between the driver's door and the windows in the passenger accommodation, and the following, shorter length of bench seating had windows arranged to give large, droplight, large, and two droplights. Next, there was a panel. Serving the walkover seats, there was a large window, a smaller one, two droplights and three more large windows. The longer length of bench seating had one large window, two droplights and two further large lights. In its conversion, No.126 was turned around relative to its parent SRM, an unusual operation in which the SRM power unit end became the trailer's driving end. The side window arrangement at the end of fixed light/droplight/fixed light replaced the SRM power unit panelling, and the first pair of droplights replaced the SRM luggage doors. The rest of the coach was largely unchanged from the SRM design.

On No.127, there were retractable steps below the end vestibule doors, but not below the luggage compartment doors. The window arrangement was reversed; with the longer length of bench seating coming first, the adjacent windows were provided as one large, two droplights and one more large. There was one pair of walkover seats less than in No.126 so the windows were arranged to give three large, two droplights, a small fixed light and large one. There was then a small panel and what appeared to be two droplights from the SRM luggage compartment, followed by two more large windows to cover the longitudinal benches at that end of the coach.

When compared with its SRM ancestor, No.127 had a traditional conversion with the power unit becoming the luggage compartment end, as usual. The luggage compartment and the first two windows of the saloon at that end were the original power unit section, and the SRM luggage compartment doors with their droplights were replaced by the trailer's double droplights.

The gangwayed ends of the trailers retained their end windows, and the luggage compartment end of No.127 kept its three large windows.

It is believed that these two trailers ran together as Plymouth area coaches until withdrawal. Further, it is interesting, if not profitable, to speculate why they should be made to run together, when this meant a major rebuild to trailer No. 10, and additional effort to produce No. 127 (both of which were effectively turned round), particularly at a time when the GWR was very busy with the wartime backlog of coach repairs and building.

No.127 is recorded as being given new pattern tail lamp brackets in March 1923, whilst both received 'Swindon fireproof flooring' in May 1927. There is no record of No.126 receiving sand apparatus, but both were given blue-painted axleboxes in May 1929. The pair seem to have been in for major maintenance at the end of 1929 and the beginning of 1930, as they then received electric lighting and chain communication; at the same time, the arrangement of the smoking areas was altered (from the small saloon in each trailer), whereby the whole of No.127 was designated for smoking, with No.126 non-smoking. Several other Plymouth area trailers were given electric light at about this time. Neither No.126 nor No.127 are recorded as having been painted in cream and brown with gold lines.

The end windows of No.127 were painted black in February 1935, but those of No.126 were not done until October of that year, after a reminder was sent out. Someone perhaps had reasoned that this work was unnecessary, as the end windows of No.126 were not normally next to a locomotive, so there should be no problems from reflections. Both received ATC in 1946.

They were condemned together in January 1955. No.127 was still extant in October 1956 when it was transferred into service stock, and renumbered DW079017. A photograph shows it in a monochrome livery, presumably maroon, unlined. It appears to have 7 ft bogies although these are not recorded in the register.

SRM No.	Built	SRM Diagram	To trailer	Trailer No.	Trailer Diagram
59	Nov. 05	P/T	Jun. 20	126	A13
60	Oct. 05	P/T	Jun. 20	127	A14

Summary

Trailer No.	Blue axleboxes	Chain comm.	Smoking cmpts rearranged	Electric lighting	End windows black	ATC	Cond.
126	May 29	Yes	Nov. 29	Nov. 29	Oct. 35	Feb. 46	Jan. 55
127	May 29	Jan. 30	Jan. 30	Jan. 30	Feb. 35	Feb. 46	Jan. 55 (see text)

70 ft. Trailers Nos.134–137 and 148, Diagrams A15, A17, A18 and A25

These trailers were conversions of SRMs to Diagrams M and M1. The difference between the Diagram M and M1 units was in the window arrangements. The conversions took place in 1922/3, and 1928. SRM No. 48 (Diagram M) was destroyed by fire and condemned in January 1916.

SRM 45 was loaned to the Highland Railway between 1918 and 1920. On its return it was overhauled at Swindon and not converted until 1928.

Diagram M and M1 SRMs had been equipped with standard gangways in 1910–11 at the non-power unit end, and could therefore run with gangwayed trailers, presumably Diagrams T and U, and Diagram L, No. 32. On conversion to trailers, they did not all keep their gangways, since the usual procedure for converting an SRM to a trailer was for the power unit end of the SRM to become the luggage/non-driving end of the trailer. In consequence, these conversions were somewhat complicated and produced four new trailer diagrams, as follows.

SRM	SRM Diag.	To Trailer	Trailer No.	Trailer Diag.	Notes
43	M1	Apr. 23	134	A17	Gangwayed, Intermediate Trailer
44	M	Apr. 23	135	A18	Gangwayed, Driving Trailer
45	M	May 28	148	A25	See text.
46	M	Nov. 22	136	A15	
47	M	Oct. 22	137	A15	
48	M	–	–	–	Destroyed and condemned in 1916.

1. **Diagram A15 trailers (Nos.136 & 137):** Non-gangwayed, standard driving trailers with no luggage compartment. This was a normal conversion, except that the end wall of the driving end of the trailer had to be made good on conversion where the gangway was removed.

On the right of this view of diesel railcar No. 1 at Reading is trailer 137 of Diagram A15. It is gas-lit, has 9ft American bogies and is in 1948 BR brown and cream livery. The trailer behind the railcar is one of the electrically-lit Diagram A26 trailers 181–185, also in brown and cream.

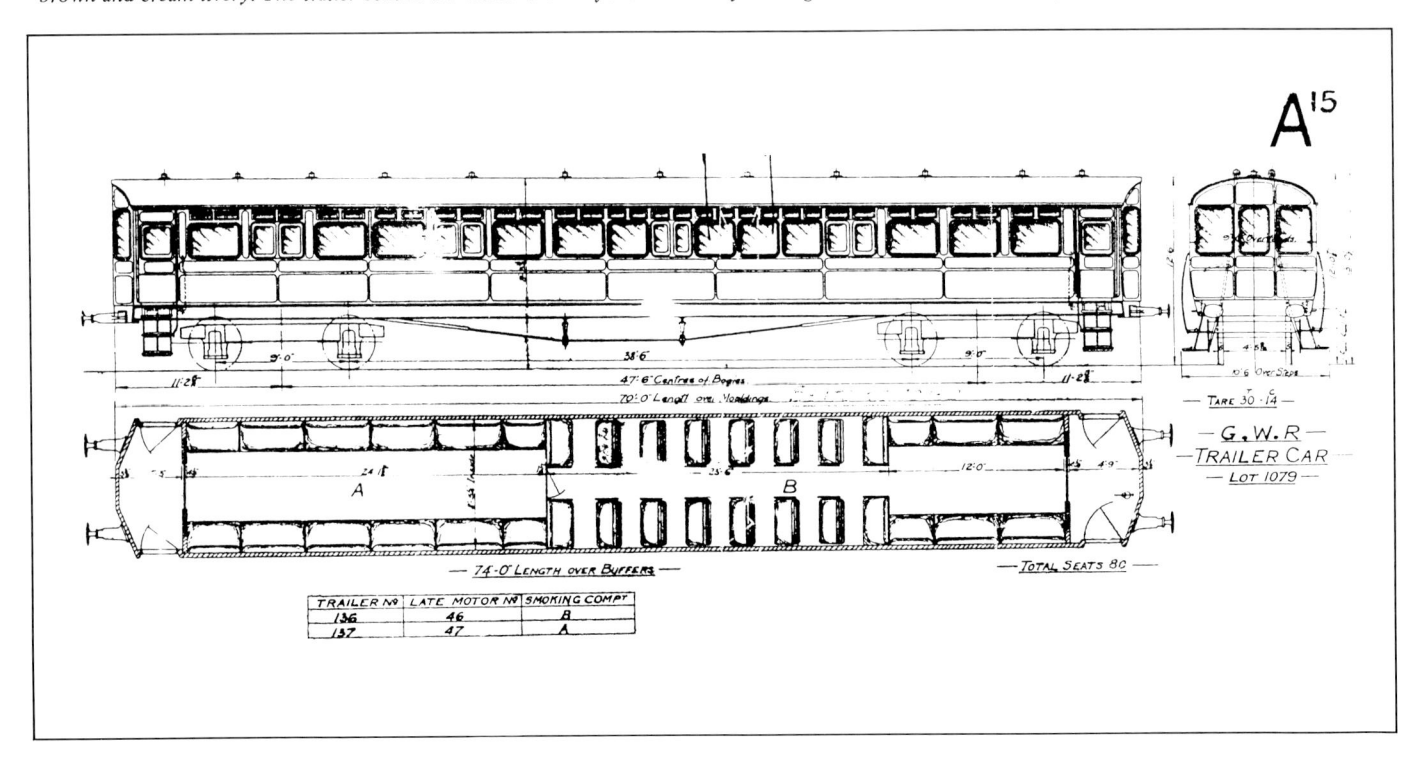

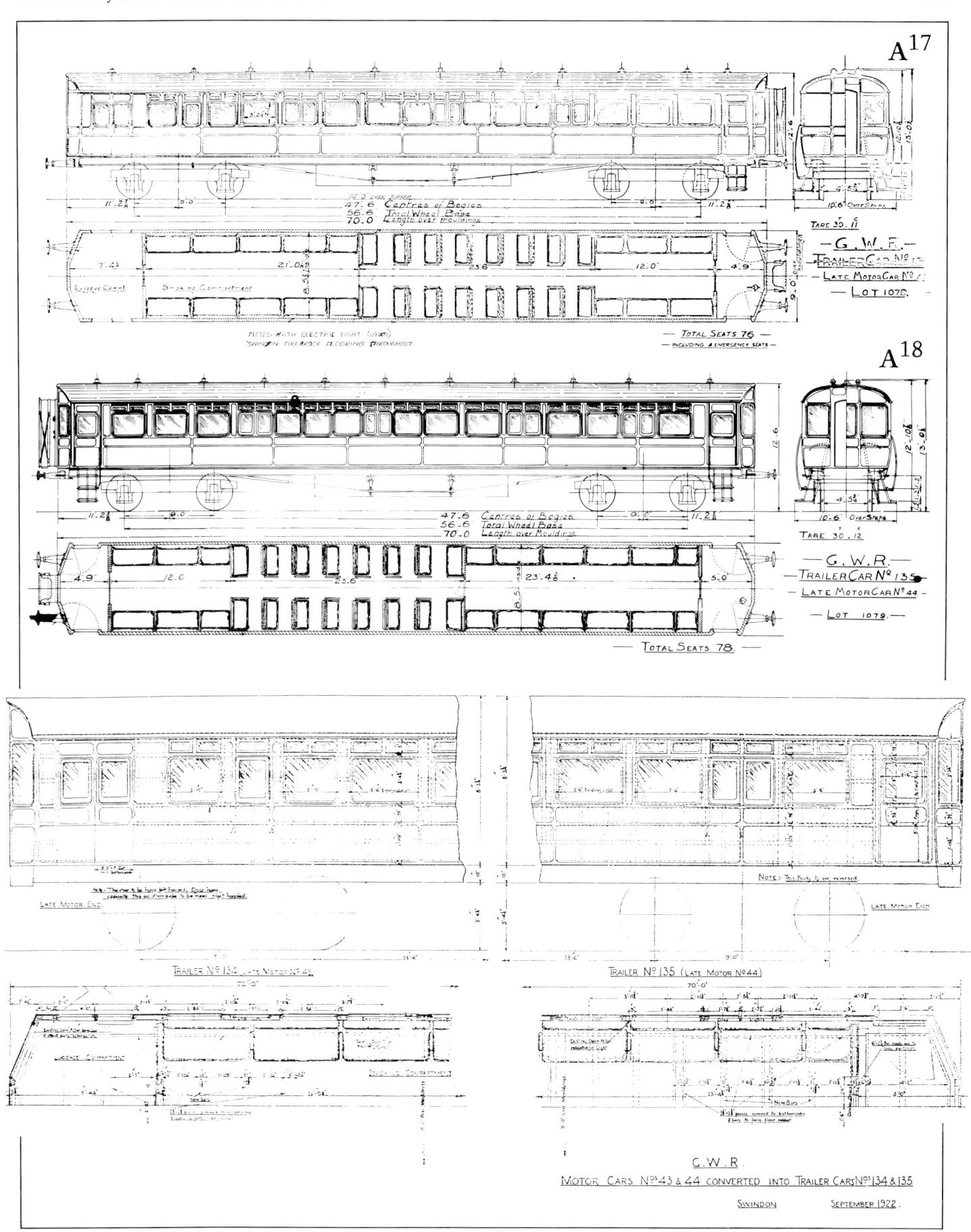

Conversion of Wood Panelled SRMs to Trailers   171

The leading coach of the Plymouth area suburban auto train is No. 135 of Diagram A17. It is in the 1927 simple livery with the garter crest and supporters, so the photograph can be dated to the period spring–autumn 1927. The coach still has 9ft coil spring bogies and gas lighting. The second coach is No. 134 of Diagram A18 and they are gangwayed together. No. 134 is in the same condition as 135. The loco is recorded as being 0–6–0PT No. 1284, and a Diagram Q and Diagram R pair of trailers brings up the rear.
F. D. AGAR

2. **Diagram A17 trailer (No.134):** Gangwayed at 'forward end' (i.e. not the luggage compartment end). Intermediate trailer, with luggage compartment made out of the small saloon (which was correspondingly reduced). Normally ran connected to No. 135. This conversion was fairly standard.
3. **Diagram A18 trailer (No.135):** Gangwayed at 'trailing end'. Driving trailer, without a luggage compartment – normally ran coupled to No. 134. Except for the gangway, the A18 design was a mirror image of A15; the conversion involved removing the gangway connector from what had been the non-power unit end of the SRM to what had been the proper unit end.
4. **Diagram A25 trailer (No.148):** This appears to have been the same conversion as the A18 trailer, but without a gangway being fitted at the non-driving end. This also gave a mirror image trailer to the A15 design.

Externally, these trailers were all 70 ft long, 9 ft wide and 12 ft 6 in from rail to roof. Their total wheelbase was shown as 56 ft 6 in with 9 ft bogies on the diagrams, the latter being of the 9 ft coil spring type in the case of all except No. 148 (A25). No. 148 had 9 ft American bogies. The underframes had the usual flat rod queenpost trusses with I beams across the tops of the queenposts. The truss rods are shown on the diagrams as having equal twists at each end, and photographs of No. 135 confirm this feature.

All received 9 ft American bogies although this is only recorded in the case of 136 (Oct.24) and 148 (on conversion).

Internal Arrangement Table

A15	A17	A18	A25
End Vestibule	Luggage Compt.	End Vestibule	End Vestibule
4 ft 3 in wide (max) Single, flat, inward-opening door each side, recessed slightly Retractable steps Gangway	7 ft 4⅜ in wide Double doors opening outwards, flush to bodyside No retractable steps	4 ft 9 in wide Single, flat, inward-opening door each side, recessed slightly Retractable steps	4 ft 9 in wide Single, flat, inward-opening door each side, recessed slightly Retractable steps
Small Saloon	Small Saloon	Large Saloon	Large Saloon
24 ft 1⅜ in long Longitudinal bench seating	21 ft 0⅛ in long Longitudinal bench seating	12 ft bench seats + 23 ft 6 in walk-over seats, 8 each side	12 ft bench seats + 23 ft 6 in walk-over seats, 8 each side
Large saloon	Large saloon	Small saloon	Small saloon
23 ft 6 in walk-over seats, 8 each side + 12 ft bench seats	23 ft 6 in walk-over seats, 8 each side + 12 ft bench seats	23 ft 4⅜ in long Longitudinal bench seating	23 ft 4⅜ in long Longitudinal bench seating
Driver's Cmpt	End Vestibule	Driver's Cmpt	Driver's Cmpt
4 ft 9 in wide Flat, slightly recessed inwardly-opening doors Retractable steps	4 ft 9 in wide Flat, slightly recessed inwardly-opening doors Retractable steps Gangway	5 ft wide Flat, slightly recessed inwardly-opening doors Retractable steps	5 ft wide Flat, slightly recessed inwardly-opening doors Retractable steps

Conversion of Wood Panelled SRMs to Trailers

Window Arrangement Table
(D = door; d = droplight; F = large fixed window)

A15:	D F ddF F ddF F F ddF F F ddF F F D	
	(guard)	(driver)
A17:	DD F dF F ddF F F ddF F F ddF F F D*gangway	
	(luggage)	(vestibule)
		*2 ft. door
A18:	gangway D F F F ddF F F ddF F F ddF F ddF D	
	(vestibule)	(driver)
A25:	D F F F ddF F F ddF F F ddF F ddF D	
	(driver)	(guard)

Subsequently, Nos.134, 135 and 148 received electric lighting in 1930/1. As a pair, Nos.134 and 135 had their smoking/non-smoking accommodation rearranged in January 1931 so that 134 was for smokers and 135 for non-smokers. No. 135, which was the driving trailer of the pair, did not have its end windows painted black until after the reminder in October 1935.

No.134 was photographed at Plymouth (with No.135) in the 1948 brown & cream livery, with twin waist lines; both had their toplights plated over.

No.135 was photographed on a Plymouth suburban train in what appears to be the spring 1927 livery. It had 9 ft coil spring

No. 134 of Diagram A17 coupled to No. 135 of A18 at Laira Junction, Plymouth. Both are electrically lit and have 9ft American bogies. They have also had their toplights plated over, but are in 1948-style brown and cream with twin waist lines.
H. C. CASSERLEY

The Ashburton branch train at Totnes in July 1954 with 0–4–2T No. 1470 and trailer No. 135 of Diagram A18. This trailer is in the 1948 double-lined brown and cream livery but with the 'W' suffix.
COLLECTION R. C. RILEY

Collett 0–4–2T No. 1439 at Moretonhampstead with the 1.35 p.m. to Newton Abbot. The leading trailer, No. 148 of Diagram A25, has 9ft American bogies and is in the 1949 crimson and cream livery. The rear trailer is a matchboarded one, possibly A6 No. 104. 14th October 1950.

W. A. CAMWELL

Conversion of Wood Panelled SRMs to Trailers

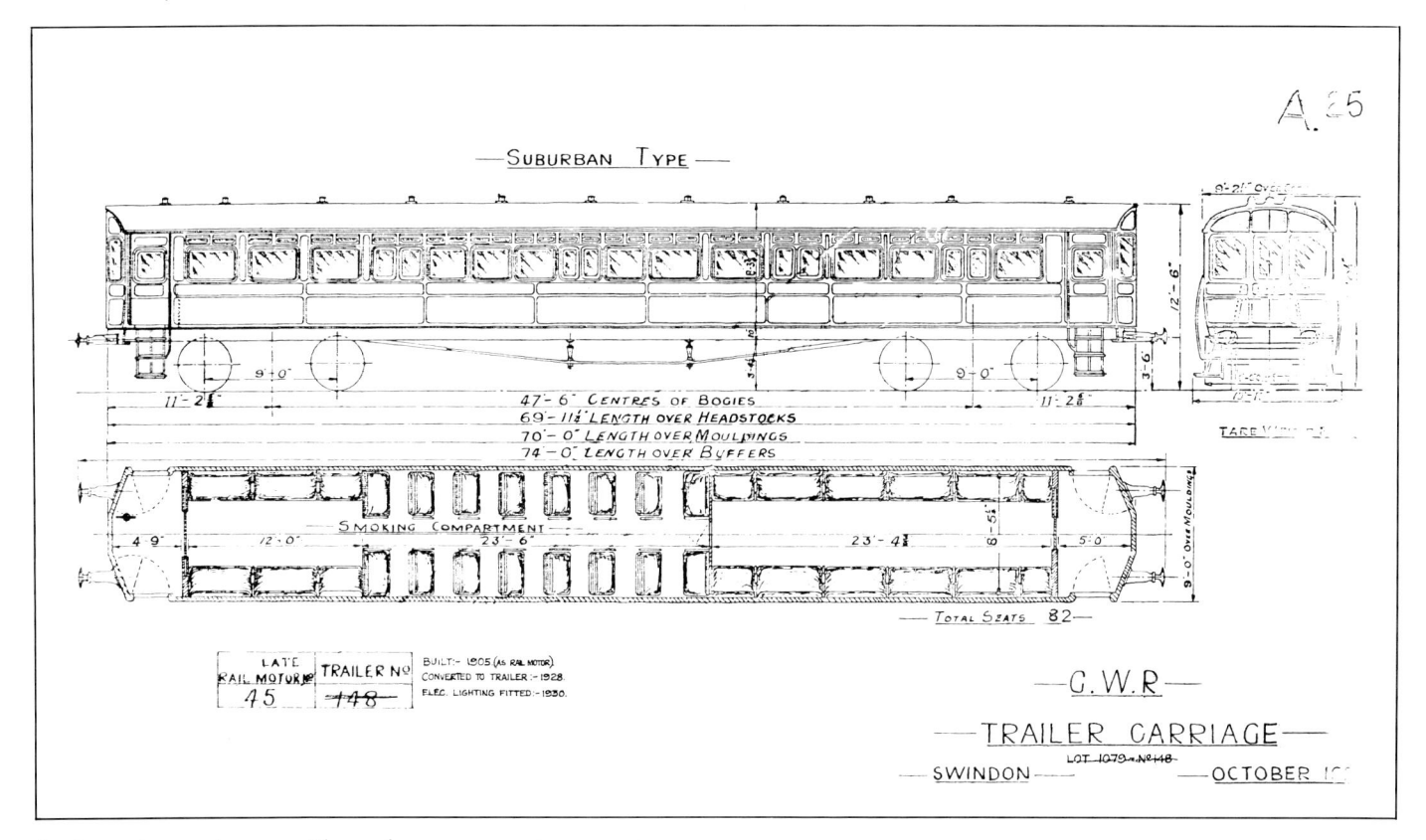

bogies, and a warning gong. The roof appears white, so the picture may have been taken in the summer of 1927, although a date between the spring of 1927 and the end of 1928 is possible. No. 135 eventually ran as W135W, 1949 style but probably still in brown and cream with COMMERCIAL DEPT. written on the side. The photograph shows it to have had sanding apparatus.

No. 136 was condemned as early as July 1939.

In 1927, No. 137 was in the London area, and was involved in a collision with a clerestory coach at Old Oak Common. It still had coil spring bogies, and was in the early 1927 livery. In 1938, it was photographed at Newton Abbot on a Bovey Tracey service. It was at Reading in early BR days as W137, probably in brown and cream.

No. 148 was photographed as W148 in the 1949 carmine and cream livery.

Apart from No. 136, all were equipped with ATC, and survived until 1954–1958.

No. 148 of Diagram A25, electrically lit and with 9ft American bogies, seems to be in BR maroon and cream with the toplights all painted over. However, there is no maroon below the roof except on the end.
H. C. CASSERLEY

Summary

Trailer No.	Diagram	Sand boxes	Blue a/boxes	Chain comm.	Smoking cpts. altered	Electric lighting	Cream brown & gold	End windows black	ATC	Cond
134	A17	Jul. 27	Feb. 29	Feb. 29	Jan. 31	Jan. 31		Feb. 35	Apr. 41	Sep. 57
135	A18	+	Feb. 29	Feb. 29	Jan. 31	Jan. 31		Oct. 35	Apr. 41	Mar. 58
136	A15		Jul. 27	Sep. 30	Mar. 30	–		Feb. 35	–	Aug. 39
137	A15			Aug. 30	Aug. 30	–	Aug. 30	Apr. 35	Oct. 43	Oct. 54
148	A25			Oct. 30	May 28	Oct. 30	Aug. 30	Feb. 35	May 46	Mar. 56

No. 140 of Diagram A19 in 1947 livery at Swansea High Street. This picture shows the dual bells wiring on the front. The single thick cable is the old bells communication wiring, the double, thin cables are for the new ATC and bell. An A34 trailer and possibly No. 48 of Diagram S are at the far end.
W. A. CAMWELL

70 ft Trailers Nos.138–140, Diagram A19

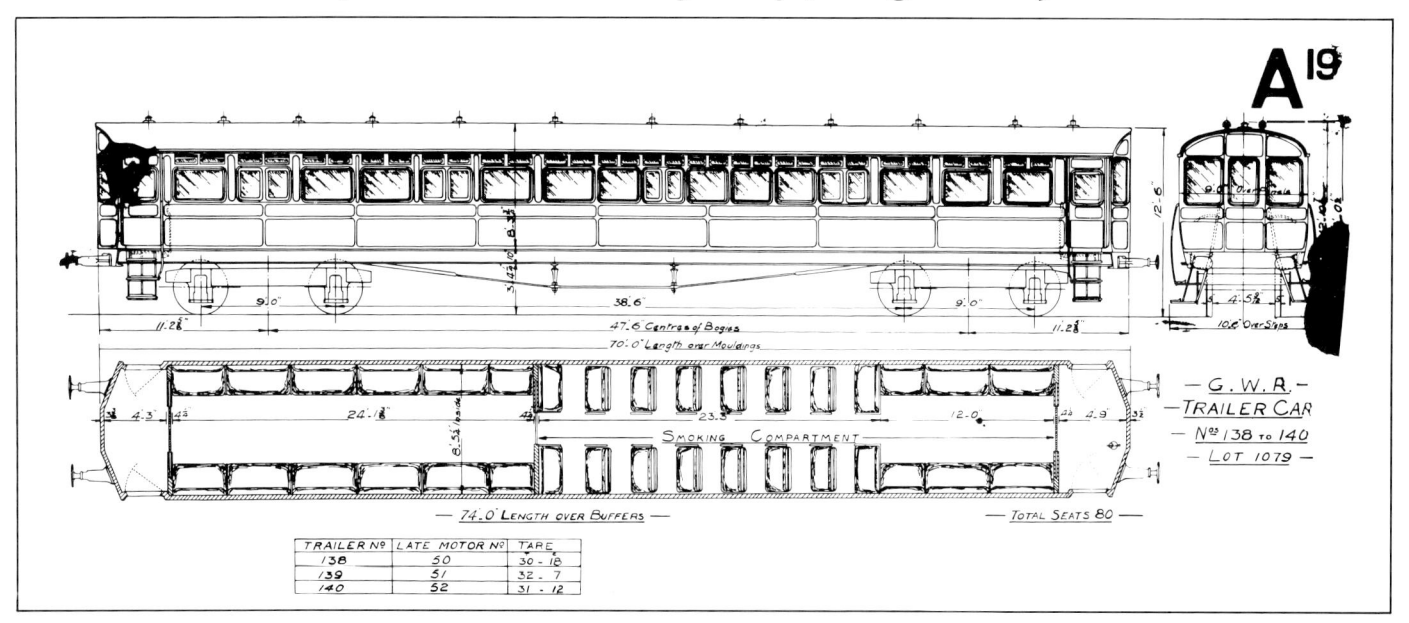

No. 139 of Diagram A19, probably in the 'full' 1922 livery (the mouldings appear to be black above the waist). This trailer is not fitted with a warning gong or sandboxes. The second trailer is one of Diagram L. R. SOUTHERDEN

These three trailers were conversions from SRMs Nos.50–52 of SRM Diagram N. All three conversions took place in April 1923.

The A19 trailers were non-gangwayed, and were without a passenger vestibule. They were the standard 70 ft long, 9 ft wide, and 12 ft 6 in tall, and were originally carried on 9 ft bogies with a symmetric overall wheelbase of 56 ft 6 ft. The underframe had the usual flat bar truss rods with a twist at each end of them.

The accommodation was arranged with a driver's vestibule (4 ft 9 in max.) at the leading end. In the large saloon, there was a 12 ft length of longitudinal bench seating, and a 23 ft 3 in length of 8 pairs of walkover seats. The small saloon had a 24 ft 1⅜ in length of longitudinal bench seating only. The guard's vestibule was 4 ft 3 in in length.

The driver's and the guard's external doors were flat and slightly recessed, and opened inwards. The large saloon had three large fixed lights by the longitudinal seating; the walkover seats were served by two droplights, three fixed lights, two more droplights and another pair of fixed lights. The small saloon had a fixed light, two droplights, two fixed lights, two more droplights and another fixed light.

Initially, No.138 still had 9 ft coil spring bogies, but these were exchanged for Collett 7 ft heavy duty units in October 1929; it acquired blue-painted axleboxes at the same time. The other two vehicles had 9 ft 'American' bogies.

Chain communication was fitted to all three trailers. The large saloon was designated the smoking compartment between November 1928 and December 1931. Nos. 138 and 140 were painted in cream and brown with gold lines in 1932; all three had their luggage end windows painted black in 1935.

All the vehicles received ATC apparatus with No.140 receiving the dual bells arrangement in February 1945. A 1959 photograph shows it with only ATC circuitry.

No.140 was photographed at Swansea High Street in the 1947 livery, working with No. 48 and a Diagram A34 trailer; it was also photographed in the same livery at Reading in 1948. It had been fitted with sandboxes at the driver's end, although this is not recorded in the register.

They were condemned in 1956; No.140 at Slough, whilst No. 138 became internal user service stock No. DW079019 after condemnation, but no other details are available.

Summary

SRM No.	To Trailer	Trailer No.	Sand	Chain comm.	Smoking compts altered	Cream, brown & gold	End windows black	ATC	Cond
50	Apr. 23	138		Oct. 29	Jun. 32	May 32	Feb. 35	Feb. 46	May 56
51	Apr. 23	139		Feb. 29	Dec. 31		Dec. 35	Jan. 49	Sep. 56
52	Apr. 23	140	+	Sep. 30	Nov. 28	Jan. 32	Jun. 35	Feb. 45db	Dec. 55

70 ft Trailers 146, 197 & 198, Diagram A23

'517' class 0–4–2T No. 1431 and trailer No. 146 of Diagram A23 at Exeter St. David's on 26th July 1928. The trailer is in the 1927 autumn livery with twin shields crest, no supporters, and only black waist lining below the windows. The steam railmotor alongside is No. 77.

G. N. SOUTHERDEN

The conversions of SRMs Nos.38–40 shown on Diagram K took place in 1928, 1933 and 1934 respectively, and trailers Nos.146, 197 and 198 were the outcome; they were shown on trailer Diagram A23. Originally, the SRMs had been built in 1905 on Lot 1078, which also included 59 ft 6 in SRMs Nos.29–36, and 70 ft SRM No.37 (which was not converted to a trailer).

Trailers Nos.146, 197 and 198 were of a conventional design, with a central passengers' vestibule; they were 70 ft long, 9 ft wide and 12 ft 6 in high from rail to roof. The vehicles are shown on the diagram as having 7 ft bogies, but No.198 is known from photographs to have had 9 ft 'American'. The underframe was the usual 69 ft $11\frac{1}{4}$ in over headstocks, and bogies were shown on the diagram as being at 49 ft $3\frac{1}{2}$ in centres; the bogie centre–headstock distance at the driver's end was 11 ft $2\frac{5}{8}$ in, and that at the luggage end was 9 ft $5\frac{1}{8}$ in.

Internally, there was a driver's compartment (with a maximum depth of 4 ft 9 in), then a large saloon with a 12 ft length of bench seating, and a 16 ft 9 in length containing six pairs of walkover seats. The passengers vestibule was 3 ft 4 in wide, and the small saloon was 23 ft $9\frac{7}{8}$ in long, with longitudinal bench seating. The luggage compartment was 7 ft $7\frac{1}{4}$ in long. No. 146 seated 76, whilst the others seated 81 (including 9 emergency seats).

Externally, the layout from the driver's end gave the usual flat, recessed driver's door that opened inwards. The bench seats in the large saloon were served by a pair of large fixed lights followed by a pair of droplights, while the walkover seating was provided with three fixed large lights, a pair of droplights and another large fixed light. The passengers' door was the same as the driver's, but with retractable steps under it. The small saloon had a fixed light, a pair of droplights, three more fixed lights, another pair of droplights and a final fixed light. There was a fairly wide panel between the windows and the pair of doors to the luggage compartment; these doors had droplights, and opened outwards. No.198 (at least) retained the SRM-design very wide waist panel at its luggage end (originally the SRM's power unit end), though this is not shown on the diagram.

Collett 0–4–2T No. 4848 and A23 trailer No. 198 at Windsor in June 1935. The small end windows and deep waist panel are not shown on the diagram.

A. W. CROUGHTON

These trailers were all produced with the large saloon designated as 'smoking' and, it is thought, sanding apparatus. No.146 was given blue-painted axleboxes and chain communication in November 1930, the other two on their conversion. Nos.197 and 198 were given the cream, brown and gold livery when rebuilt, but there is no record of No.146 receiving it.

Nos.197 and 198 had their end windows at the luggage end painted black in February 1935; No. 146 was similarly treated during that year. Nos. 197 and 198 both received dual bells ATC wiring in February 1945, whilst No. 146 was fitted in October 1947.

Conversion of Wood Panelled SRMs to Trailers

The interior of Diagram A23 trailer No. 197 complete with gas lighting at Cinderford in July 1956.   H. C. CASSERLEY

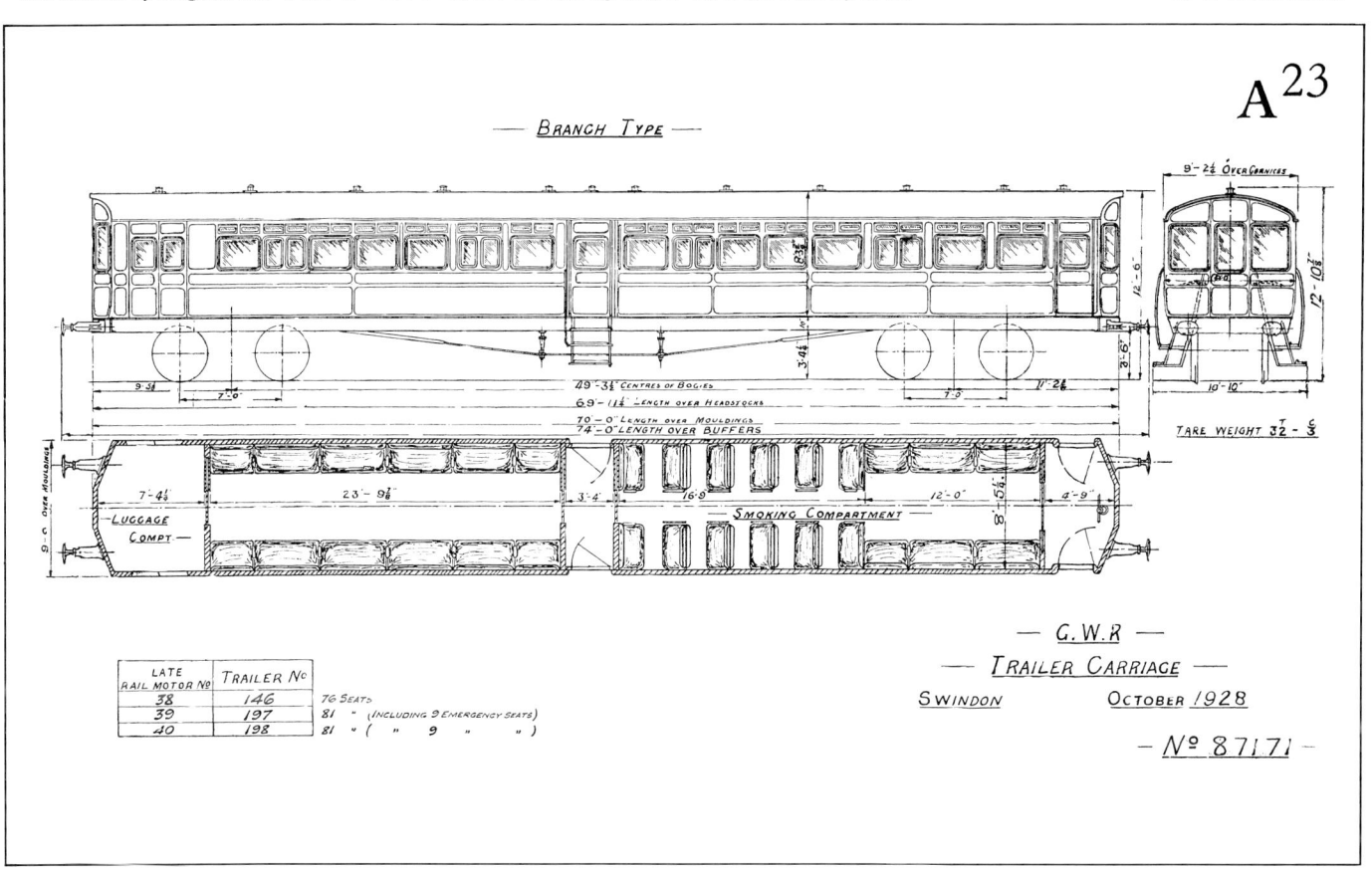

One of these trailers, possibly No. 197 which was known to have been on this service in 1956 (it had 7 ft bogies), was photographed on the Cinderford–Gloucester service in BR days, painted in brown or maroon with the toplights plated over. The luggage end showed no signs of a deep waist panel (cf No. 198). No. 146 was photographed at Exeter in 1928 and again there in BR days in carmine and cream with 1949-style lettering.

No. 198 was in use on the Windsor–Slough service in June 1935, and in 1952 it was in the London area with the lettering in 1949 style as 'W198'. Photographs do not show any twist to the underframe truss rods at the driver's end, which is curious as SRM 40 had 'twist' at both ends of the truss rod. The SRM register says of SRM 40 'Recovered parts used in Trailer 198'. It looks as if there was an exchange of underframe with another condemned SRM.

No. 146 was condemned in August 1953, the other two lasting officially until January 1957 and December 1956 respectively.

Summary

SRM No.	Built	Lot	SRM Diag	Rebuilt to Trailer	Trailer No.	Blue a/boxes	Chain comm	Cream, brown & gold	End windows black	ATC	Cond
38	Mar. 05	1078	K	May 28	146	Nov. 30	Nov. 30		1935	Oct. 47	Aug. 53
39	Apr. 05	1078	K	Dec. 33	197	Dec. 33	Dec. 33	Dec. 33	Feb. 35	Feb. 45 d/b	Jan. 57
40	Mar. 05	1078	K	Mar. 34	198	Mar. 34	Mar. 34	Mar. 34	Feb. 35	Feb. 45 d/b	Dec. 56

No. 146 of Diagram A23 at Exeter with 7ft Collett bogies and plated-over toplights. The underframe truss rod has 'twists' at both ends.

H. C. CASSERLEY

No. 198 of Diagram A19 at Paddington in 1952. This picture shows the deep waist panel at the end, and the 9ft American bogies. The truss rod on this side is only twisted at one end.

M. LONGRIDGE

70 ft Trailers Nos.149–158, 181–186, 199–201, 206, 210, 212–218, Diagrams A26 & A29

According to official records, trailer 200 of Diagram A26 was converted from SRM 58 in December 1933, yet this photo was taken in November 1933. It shows Collett 7ft bogies whilst the register indicates 8ft American bogies! A26 is similar to A29 but has only a single passengers' vestibule door, whereas A29 had double doors.
NATIONAL RAILWAY MUSEUM

These 28 trailers formed a near-standard class on their conversion from steam rail motors between 1928 and 1936. In fact, the Diagram R SRMs, from which some of these were produced, are described as 'standard' in the Lot list. The conversions were from two types of SRM, to diagrams O to R. The second Lot of the Diagram O SRMs were built by Kerr, Stewart & Co. for the GWR (to GWR designs) and had rather narrow double doors which opened inwards, whilst the original lot of the Diagram O SRMs and the Diagram R SRMs were built at Swindon, and had the usual single, inward opening doors. Kerr Stewart subcontracted the building of the bodies of SRMs 61–72 to Hurst Nelson.

It is believed that, originally, Diagram A26 was intended to cover all these trailers. It would appear that Diagram A29 was subsequently produced to include those trailers originating from the second Lot of SRMs to Diagram O with their twin doors, leaving Diagram A26 for the remainder with the single doors to the passenger vestibule.

One feature not shown on the diagrams is that some of these trailers retained the shallow end windows (and corresponding deep waist panels) of the SRM power unit ends at their luggage ends. Examples known from photographs are: No.210 (A26), 214 (A26) and 216 (A29).

Trailer No. 214 was the last to be altered from an SRM, in February 1936. The GWR started to issue coaching stock Lots for the conversions after 1930.

The SRMs shown in the table as not being altered to trailers were all condemned in October 1935 at the end of SRM working on the GWR.

The interior accommodation was arranged to give a driver's compartment, 3 ft 9 in deep (maximum), with 2 ft wide outward opening doors that followed the body side profile. The large saloon was a 14 ft 9 in length of 5 pairs of walkover seats, served by 3 fixed large windows and 2 droplights, plus a 12 ft $0\frac{1}{2}$ in length of longitudinal bench seating with 3 fixed lights, larger than those by the walkover seats. The passenger's vestibule was 3 ft 9 in wide, with flat recessed inward-opening doors and retractable steps below. Next came the small saloon, an 11 ft 6 in length of 4 pairs of walkover seats, with 2 fixed lights and double droplights. A further partition (with door) gave access to a 14 ft $6\frac{1}{8}$ in length of longitudinal bench seats, with 5 fixed large size lights; one was about half the width of the others. Finally came a luggage compartment, 7 ft $4\frac{1}{4}$ in long (max).

Within the two diagrams, there were a number of variations. Most had either the 9 ft 'American' or 7 ft heavy duty bogies. Lot 1088 SRMs (SRM Diagram O, first Lot) had droplights without bolection mouldings; the others had bolection mouldings. These trailers all had a standard underframe with queenpost trusses and flat truss rods, but on Lots 1088 and 1100, the truss rods had a twist at both ends, whilst on the others there was only a twist at the power unit end. The wheelbase is shown as asymmetric on the diagrams, the bogie centres being 9 ft $5\frac{1}{2}$ in from headstock to the centre pin at the luggage end, and 8 ft $11\frac{5}{8}$ in at the driver's end. Six were given electric light on conversion; No.158 was also considered for electric lighting in 1950, but was declared to be too old by that time.

SRM Nos.	Lot	SRM Diag.	Builder	Built	Passenger Doors	Underframe Twist	Original Bogies	Trailer Diag.	SRMs not converted
53 – 58	1088	O	GWR	Jly–Oct.05	Single	Both ends	9' Volute	A26	55
61 – 72	1100	O	KS/HN	Mar–Jne.06	Double	Both ends	9' F/b	A29	65, 70, 71
84 – 90	1140	R	GWR	Dec.07–Jan.08	Single	One end	9' American	A26	88
91 – 99	1142	R	GWR	Jan–Feb.08	Single	One end	9' American	A26	92

They all received ATC in the 1940s, and lasted on passenger services until the mid-1950s; two were subsequently taken into internal user service stock (DW079xxx series).

These trailers saw service throughout the GWR system, and several have been noted on photographs. No.149 was recorded at Exeter St David's in BR carmine and cream livery, with 1949-style lettering; it had sand apparatus. No.152 was used on a Nelson–Pontypool Road auto in July 1929 when it was involved in an accident at Pontypool Road West Junction. In BR days, it was photographed in a two colour livery with 1949-style lettering. It was mostly steel panelled. Nos. 154 and 155 were allocated to the Taunton division in late 1935; No.155 (in 1934 livery) was being used on the Yeovil Town–Yeovil Pen Mill service in 1935.

Nos.156 and 158 were allocated to Exeter in the winter of 1937/8, and were diagrammed for services to:

No. 156
07.45 Exeter–Sampford Peverell
08.27 S.P.–Exeter
09.25 Exeter–Heathfield
11.00 Heathfield–Exeter
12.50 Exeter–Heathfield
14.25 Heathfield–Chudley Knighton (WSO)
14.35 C.K.–Heathfield (WSO)
14.40 Heathfield–Newton Abbot (WSO)
15.00 Newton A–Heathfield (WSO)
15.26 Heathfield—Exeter
16.38 Exeter–Tiverton
18.20 Tiverton–Tiverton Junc.

Interior view of No. 200, Diagram A26, showing the bench seating, the leather straps to hold the droplights partially open, the straps for 'straphangers', gas lamps and the ventilators in the ceiling.
NATIONAL RAILWAY MUSEUM

Conversion of Wood Panelled SRMs to Trailers

'Walkover' seats in No. 200. NATIONAL RAILWAY MUSEUM

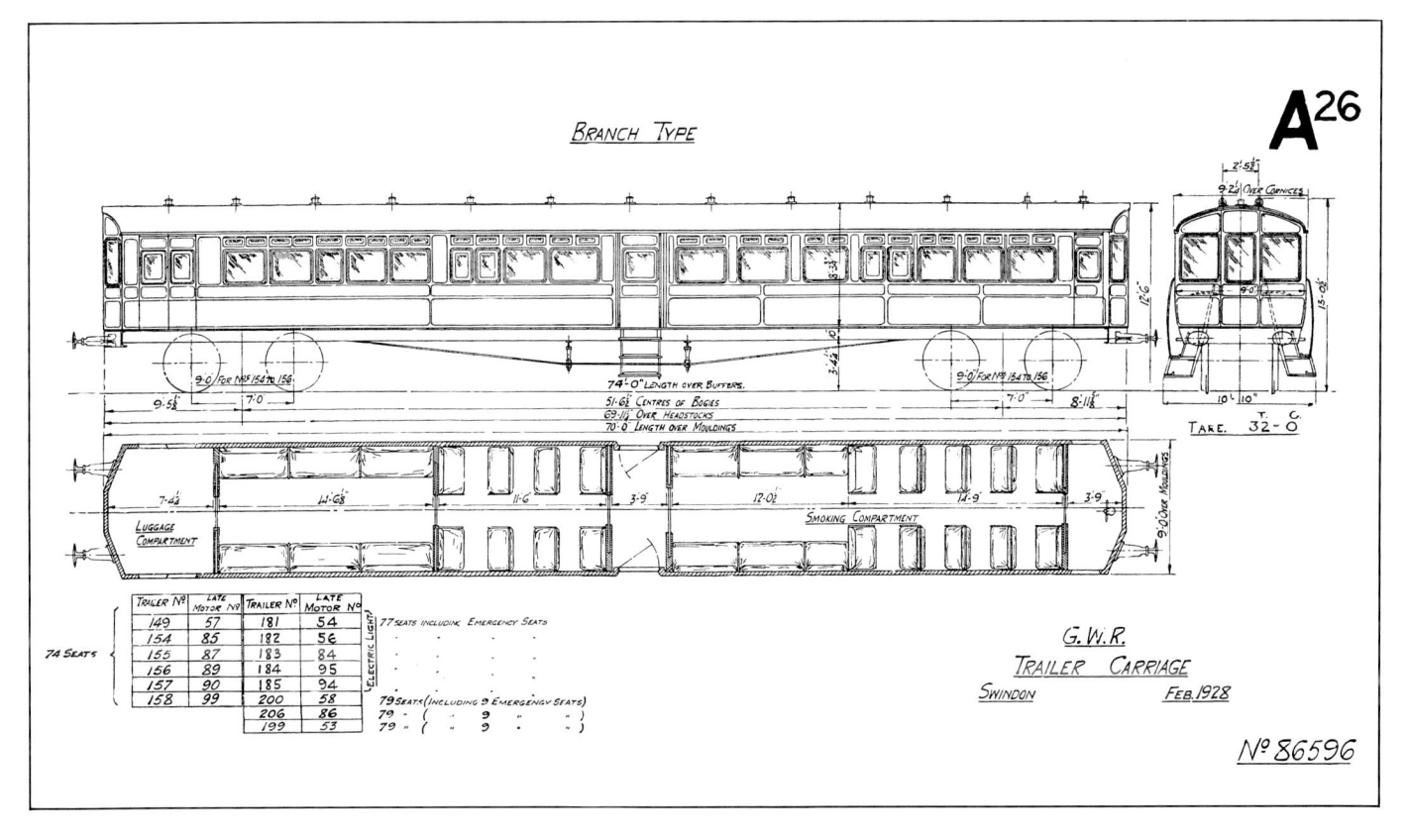

BRANCH TYPE

A26

G.W.R.
TRAILER CARRIAGE
SWINDON   FEB. 1928

N° 86596

Trailer N°	Late Motor N°	Trailer N°	Late Motor N°
149	57	181	54
154	85	182	56
155	87	183	84
156	89	184	95
157	90	185	94
158	99	200	58
		206	86
		199	53

74 Seats

77 Seats including Emergency Seats

Electric Light

79 Seats (including 9 Emergency Seats)
79 " (" 9 " ")
79 " (" 9 " ")

Metro class 2–4–0T No. 975 at Newton Abbot with Diagram A26 trailer No. 157. Converted in June 1928, it appears to be in the autumn 1927 livery with coat of arms and no gold lines. It has 9ft American bogies and 'full size' luggage end windows.
COLLECTION J. E. KITE

No. 181 of Diagram A26, leaving Poyle Halt on the Staines branch, is believed to be in the 1929 livery (it was rebuilt in January 1930) although this view c.1930 seems to show it carrying the pre-1927 supporters to the garter livery. It was electrically lit and mounted on Collett 7ft bogies. The clerestory coach might have been a trailer but not enough is visible to be certain.
HMRS

A26 No. 155, at Yeovil in May 1935, is fitted with 9ft 'fish-belly' bogies. It is in 1934 livery with one waist line and once again the underframe truss rod has a twist at one end only.
H. C. CASSERLEY

Conversion of Wood Panelled SRMs to Trailers

18.50 Tiverton Junc–Tiverton
19.05 Tiverton–Exeter

No. 158
07.00 Exeter–Heathfield
08.23 Heathfield–Exeter
10.55 Exeter–Heathfield
12.55 Heathfield–Exeter
14.45 Exeter–Trusham
15.45 Trusham–Chudleigh
15.53 Chudleigh–Christow†
16.12 Christow–Heathfield
17.15 Heathfield–Exeter

† Empty working
WSO Wednesdays and Saturdays only

No.181 was photographed in the 1929 brown and cream livery, with one waist line. The train consisted of No.181 leading, locomotive, and a clerestory carriage in a new-looking brown and cream livery trailing. It also ran on the Woodstock branch during the early 1950s in BR carmine and cream, as W181W (like 183) with lettering in 1949-style, and without toplights.

No.182 is thought to have been in the London Division (in 1927 livery) about 1929.

No.183 ran without toplights in BR carmine and cream livery as W183W in 1949-style lettering. It was used thus on the Woodstock branch on the last day of the service, 27th February 1954.

No.185 was photographed in the 1930s on the Greenford Loop service. In BR days, it was used on the Windsor and Woodstock branches as W185, apparently in brown and cream with 1949-style lettering, as late as 1954. No. 185 was also used on the Abingdon branch in BR days (unfortunately the picture is not dated) as W185W in BR plain red livery.

No.186 was at Southall in May 1933 in the 1929 double-lined livery, with sanding and chain communication apparatus. It was being used on a train with another A26/A29 trailer and loco No. 5419.

No.200 had its official portrait taken when new in December 1933; this shows it in the

'517' class 0–4–2T No. 1487 on an Ashburton train at Totnes with trailer No. 213 of Diagram A26. The photograph was taken on 10th August 1935 three months after No. 213 was 'rebuilt'. The luggage end windows are a relic of its days as an SRM. It is in 1934 brown and cream livery, but does not seem to have a lower gold line at the waist. It has 9ft American bogies. Behind No. 213 is Diagram A10 trailer No. 130 with Collett 7ft bogies.
G. N. SOUTHERDEN

0–6–0PT No. 5401 at Old Oak Lane Halt with Diagram A26 No. 185. One of the electrically-lit examples and fitted with Collett 7ft bogies, the trailer is in 1930 livery with double gold lines at the waist. The underframe truss rod has a twist only at the luggage end. The chain apparatus is presumably at the driver's end.
C. R. GORDON STUART/LENS OF SUTTON

No. 210 of Diagram A26, seen here at Gloucester about 1936, has the 1934 livery, although the axleboxes of the 9ft 'fish-belly' bogies are not painted blue.
L. E. COPELAND

contemporary two colour livery with double gold lines. It had lost its toplights by the BR era, and ran thus as W200W (1949-style lettering) in the BR carmine & cream livery. It was still in the same livery after withdrawal in 1959, although by then the exterior paintwork was in very poor condition.

No.201 was specified in the September 1937 (and until further notice) *Local Coach Working Programme* as being used on the Yatton–Clevedon branch service with No.62 of Diagram L. Both are described as 'chain fitted', although by then chain communication apparatus was a standard feature of trailers. No. 201 was photographed at Bourne End on a Marlow train in July 1949; it was in brown and cream, but the photograph does not indicate exactly which livery. Later, No.201 lost its toplights, and ran in maroon livery as W201W in 1951-style lettering. It had the deep waist panel at the luggage end, a legacy from its SRM days.

No.210 was pictured at Gloucester (in the 1934 livery) about 1936. It had one waist line, and the axleboxes were still painted black. In 1951, it was photographed at Gobowen on the Oswestry auto train, in brown and cream livery, in company with Diagrams A38 No. 231 and A32 No.6820. It was subsequently photographed in plain maroon livery with the running number as 'W210W' in the 1951 position, but in large size characters. It is thought to have been used on the Marlow branch in August 1955.

No.212 was photographed at Wolverhampton as No.079014, in a single colour livery (probably maroon) with the running number at the left-hand end in 1949-style, but using small size characters. It had a deep waist panel at the luggage end.

No.213 was being used with another (unidentified) trailer on the Totnes–Ashburton service in August 1935.

Collett 0–4–2T No. 1439 propelling a Moretonhampstead–Newton Abbot auto out of Heathfield in April 1948. The trailer nearest the loco is an A26 in a wartime all-brown livery, and the leading trailer is an A15 or A19 type (externally the same) in 1943 brown and cream.
C. H. S. OWEN

No.215 also lost its toplights, and was photographed at Exeter as W215W in BR plain maroon livery, in the 1951-style.

No.217 was photographed at Leamington Spa in a monochrome livery, probably maroon, as No.079020, with the number in what appears to be white, small block characters at the left-hand end of the trailer side.

No.218 was photographed in maroon livery as W218W, in 1951-style.

Conversion of Wood Panelled SRMs to Trailers

Trailer 182 of Diagram A26, at Haddenham in July 1948, has Collett 7ft bogies and is in 1947 brown and cream livery. As can be seen on the left, the driver's doors opened outwards so they could conform to the body side profile.
P. J. GARLAND

Trl No.	Trl Diag altered	ex SRM	Conv. date	Sand boxes	Bogies	Blue a/boxes	Chain comm.	Elec light	Cream brown & gold	End windows black	ATC	Cond	Notes
149	A26	57	May 28	–	7ft CHD*	Sep. 30	Feb. 32	–		Feb. 35	Oct. 47	Sep. 56	
150	A29	61	Jun. 28	–	7ft CHD*	Jul. 30	Jul. 30	–	Sep. 31	Feb. 35	Nov. 40	Jan. 56	
151	A29	63	Jun. 28	–	7ft CHD	Jul. 30	Jul. 30	–	Dec. 31	Feb. 35	Jul. 41	May 55	
152	A29	67	Jun. 28	–	7ft CHD	Sep. 29	Sep. 29	–	Mar. 32	Feb. 35	Feb. 45db	Dec. 55	
153	A29	68	Jun. 28	–	7ft CHD*	May 30	May 30	–		Oct. 35	Aug. 46	Dec. 54	
154	A26	85	Jun. 28	–	9ft F/b*	–	Apr. 30	–		Feb. 35	Aug. 46	Dec. 56	
155	A26	87	Jun. 28	–	9ft F/b*	–	Mar. 30	–	Jun. 31	Feb. 35	Aug. 40	Sep. 57	9ft Am originally?
156	A26	89	Jun. 28	–	9ft Am*	Jun. 28	Feb. 33	–		Feb. 35	Aug. 47	Dec. 56	
157	A26	90	Jun. 28	–	9ft Am*	–	Feb. 31	–	Jan. 31	Feb. 35	May 46	Aug. 57	
158	A26	99	May 28	–	7ft CHD	Jul. 30	Jul. 30	–		Feb. 35	Jun. 45	Nov. 57	
181	A26	54	Jan. 30	Jan. 30	7ft CHD*	Jan. 30	Sep. 30	Jan. 30	Jul. 32	Nov. 35	Jan. 42	Oct. 58	
182	A26	56	Jan. 30	Jan. 30	7ft CHD*	Jan. 30	Sep. 30	Jan. 30	May 32	Apr. 35	May 40	May 56	
183	A26	84	Mar. 30	Mar. 30	7ft CHD*	Mar. 30	Sep. 30	Mar. 30		Apr. 35	Feb. 46	Oct. 54	
184	A26	95	Mar. 30	Mar. 30	7ft CHD*	Mar. 30	Sep. 30	Mar. 30	Aug. 32	Apr. 35	Feb. 41	Sep. 57	
185	A26	94	Mar. 30	Mar. 30	7ft CHD*	Mar. 30	Sep. 30	Mar. 30		Apr. 35	Feb. 45db	Mar. 59	
186	A29	62	Jun. 30	Jun. 30	7ft CHD*	Jun. 30	Sep. 30	Jun. 30		Mar. 35	Feb. 46	Jan. 55	
199	A26	53	Dec. 33	Dec. 33	9ft Am	Dec. 33	Dec. 33	–	Dec. 33	Apr. 35	Feb. 45db	Apr. 58	
200	A26	58	Dec. 33	Dec. 33	7ft CHD*	Dec. 33	Dec. 33	–	Dec. 33	Feb. 35	Jun. 49	Feb. 59	See below.
201	A29	69	Mar. 34	Mar. 34	7ft CHD*	Mar. 34	Mar. 34	–		Feb. 35	Jul. 45	Oct. 58	Painted brown May. 42
206	A26	86	Dec. 33	Dec. 33	7ft CHD	Dec. 33	Dec. 33	–		Nov. 35	Mar. 41	Sep. 56	
210	A26	91	Aug. 35	Aug. 35	9ft F/b*	Aug. 35	Aug. 35	–		Aug. 35	Feb. 45db	Nov. 56	Painted brown May. 42
212	A26	93	May 35	May 35	9ft Am	May 35	May 35	–		May 35	Feb. 45db	May 56	See below.
213	A26	96	May 35	May 35	9ft Am*	May 35	May 35	–		May 35	Feb. 45db	Jun. 56	
214	A26	97	Feb. 35	Feb. 35	9ft Am	Feb. 35	Feb. 35	–		Feb. 36	Aug. 45	Nov. 56	
215	A26	98	Jan. 36	Jan. 36	9ft Am	Jan. 36	Jan. 36	–		Jan. 36	Dec. 45	Nov. 57	
216	A29	64	Dec. 35	Dec. 35	9ft F/b*	Dec. 35	Dec. 35	–		Dec. 35	Feb. 45db	Sep. 57	
217	A29	66	Jan. 36	Jan. 36	9ft Am	Jan. 36	Jan. 36	–		Jan. 36	Feb. 45db	Oct. 56	See below.
218	A29	72	Nov. 35	Nov. 35	9ft F/b*	Nov. 35	Nov. 35	–		Nov. 35	Jun. 45	Nov. 57	

*Photographic evidence

No.200: When condemned, became No.079132 (Jun. 63). Staff accommodation, R & M Carmarthen. Finally condemned & sold to Briton Ferry for breaking up Sep. 64.

No.212: To No.079014 Work Study Office C & W Dept, Swindon. NWO 7881 (May 56.) Based at Wolverhampton. Preserved GWS, Didcot.

No.217: To No.079020 Mobile Office, Industrial Consultants, Leamington.

The trailer register gives the condemned dates of Nos. 151, 157 and 183 as one month later than shown.

Collett 0-4-2T No. 1413 at Cheltenham (St. James) on 6th May 1953, with No. 200 of Diagram A26. The trailer has Collett 7ft bogies, narrow (standard) end waist panel (evidenced by the handrails) and has lost its toplights. It is in BR carmine and cream 1949 livery, but with the 'W' suffix.
COLLECTION
R. C. RILEY

A26 No. 185 at Abingdon in 1951 BR livery. This was an electrically-lit example.
PHOTOSCRIPT, DEDDINGTON

0–6–0PT No. 6414 with the 1.48 p.m. Plymouth North Road–Tavistock motor train passing Mutley on 27th June 1955. The trailer is No. 157 of Diagram A26 in BR 1951-style plain maroon livery.

R. E. VINCENT

No. 186 of Diagram A26, one of the electrically-lit examples, at Southall on 20th May 1933.

W. POTTER

Conversion of Wood Panelled SRMs to Trailers

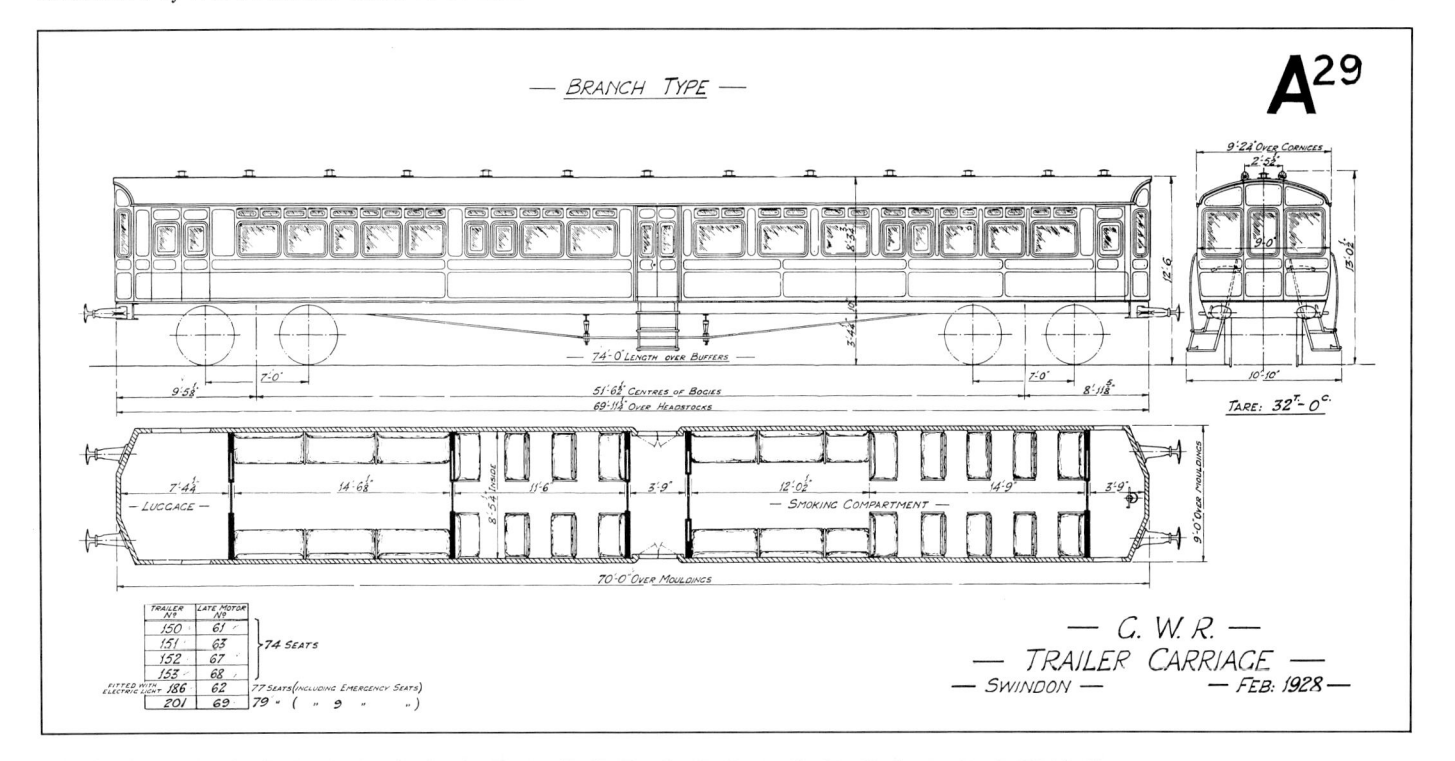

A29

— BRANCH TYPE —

— G.W.R. —
— TRAILER CARRIAGE —
— SWINDON — — FEB: 1928 —

TRAILER Nº	LATE MOTOR Nº	
150	61	74 SEATS
151	63	
152	67	
153	68	
186	62	77 SEATS (INCLUDING EMERGENCY SEATS) FITTED WITH ELECTRIC LIGHT
201	69	79 " (" 9 " ")

Trailer 150 of Diagram A29 in the 1929 livery with one gold/black waist line. No. 150 has Collett 7ft bogies. The loco is an unidentified 'small Metro' 2–4–0T.
L & GRP
CTY. DAVID & CHARLES

A29 trailer 201 in BR 1951 plain maroon with Collett 7ft bogies, the deep end waist panel, and without toplights.
COLLECTION
R. C. RILEY

Collett 0–4–2T No. 4865 at Totnes in June 1936. The trailer is in 1934 livery, having one gold/black line at the waist. There is no sign of the whistle cord being connected. W. POTTER

59ft 6in Trailers ex-SRMs 193

CHAPTER NINE
59 FT 6 IN TRAILERS: EX-SRMs
59 ft 6 in Trailers Nos.125, 128–133, Diagram A10

THESE seven trailers included the first conversions of wood panelled SRMs. As SRMs, they had been built as part of Lot 1078 in December 1904 and January 1905. Originally, they had been shown on Diagrams H, J and J1, which had only minor differences between them. By the time they were altered to trailers, all were covered by Diagram H.

This time, the conversion work was spread over nearly three years, and was in parallel with the alteration of four 70 ft SRMs to trailers (Trailer Diagrams A13–A15). Unlike the matchboarded trailers converted from SRMs, the trailers to Diagram A10 were not numbered in the same sequence as the original SRMs, but in the order in which they were rebuilt. The numbering sequence was interrupted by the conversions of SRMs 59 and 60, which became trailers Nos.126 and 127. One SRM omitted from the programme, was No.30, which was one of the last on the GWR, being withdrawn in October 1935.

When built as steam rail motors, these particular vehicles had a size of luggage compartment which cut the passenger accommodation to only 49 seats. Unlike the earlier (matchboarded) SRMs, these had an area of walkover seats in place of seating bays. They were also built with 8 ft wheelbase bogies, shown on the diagram as the plate frame design with bolster, having coil or elliptic springs. These bogies were not very successful under passenger stock, and were usually removed by the 1920s, and even earlier in the case of main line stock. The A10 diagram indicated 9 ft bogies (without specifying type), but there is a note that No.125 had 8 ft bogies and a 46 ft wheelbase.

'517' class 0–4–2T No. 1482 at Handsworth in 1925 with Diagram A10 (nearest the camera) and Diagram L trailers. The A10 has 9ft 'fish-belly' bogies. LENS OF SUTTON

The standard dimensions were: 59 ft 6 in long, 9 ft wide, 12 ft 2½ in high (Nos.125, 130 and 132 seem to have been a fraction of an inch different) and a wheelbase of 47 ft (No.125 – 46 ft). The underframe was still the Dean type, with cast queen posts for the truss, and round section truss rods with a central adjustable turnbuckle.

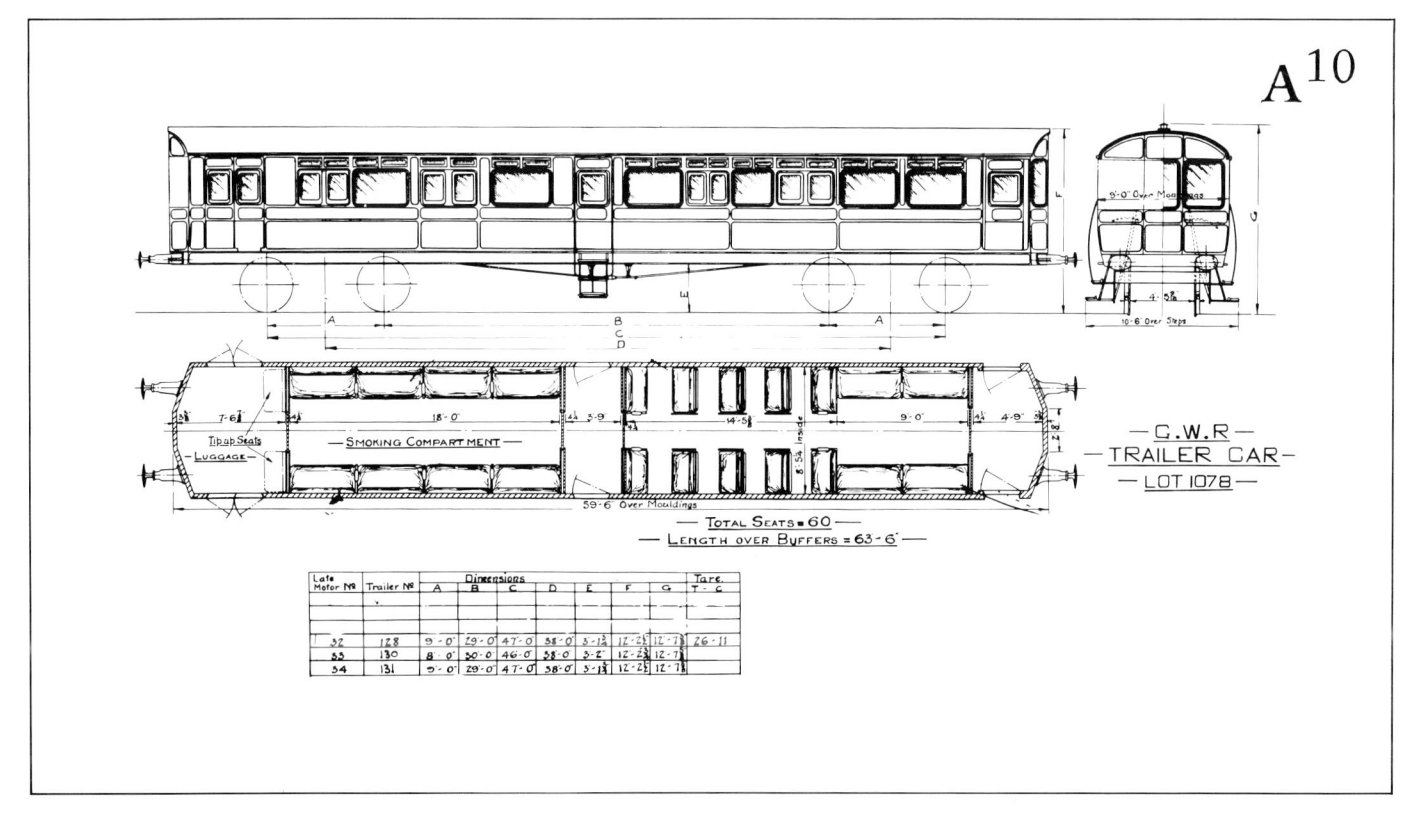

The records of the bogies are incomplete and the register, the notes on the diagram, and photographs are not always in agreement:

SRM No.	Built	Initial Diag.	Final Diag.	To trailer	Trailer No.	Trailer Bogies
29	Jan.05	H	H	Mar.20	125	* 8ft American
30	Jan.05	H	H	Not converted	—	—
31	Dec.04	J	H	Dec.22	129	* 7ft Collett
32	Dec.04	J1	H	Apr.20	128	* 9ft F/B
33	Dec.04	H	H	Dec.22	130	* 7ft Collett
34	Jan.05	H	H	Dec.22	131	9ft F/B?
35	Dec.04	J	H	Dec.22	132	* 9ft F/B
36	Dec.04	H	H	Jan.23	133	* 9ft F/B

Notes – Bogies

* Photographic evidence
Trailer 129 probably had 8ft American bogies originally (Register)
Trailer 130 may have had 8ft coil spring bogies originally.

On conversion, the accommodation was arranged to give a guard/luggage compartment, which was 7 ft 6⅜ in long, with external double doors opening outwards, and an internal sliding door to the passenger accommodation. The Diagram shows this luggage compartment as having two tip-up seats, seating four passengers, one either side of the sliding door. Next was the small saloon, which was 18 ft long and had longitudinal bench seating; then came the central vestibule (3 ft 9 in between partitions). The large saloon was unaltered from SRM days, and was divided into two areas. It had five 'walkover' seats each side of the central corridor, occupying a length of 14 ft 5⅜ in, followed by a 9 ft length of bench seating. The driver's compartment was 4 ft 9 in (maximum) width between the end of the coach and the partition, with external doors which were flat, slightly recessed and opened inwards.

Externally, there was a fairly wide panel on either side of the guard's compartment double doors. The small saloon had windows arranged to give two droplights, large fixed light, two droplights, large fixed light, with

'517' class No. 1163 at Totnes, with A10 trailer No. 130, newly painted in the 1930 livery with twin waist lines and mounted on 7ft Collett bogies.
LENS OF SUTTON

Diagram A10 trailer No. 125, at Llantrisant, appears to be in 1948 brown and cream livery, possibly with double waist lining. It has 8ft 'American' bogies. The panelling above two of the droplights is a relic from its SRM days and a feature shared with 128, but not all others.
M. LONGRIDGE

59ft 6in Trailers ex-SRMs

2–6–2T No. 4593 at Pontypool Road with two auto trailers. Although some of the 45XX locos were given auto gear in BR days, 4593 shows no signs of it and in any case the trailers are the wrong way round. The leading trailer is an A27 in 1948 brown and cream with two waist lines, but no white line across the driver's windows. The rear trailer is an A10 in a similar livery, although it may not have the lower gold waist line. The A27 may be No. 163.
DEREK CLAYTON

No. 128 of Diagram A10 at Craven Arms with 9ft 'fishbelly' bogies and the remains of what might have been 1934 brown and cream livery.
J. H. RUSSELL

the usual toplights. The door to the passenger vestibule opened inwards, and had retractable steps under it. The large saloon had windows in the format of large fixed light, two droplights, large fixed light; two droplights, two large fixed lights; again, all with toplights.

The recorded subsequent history is:

Trailer No.	Sand boxes	Blue a/boxes	Chain comm.	Smoking cpts changed	Cream, brown & gold	Black end windows	ATC	Cond
125	Nr	Nr	Sep. 30	May. 30	—	May 35	Jan. 41	Oct. 53
128	+	Nr	Oct. 31	Jul. 28	—	Feb. 35	Jan. 49	Aug. 57
129	Nr	Nov. 28	Nov. 28	Nov. 28	Dec. 31	Feb. 35	Feb. 46	May 54
130	Apr. 27	Mar. 28	Mar. 29	Apr. 29	—	Feb. 35	Oct. 44	Jul. 56
131	Nr	Nr	Jun. 29	Jun. 29	Apr. 32	Oct. 35	Mar. 50	Jun. 61
132	Nr	Nr	Sep. 30	May 30	—	Feb. 35	Mar. 48	Oct. 54
133	+	Nr	Sep. 30	Nov. 28	May 32	Feb. 35	May 45	Apr. 51 See below

No.125 was photographed at Llantrisant during 1948, in brown and cream with 'TRAILER' at the bottom right-hand corner of the side. It also later ran in BR carmine and cream as W125, 1949-style. It had 8 ft 'American' bogies.

No.128 was at Craven Arms in very poor external condition in the late 1940s, apparently still in 1934 livery. It was fitted with sandboxes and 9 ft 'fishbelly' bogies.

No.130 was at Swindon in 1932. It was also photographed at Totnes in the 1930 livery with two gold waist lines and was fitted with Collett 7 ft bogies.

No.131 was amongst the last survivors of GWR (re-)built trailers in revenue-earning service.

No.132 received the 1949 BR carmine and cream livery.

It is known that No.133 was painted brown in 1942. It was originally condemned in June 1949, reinstated in November 1949, and was finally condemned in April 1951.

59 ft 6 in Trailer No.147: Diagram A24 (ex-SRM Diagram L)

No. 147 of Diagram A24 in wartime all-brown livery at Newton Abbot in 1947. ATC is fitted but sand pipes are not very evident. Although 'GWR' should be visible in the waist panel, there is no sign of it.
P. J. GARLAND

There were originally two short SRMs to Diagram L: Nos.41 and 42. SRM No.41 was withdrawn in December 1927 and converted into trailer 147, which was shown on Diagram A24; SRM No.42 was sold in July 1920 to the Port of London Authority.

Trailer No.147 appeared in June 1928. It was 59 ft 6 in long, 9 ft wide and 12 ft 2$\frac{3}{8}$ in high (slightly less than usual). It was unique amongst ex-SRM wood panelled short trailers in not having a passengers' vestibule. In this respect, it was like the original Diagram J and J1 trailers (Nos.19–24).

It ran on Collett 7 ft 'light duty' bogies, and had a total wheelbase of 45 ft 6 in. As was sometimes the case with conversions from SRMs, this was not symmetric; the distance between the headstock and the bogie centre pin at the driver's end being 10 ft 8$\frac{5}{8}$ in, and at the other end 6 inches less. (The front of wood panelled bow-ended trailers overhung the headstocks by the depth of the mouldings: $\frac{3}{8}$ in). The axleboxes were painted blue at the conversion.

The accommodation of this trailer was arranged to give seats for 66 passengers. The driver's vestibule was 4 ft 9 in deep (maximum), whilst the large saloon contained a 12 ft length of longitudinal bench seating, plus a 14 ft 3 in length with 5 pairs of walkover seats. The small saloon measured 21 ft 10$\frac{3}{8}$ in long, with longitudinal bench seating, and the guard's vestibule was 5 ft deep (maximum).

Externally, both vestibules had flat, inwardly opening doors with retractable steps below each. The longitudinal bench seating

Diagram A24 No. 147, in 1951 maroon livery, still has its luggage end windows intact although by now its side and end are steel-panelled, up to the waist in the former case. H. C. CASSERLEY

in the large saloon had two fixed lights and a pair of droplights, whilst the walkover seats had one fixed light (a little wider than the others), a pair of droplights, and two fixed lights, the second one being of the wider size. The small saloon had a pair of fixed lights either side of a pair of droplights, followed by the same arrangement again, but with the wider size of fixed lights.

The small saloon had originally been designated 'smoking', although before the trailer had been released to traffic (or just after it had been released) the large saloon was made 'smoking' instead, and the small one became 'non-smoking' (August 1928). The trailer was painted in cream and brown, with gold lines, in March 1931; it was fitted with chain communication gear in February 1933 and had the guard's end windows painted black in March 1935. ATC apparatus was fitted in October 1944. Trailer No.147 was condemned in November 1957.

59ft 6in Trailers ex-SRMs

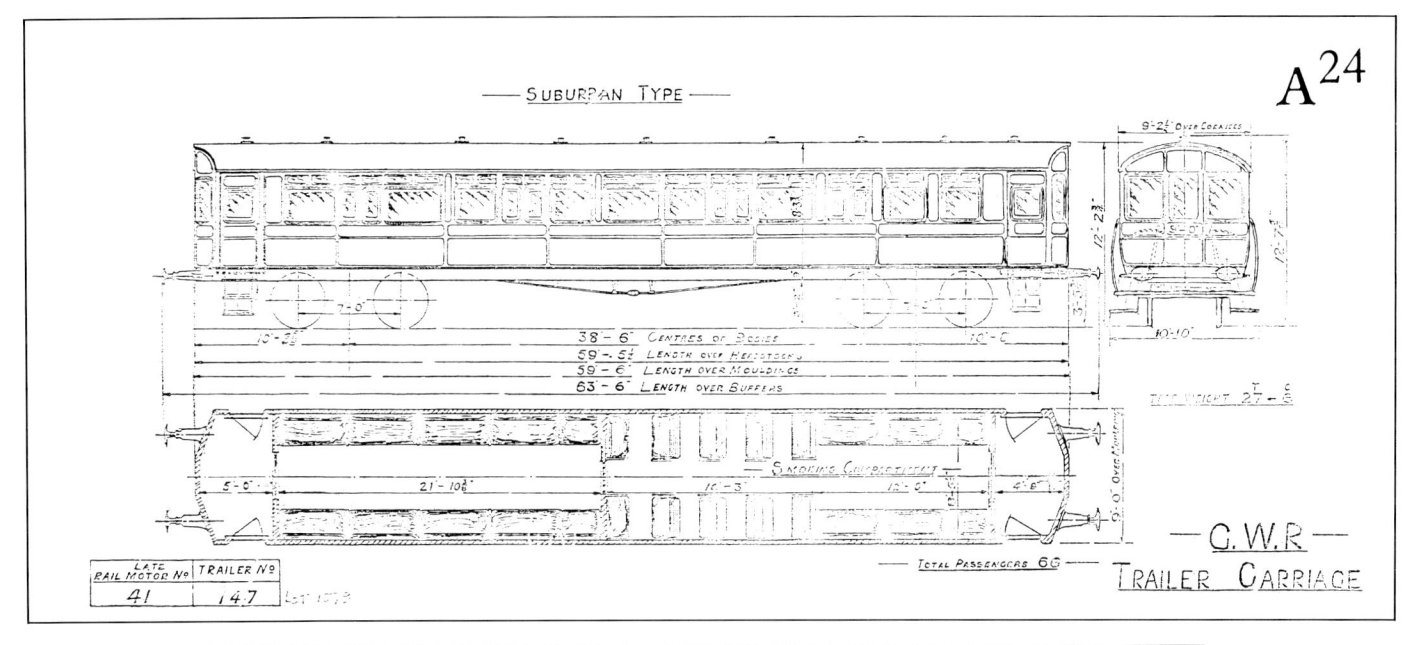

A24 — GWR Trailer Carriage — Suburban Type

Summary									
SRM No.	SRM w'drn	To Trlr	Trlr No.	Smoking cpts changed	Cream, brown & gold	Chain comm.	End windows black	ATC	Cond
41	Dec. 27	Jun. 28	147	Aug. 28	Mar. 31	Feb. 33	Mar. 35	Oct. 44	Nov. 57
42	Jul. 20	NOT – Sold as SRM							

59 ft 6 in Trailers Nos.202–205, 207–209, 211 and 219: Diagram A31

Trailer Diagram A31 covered 9 short, wood panelled trailers converted from Diagram Q and Q1 SRMs between 1934 and the end of 1935. Diagram Q covered SRMs Nos.73–80, built on Lot 1101 in 1906, which had bodies built by the Gloucester Carriage & Wagon Co., and engine units by Swindon. Diagram Q1 was for Nos.81–83, which were built in their entirety by Swindon on Lot 1129, in May 1907. The difference between the two types was that the Gloucester-built examples had double doors opening inwards to the passenger vestibule, like the ones built by Messrs Kerr, Stewart (see Diagrams A26 and A29) page 181, whilst the GWR-built trio had the usual single door.

All except two (SRMs Nos.77 and 80) were converted to trailers, and four carriage lots were issued to cover the alterations.

According to the diagrams, the A31 trailers were unique in retaining the short windows and deep waist panels at what had been the power unit end of the coach, and which was now the luggage compartment end; however, photographs of some 70 ft SRM conversions show these features to be or have been present. Even when the luggage end windows had been plated over, the wide waist panel at this end tended to show. One odd result of it was that the dividing line between the brown and cream paint, and, in later years, between carmine and cream, came part way up this panel.

The coaches measured 59 ft 6 in long, 9 ft wide, and 12 ft 5 in high. They ran on a variety of bogies of both 7 ft and 8 ft wheelbase, and their total wheelbase depended on the bogies fitted: 48 ft 6½ in when fitted with 7 ft units, or 1 ft greater if 8 ft bogies were used. The underframe was the usual type with flat bar trusses. The truss rods are shown on the diagram with equal twists at both ends, and photographs of Nos.209 and 211 show this to have been so, but No.204 is shown in a photograph to have had the twisted lengths unequal, raising questions as to the provenance of its underframe! The diagram shows the wheelbase to have been offset; the headstock–bogie centre distance at the driver's end was 8 ft 5⅝ in, and at the luggage end it was 9 ft 5⅛ in.

SRM	SRM Diag.	SRM w'drawn	To Trailer	Trailer No	Conversion Lot	Pass. doors	Bogies
73	Q	Jun. 33	Feb. 34	202	1511	Double	*8 ft 'Fishbelly'
74	Q	Jun. 33	Feb. 34	203	1511	Double	*7 ft Light Duty
75	Q	Jun. 34	Sep. 34	207	1521	Double	*8 ft 'Fishbelly'
76	Q	Jan. 35	Oct. 35	219	1545	Double	8 ft 'Fishbelly'
77	Q	Oct. 35	NOT				
78	Q	Jun. 34	Sep. 34	208	1521	Double	7 ft Light Duty
79	Q	Jun. 34	Sep. 34	209	1521	Double	*7 ft Light Duty
80	Q	Oct. 35	NOT				
81	Q1	Nov. 34	Aug. 35	211	1542	Single	*7 ft Light Duty
82	Q1	Jun. 33	Jan. 34	204	1521	Single	*8 ft 'American'
83	Q1	Jun. 33	Jan. 34	205	1521	Single	7 ft Light Duty

* Photographic confirmation

The internal arrangement of these coaches gave the format of a driver's compartment, 3 ft 9 in (maximum), followed by the large saloon, with an 11 ft 6 in length of 4 pairs of walkover seats and a 9 ft length of longitudinal bench seating. The passengers vestibule was 3 ft 9 in long, with inward opening doors, and the small saloon consisted of an 8 ft 6 in length with 3 pairs of walkover seats, and a 13 ft 6 in length of bench seating (13 ft 3 in Nos.202 & 203 where there was a sliding door between the different kinds of seat). Finally, the luggage compartment, 7 ft $4\tfrac{7}{8}$ in (maximum) length, was equipped with 9 tip-up 'emergency' seats. With the 'emergency seats', these trailers seated 67 passengers.

The driver's doors opened outwards, were flush with the body sides, (following the body-side profile) and were only 2 ft wide. The large saloon (which was unaltered from SRM days) had a large fixed window (3 ft 6 in wide), a smaller one 2 ft $6\tfrac{1}{4}$ in wide, a pair of droplights, and two more large-sized fixed lights. The passengers' doors – which were flat, recessed, and opened inwards – had the usual steps below. The trailers that originated with the Gloucester C&W Co. retained their double passenger doors each side, whilst the Swindon-built examples had single doors, as shown on the diagram. The larger saloon had a large fixed light and a pair of droplights next to the walkover seats, unchanged from the SRM design, whilst the bench seats had a

No. 204 of Diagram A31 retains the small luggage end windows – a carry-over from SRM days. It is fitted with 8ft American bogies and displays the 1934 'shirt-button' monogram.
G. HEMMINGWAY

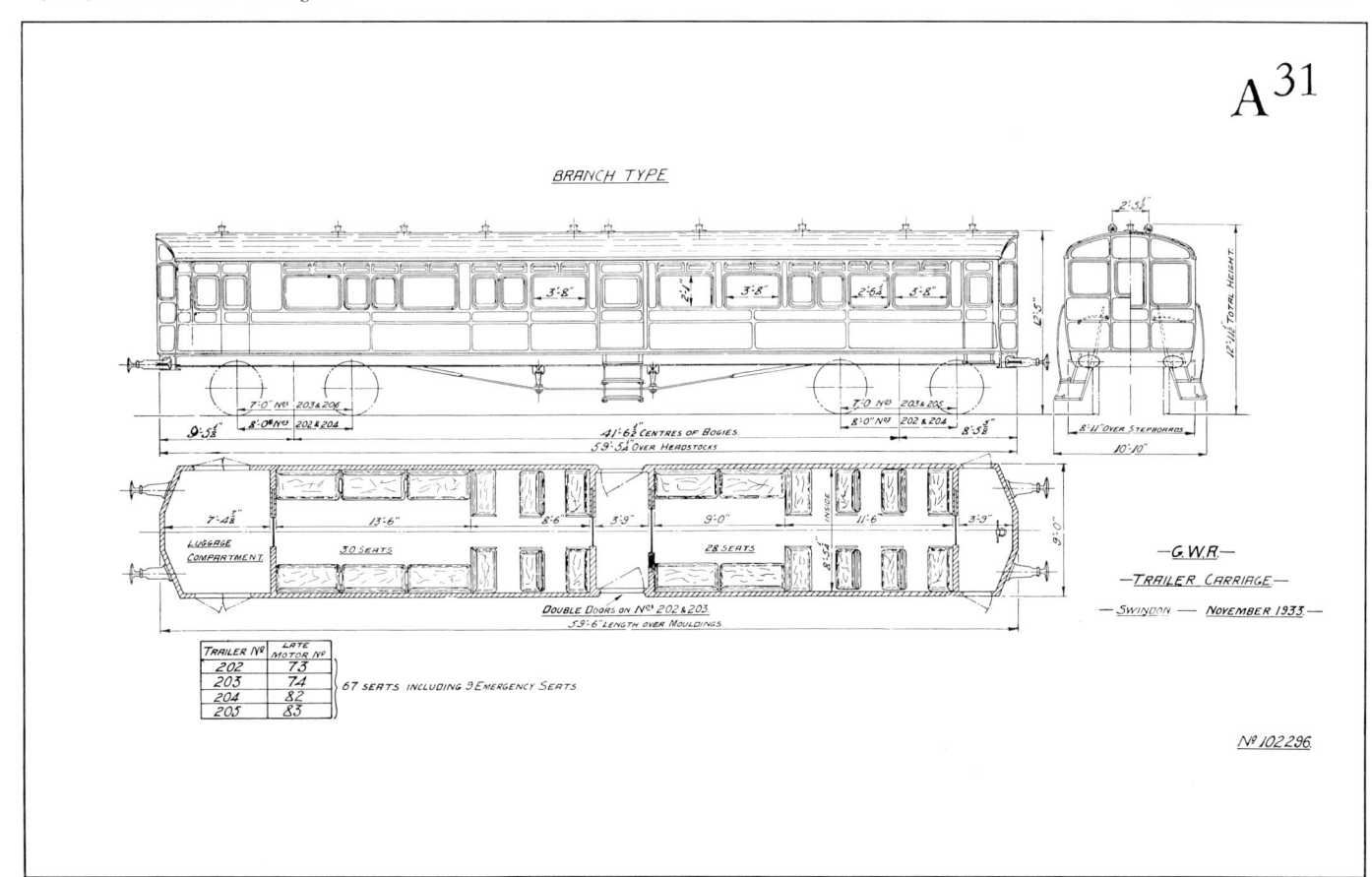

59ft 6in Trailers ex-SRMs

No. 203 of Diagram A31, thought to be in 1942 or 1943 all-brown livery newly applied. Note that the waist line is continued round the blank luggage end where it divides what had been the waist panel into two. Presumably the end windows had recently been plated over.
R. H. G. SIMPSON

Trailer 209 of Diagram A31, in 1948 brown and cream livery, has 7ft 'light' Collett bogies and double doors to the passengers' vestibule. The driving end of Diagram N No. 38 is also visible. D. M. LEE

No. 211 of Diagram A31 in BR maroon and cream livery, is fitted with 7ft light duty bogies and, in spite of the luggage end windows being plated over, the deep waist panel at this end still survives. Wiring for 'dual bells' ATC can be seen above the buffer. J. E. CULL

An A31 trailer No. 207 at Monmouth Troy in BR plain maroon livery with 8ft bogies, ATC and sanding gear. In the distance is an A38 trailer.
R. H. G. SIMPSON

pair of droplights flanked either side by large fixed lights. There was then a wide panel, followed by the usual pair of flush, outward-opening luggage doors that adopted the bodyside profile.

Since these trailers were rebuilt so late in the conversion programme, the only subsequent modifications recorded are that the end windows were painted black in 1935, and ATC was fitted from the mid-forties onwards.

No.204 was at Plymouth in 1934 (or early 1935) in the 1934 livery, with double gold lines and the shirtbutton monogram. (Presumably the latter had been specially applied without the trailer being due for painting.)

No.207 was photographed at Monmouth (Troy) in brown livery, in May 1948.

No.209 ran in brown and cream, without gold or orange lines, as W209 in the 1949-style; it was later noted in maroon, as W209W in the 1951-style, but with large characters for the running number.

No.211 was involved in an accident at Ealing Broadway on 16th November 1937 when, in thick fog, it started off prematurely for Denham, and was propelled through buffer stops into a signal box; it was not fitted with ATC at the time. Since it was only two years since it had been converted into a trailer, it was repaired and returned to traffic. In BR days, it ran in brown and cream (possibly with orange lines) as W211 in the 1949-style. It later ran in maroon as W211W, 1951-style.

One example of a Diagram A31 trailer was being used on the Lostwithiel–Fowey service in May 1935, and another on the Abbotsbury branch, probably around the same period.

No. 201 of Diagram A31, in BR maroon livery, has lost its toplights, but the broad waist panel at the luggage end is indicated by the horizontal handles. It is mounted on 8ft 'fish-belly' bogies.
H. C. CASSERLEY

Summary

Trailer No.	Black end windows	ATC	Cond.	Notes
202	Oct. 35	Mar. 45	Mar. 56	
203	Oct. 35	Mar. 50	Mar. 58	Temporarily used by Commercial Dept. Dec. 58
204	Oct. 35	?	Apr. 49	Reinstated Nov. 49 Cond. Apr. 51
205	Oct. 35	Oct. 49	Aug. 54	
207	Dec. 35	Jul. 45	Dec. 56	
208	Feb. 35	May 45	Mar. 57	
209	Apr. 35	May 46	Aug. 57	
211	Aug. 35	Feb. 45db	Mar. 59	
219	Oct. 35	Oct. 44	Apr. 56	